Aiiieeeee!

An Anthology of
Asian-American Writers

Aiiieeeee!

An Anthology of
Asian-American Writers

Edited by

FRANK CHIN

JEFFERY PAUL CHAN

LAWSON FUSAO INADA

SHAWN HSU WONG

HOWARD UNIVERSITY PRESS

Washington, D.C. 1974

LIBRARY OF CONGRESS CATALOGING
IN PUBLICATION DATA

Main entry under title:

Aiiieeeee! An anthology of Asian-American writers.

1. American literature—Asian-American authors.
2. American literature—20th century. I. Chan, Jeffery Paul, 1942–   -comp.
PS508.A8A4   810'.8'0895   73–88968
ISBN 0–88258–008–6
Printed in the United States of America.

Grateful acknowledgment is made to:

Caxton Printers, Ltd. for permission to reprint "The Lady Who Makes Swell Doughnuts" by Toshio Mori from *Yokohama, California*, 1949.

Frank Chin for permission to reprint Act I of *The Chickencoop Chinaman*, Copyright © 1973, 1974 by Frank Chin.

The Giligia Press for permission to reprint "Chinks" and "Japs" by Lawson Inada from *Down at the Santa Fe Depot: 20 Fresno Poets*, Copyright © 1970 by David Kherdian and James Baloian.

Harcourt Brace Jovanovich for permission to reprint excerpts from *America is in the Heart* by Carlos Bulosan, Copyright © 1946 by Harcourt Brace Jovanovich.

Momoko Iko for permission to reprint Act I of *Gold Watch*, Copyright © 1969 by Momoko Iko. Full text of the play *Gold Watch* is available through Inner City Press.

Rafu Shimpo for permission to reprint "And the Soul Shall Dance" by Wakako Yamauchi, Copyright © 1974 by Wakako Yamauchi.

Random House, Inc. for permission to reprint excerpts from *The Frontiers of Love* by Diana Chang, Copyright © 1956 by Diana Chang.

Lyle Stuart Inc. for permission to reprint excerpts from *Eat a Bowl of Tea* by Louis Chu, Copyright © 1961 by Louis Chu.

Charles E. Tuttle Co. for permission to reprint excerpts from *No-No Boy* by John Okada, Copyright © 1957 by Charles E. Tuttle Co.

Hisaye Yamamoto for permission to reprint "Yoneko's Earthquake" from *Furioso*, Copyright © 1951, 1952, 1974 by Hisaye Yamamoto.

To the Memory of
John Okada and Louis Chu

PREFACE

ASIAN-AMERICANS are not one people but several—Chinese-Americans, Japanese-Americans, and Filipino-Americans. Chinese- and Japanese-Americans have been separated by geography, culture, and history from China and Japan for seven and four generations respectively. They have evolved cultures and sensibilities distinctly not Chinese or Japanese and distinctly not white American. Even the Asian languages as they exist today in America have been adjusted and developed to express a sensitivity created by a new experience. In America, Chinese- and Japanese-American culture and history have been inextricably linked by confusion, the popularization of their hatred for each other, and World War II.

Filipino America differs greatly from Chinese and Japanese America in its history, the continuity of culture between the Philippines and America, and the influence of western European and American culture on the Philippines. The difference is definable only in its own terms, and therefore must be discussed separately.

Our anthology is exclusively Asian-American. That means Filipino-, Chinese-, and Japanese-Americans, American born and raised, who got their China and Japan from the radio, off the silver screen, from television, out of comic books, from the pushers of white American culture that pictured the yellow man as something that when wounded, sad, or angry, or swearing, or wondering whined, shouted, or screamed "aiiieeeee!"

Asian America, so long ignored and forcibly excluded from creative participation in American culture, is wounded, sad, angry, swearing, and wondering, and this is his AIIIEEEEE!!! It is more than a whine, shout, or scream. It is fifty years of our whole voice.

Seven generations of suppression under legislative racism and euphemized white racist love have left today's Asian-Americans in a state of self-contempt, self-rejection, and disintegration. We have been encouraged to believe that we have no cultural integrity as Chinese- or Japanese-Americans, that we are either Asian (Chinese or Japanese) or American (white), or are measurably both. This myth of being either/or and the equally goofy concept of the dual personality haunted our lobes while our rejection by both Asia and white America proved we were neither one nor the other. Nor were we half and half or more one than the other. Neither Asian culture nor American culture was equipped to define us except in the most superficial terms. However, American culture, equipped to deny us the legitimacy of our uniqueness as American minorities, did so, and in the process contributed to the effect of stunting self-contempt on the development and expression of our sensibility that in turn has contributed to a mass rejection of Chinese and Japanese America by Chinese- and Japanese-Americans. The Japanese-American Citizens League (JACL) weekly, the *Pacific Citizen,* in February, 1972, reported that more than 50 percent of Japanese-American women were marrying outside their race and that the figure was rising annually. Available statistics indicate a similar trend among Chinese-American women, though the 50 percent mark may not have been topped yet. These figures say something about our sensibility, our concept of Chinese America and Japanese America, our self-esteem, as does our partly real and partly mythical silence in American culture.

The age, variety, depth, and quality of the writing collected here proves the existence of Asian-American sensibilities and cultures that might be related to but are distinct from Asia and white America. American culture, protecting the sanctity of its whiteness, still patronizes us as foreigners and refuses to recog-

nize Asian-American literature as "American" literature. America does not recognize Asian America as a presence, though
Asian-Americans have been here seven generations. For seven
generations we have been aware of that refusal, and internalized
it, with disastrous effects.

Asian-American sensibility is so delicate at this point that the
fact of Chinese or Japanese birth is enough to distinguish you
from being American-born, in spite of the fact that you may
have no actual memories of life in Asia. However, between the
writer's actual birth and birth of the sensibility, we have used
the birth of the sensibility as the measure of being an Asian-
American. Victor Nee was born in China and came to the
United States when he was five. Novelist Louis Chu came when
he was nine. For both, Chinese culture and China are not so
much matters of experience as they are of hearsay and study.
Victor and his wife Brett have written the first Chinese-American history of Chinese America, *Longtime Californ': A Documentary Study of an American Chinatown* (1973). Louis Chu's
Eat a Bowl of Tea (1961) is the first Chinese-American novel
set in Chinese America. Here we get sticky, however, for the
first novel published by an American-born Chinese-American
is the *Frontiers of Love* (1956), by Diana Chang, a Eurasian. She
was born in America but moved to China before her first birth-
day, to be raised in the "European Compound" of Shanghai
as an American in China. She writes of that experience, while
Chu writes of Chinatown, New York. Between them so many
questions are raised as to what is or is not Chinese-American
that to save, and in another sense encourage, confusion (our
criterion of Asian-American literature and identity is not a
matter of dogma or party line), we have included them both.
Chu's book honestly and accurately dramatizes the Chinese-
American experience from a Chinese-American point of view,
and not from an exclusively "Chinese or Chinese-according-
to-white" point of view. Diana Chang in her protagonists of
mixed blood and their single-blooded parents provides us with
a logical dramatic metaphor for the conflict of cultures. Her
protagonist, Sylvia, cannot choose between her parents or
identify her blood as one thing or the other. The question of

choice is shown to be a phony one imposed on her by outside forces.

Sensibility and the ability to choose differentiate the Asian-American writers in this collection from the Americanized Chinese writers Lin Yutang and C. Y. Lee. They were intimate with and secure in their Chinese cultural identity in an experiential sense, in a way we American-born can never be. Again, unlike us, they are American by choice. They consciously set out to become American, in the white sense of the word, and succeeded in becoming "Chinese-American" in the stereotypical sense of the good, loyal, obedient, passive, law-abiding, cultured sense of the word. It is no surprise that their writing is from whiteness, not from Chinese America. Becoming white supremacist was part of their consciously and voluntarily becoming "American." Lin Yutang's *A Chinatown Family* (1948) and C. Y. Lee's *Flower Drum Song* affected our sensibility but did not express it. They come from a white tradition of Chinese novelty literature, would-be Chinese writing about America for the entertainment of Americans in books like *As a Chinaman Sees Us, Chinaman's Chance,* and *A Chinaman Looks at America.* These travel books were in the tradition not so much of de Tocqueville as of *Gulliver's Travels.* Their attraction was comic. The humor derived from the Chinese mangling of the English language and from their comic explanations of American customs and psychology. These books appeared in the early twentieth century after almost fifty years of travel books on China written by Christian missionaries and "world travelers" who cited missionaries as authorities on China. The reversal of the form, books of American adventures by Chinese travelers, was a comic inevitability. During this period the exploitation of the comic potential of Asian dialect became, forever, a part of popular American culture, giving rise to Earl Derr Biggers' series of Charlie Chan novels and Wallace Irwin's Hashimura Togo stories. The Hashimura Togo stories were featured in *Good Housekeeping* Magazine and described the adventures of a Japanese house servant who is both unintelligible and indispensible in an American household. A sample of the wit and wisdom of Hashimura Togo, from "Togo Assists in a Great Diamond Robbery," (*Good Housekeeping,* March, 1917):

> With occasional oftenness she approached up to me and report with frogged voice, "Togo where did you put my diamond broach and Mother Hubbard chamois ring when you stole it?"

The substance and imagery of these books and stories were reinforced by the whining, apologetic tone of books done by Chinese government officials giving the official explanations of Chinese culture and the nonthreatening, beneficial, humble motivations of the Chinese presence and immigration to America. Books were written as *The Real Chinese in America* (1923) by J. S. Tow, secretary of the Chinese Consulate at New York, with the rank of Consul-Eleven. The subservient character of the Chinese and the inferiority of China were major themes in works by Chinese converts to white supremacy and Christianity. Yung Wing's *My Life in China and America* (1909) is the outstanding example of early yellow white supremacy.

In 1925 Earl Derr Biggers, a distinctly non-Chinese, non-Chinese-American, and subtly racist writer, created the modern Chinese-American: Charlie Chan, the Chinese detective, who first appears in "The House Without a Key" walking with "the light dainty step of a woman." The travel format, going from one nation to another, became in Biggers' immensely popular Charlie Chan novels, an interior journey from one culture to another. Thus, the form evolved into the Chinatown book itself reinforced, and clearly articulated today's popular notion of being an Asian-American. The concept of the dual personality, of going from one culture to another, emerged.

Eleven years after the appearance of the fat, inscrutable, flowery but flub-tongued effeminate little detective, the first book by a Chinese-American about Chinese America was published. Leong Gor Yun's *Chinatown Inside Out* (1938) was a direct descendant of the Charlie Chan novels and became the prototype of what was to become the "Chinatown Book." The essence of the formula was, "I'm an American because I eat spaghetti and Chinese because I eat chow mein." The

Charlie Chan model of Chinese-Americans was developed in books like Pardee Lowe's *Father And Glorious Descendant*, Lin Yutang's novel *A Chinatown Family*, Jade Snow Wong's *Fifth Chinese Daughter*, *Inside Chinatown* by Garding Lui, and two books titled *Chinatown*, *U.S.A.*, one by Calvin Lee and the other by a white, Elizabeth Coleman.

Chinatown Inside Out was obviously a fraud. The author's name, "Leong Gor Yun," means "two men" in Cantonese. The book consists of items cribbed and translated from the Chinese-language newspapers of Chinatowns in San Francisco and New York tied together with Charlie Chan/Fu Manchu imaginings and the precise logic of a paranoid schizophrenic. Part exposé, part cookbook, the book was supremacist in its overlooking of the effect of racism on our psychology and its never missing a chance to brown-nose the white man with Charlie Chan-like observations, i.e.:

> Like chop-suey, this [unofficial Chinatown] government is an American product. It uses racketeer methods and ingenuity but it depends for its continued and prosperous existence on Chinese psychology, in this connection more precisely called passivity.

Far from giving America a big yuk, and celebrated as a classic of American humor, *Chinatown Inside Out* was accepted by everyone as the first book about Chinese America by a Chinese-American. No one, not even the scholars of Chinese America, noticed the awkward changes of voice and style, the differences between the outright lies and the rare facts. The clue of the author's pen name "two men" escaped all. *Chinatown Inside Out* was the source of Lin Yutang's 1948 novel *A Chinatown Family*. In 1962 S. W. Kung from China published *Chinese in American Life* and cited the work of another foreigner to Chinese America, Lin Yutang's *A Chinatown Family*. In 1965 Calvin Lee, a former assistant dean at Columbia University and the author of Chinese cookbooks, saw the light and testified to his successful conversion to utter white supremacy in *Chinatown U.S.A.* in which he cited Leong Gor Yun and S. W. Kung. Betty Lee Sung loosed *Mountain of Gold* in 1967. She praised the "Chinese in America" for never being "overly bitter

about prejudice." In this book, she told us, "If you make yourself obnoxious . . . that is a hindrance to acceptance." *Mountain of Gold* cited the gospel according to S. W. Kung, Lin
Yutang, and Calvin Lee. In 1971 the gospel of Leong Gor Yun
became hilarious self-parody in Francis L. K. Hsu's *The Challenge of the American Dream:*

> The Chinese in America, in common with other minority
> groups, will have a continuing problem of double identity. But
> the effective way of dealing with it is not to deny its existence
> but to face it squarely. The first step is to realize that the double
> identity of a minority group is not dissimilar to that of the
> professional woman. She is a woman and a professional. Some
> American professional women have tended to forget their sex
> identity but most have kept some sort of balance between it and
> their profession. In the latter case, their sex identity sometimes
> becomes an advantage rather than a disability.

Hsu's work may or may not give us insight into the mind of
the first-generation upper-middle-class Chinese immigrant
scholar, but in terms of the native Chinese-American sensibility,
we can only note that, in the great tradition of Charlie Chan
and Leong Gor Yun, his vision of Chinese America reinforces
white racist stereotypes and falls short of the vision Malcolm
X and other blacks had for their "minority."

The period from the late twenties through the thirties that
spawned Charlie Chan, Fu Manchu, and Leong Gor Yun also
produced a rash of popular songs, Charlestons, and fox trots
about "China boys" being stranded in America without their
women. Such a song was "So Long Oolong (How Long You
Gonna Be Gone)," that tells of a girl, "Ming Toy," pining for
her sweetheart, "Oolong," stranded in America. Songs with
titles like "Little Chinky Butterfly," "Hong Kong Dream Girl,"
and dozens of others appeared to be Tin Pan Alley's way of
celebrating America's closing of the last loopholes in the
Chinese Exclusion Act of 1923 by finding ways to exclude entry
to Chinese women into the country. Also, a series of popular
novels and movies involving passive Chinese men, worshiping
white women and being afraid to touch them, appeared in
Son of the Gods, East is West, and the Fu Manchu and Charlie
Chan series.

In the meantime Japanese-Americans cranked up an underground press and literary movement in English, publishing their own poetry magazines, literary quarterlies, and newspapers that featured, as they still do, creative writing supplements in their holiday issues.

The "Inside Chinatown" books were done by American-born Chinese for the most part, but Chinese from China capitalized on the formula, and played it for bucks and popularity. Secure in their Chinese identities and Chinese cultural values—both of which were respectable in America, in the Mandarin versions—these books were not as significant or personally affecting to them as they were to the American-born, for whom these books represented manifestoes of Chinese-American identity and assimilation. The Chinese (not Chinese-American) writers Lin Yutang and C. Y. Lee refined the "spaghetti–chow-mein" form. In Arthur T. S. Chu's *We Are Going to Make the Lousiest Chop Suey in Town* (1966), the form takes its most ridiculous shape.

During World War II the inside books became more personal and more manipulated. Patriotic Chinese-Americans wrote anti-Japanese propaganda disguised as autobiography. Pardee Lowe's *Father and Glorious Descendant* was the first. Though *Fifth Chinese Daughter* was published in 1950, it fits the propaganda-as-autobiography mold perfectly. There is reason to believe work on it actually began during the war. Chapters of it appeared in magazines in 1947. America's "anti-Jap" prejudice, as indicated by the release of new anti-Japanese war movies, continued strong until the mid-fifties, when the first sign of a change in white attitude was an announcement disclaiming prejudice against loyal Japanese-Americans before the airing of World War II "anti-Jap" movies on television.

In travel books and in music, Japanese America was indiscriminately linked in confusion with Chinese America. In America's pop mind, Japan and China, as well as Japanese America and Chinese America, were one in exotica. China and Japan and Japanese America became distinguished from each other by hatred. That hatred was not explained in the terms of culture and politics, but in the terms of the Hatfields and McCoys—we were all some kind of silly, but civilized hillbillies feuding in the hills of jade. Chinese-Americans became America's pets, were kept and groomed in kennels, while Japanese-Americans were the mad dogs who had to be locked up in pounds. The editors and writers of the Japanese-American community papers were thrown ever closer to Japanese-American artists, poets, and storytellers. The Japanese-American writing in English that had been an activity was now welded into a movement.

The tradition of Japanese-American verse as being quaint and foreign in English, established by Yone Noguchi and Sadakichi Hartman, momentarily influenced American writing with the quaintness of the Orient but said nothing about Asian America, because, in fact, these writers weren't Asian-Americans but Americanized Asians like Lin Yutang and C. Y. Lee.

The first serious creative writing by an Asian-American to hit the streets was Miné Okubo's *Citizen 13660,* an autobiographical narrative in drawings and words, describing the relocation and camp experience from an artist's point of view. It was a remarkable book given the time of its appearance, 1946, when anti-Japanese sentiment was still high. Toshio Mori's collection of stories, *Yokohama, California,* appeared in 1949. It had been scheduled for release in 1941, but World War II "anti-Jap" prejudice worked against Japanese-Americans appearing in print; however, it also spared their being shaped, used, and manipulated as Chinese-Americans.

After the war, the best way to rehabilitate Japanese America, from the white point of view, was to link it up and get it inextricably confused with Chinese America again, so from *Fifth Chinese Daughter* came son of *Fifth Chinese Daughter,* Monica Sone's *Nisei Daughter,* a book remarkable for maintaining its Japanese-American integrity in spite of its being, in the publisher's eyes, blatantly modeled on Wong's snow job.

None of the Chinese-, Japanese-, and Filipino-American works in this volume are snow jobs pushing Asian-Americans as the miracle synthetic white people that America's proprietors of white liberal pop, like Tom Wolfe, ABC television ("If Tomorrow Comes," "Kung Fu," "Madame Sin"), and such racist henchmen passing for scholars as Gunther Barth and Stuart Miller, make us out to be.

The Asian-American writers here are elegant or repulsive, angry and bitter, militantly anti-white or not, not out of any sense of perversity or revenge but of honesty. America's dishonesty—its racist white supremacy passed off as love and acceptance—has kept seven generations of Asian-American voices off the air, off the streets, and praised us for being Asiatically no-show. A lot is lost forever. But from the few decades of writing we have recovered from seven generations, it is clear that we have a lot of elegant, angry, and bitter life to show. We know how to show it. We are showing off. If the reader is shocked, it is due to his own ignorance of Asian-America. We're not new here. Aiiieeeee!!

The editors extend a special note of thanks to Kay Boyle, The Combined Asian-American Resources Project, Inc., Kai-yu Hsu, David Ishii, H. Mark Lai, Dorothy Okada, Glenn Omatsu, Ishmael Reed, Leslie Silko, Ben R. Tong, Richard Wada, and Connie Young Yu for their help and encouragement in the preparation of this anthology. Grateful acknowledgement is also made to authors, publishers, and agents for their permission to reprint the following selections.

San Francisco, 1973

Frank Chin
Jeffery Paul Chan
Lawson Fusao Inada
Shawn Hsu Wong

CONTENTS

INTRODUCTION:

Fifty Years of
Our Whole Voice

An Introduction
To Chinese- and
Japanese-American Literature

In the 140-YEAR history of Asian America, fewer than ten works of fiction and poetry have been published by American-born Chinese, Japanese, and Filipino writers. This fact suggests that in six generations of Asian-Americans there was no impulse to literary or artistic self-expression. The truth is that Asian-Americans have been writing seriously since the nineteenth century, and writing well.

Sui Sin Fah, an English-born Eurasian, wrote and published short fiction in the nineteenth century. She was one of the first to speak for an Asian-American sensibility that was neither Asian nor white American. And, interestingly enough, in her work, there is no cultural conflict between East and West. That is a modern invention of whites and their yellow goons—writers who need white overseers to give them a license to use the English language. In 1896 the California magazine *Land of Sunshine* said her stories' characters ". . . are all of Chinese characters in California or on the Pacific Coast; and they have an insight and sympathy which are probably unique. To others the alien Celestial is at best mere 'literary material': in these stories he (or she) is a human being." Working within the terms of the stereotype of the Chinese as laundryman, prostitute, smuggler, coolie, she presents "John Chinaman" as little more than a comic caricature, giving him a sensibility that was her own.

Americans' stereotypes of "Orientals" were sacrosanct and no one, especially a "Chink" or a "Jap," was going to tell them that America, not Asia, was their home, that English was their language, and that the stereotype of the Oriental, good or bad, was offensive. What America published was, with rare exception, not only offensive to Chinese and Japanese America but was *actively inoffensive* to white sensibilities.

World War II signaled the suppression of a Japanese-American writing movement that had been active since the late twenties and the sudden popularity of Chinese-Americans' writing to encourage America to "assimilate her loyal minorities," as the dust jacket of Pardee Lowe's *Father and Glorious Descendant* states. The implied worth of these first Chinese-Americans to reach mass print and enjoy a degree of popularity was that they mostly had patriotic virtues rather than literary ones. They were more manipulable. The autobiographies of Pardee Lowe and later Jade Snow Wong were treated less as works of art than as anthropological discoveries. Indeed, the dust jacket of Lowe's book said that he "enlisted in the U.S. Army shortly after delivering the manuscript of this book," as if this patriotic gesture affected its literary worth.

Much of Asian-American literary history is a history of a small minority being cast into the role of the good guy in order to make another American minority look bad. In World War II the Chinese were used against the Japanese. Today, Chinese- and Japanese-Americans are used to mouth the white racist cliches of the fifties, as evidenced by a recent *Newsweek* Magazine article (June 21, 1971) entitled "The Japanese-American Success Story: Outwhiting the Whites," and the favorable reception of Daniel K. Okimoto's *American in Disguise* and Betty Lee Sung's *Mountain of Gold: The Story of the Chinese in America.*

Betty Lee Sung's *Mountain of Gold* (1967) went through two printings of 7,500 and in 1971 was issued in a paperback edition under the title *The Story of the Chinese in America.* Hers is the only book by a Chinese-American still in print, and further enjoys the distinction of being cited by scholars in (*For-*

gotten Pages of American Literature, edited by Gerald Haslam) as an authoritative source, supporting the age-old stereotype of Chinese-Americans being culturally Chinese and only monetarily white.

"There is nothing wrong with autobiography," writes Kai-yu Hsu in his introduction to *Asian-American Authors* (1972), "except when one realizes that the perceptions of reality revealed through these works seem to continue to confirm rather than to modify a stereotyped image of the Chinese and their culture." Part One of Virginia Lee's novel *The House that Tai Ming Built* consists mostly of the retelling of the legend of "the house that Tai Ming built." This narration is supposed to be from the Chinese point of view, but we find that the point of view is surprisingly Western:

> Grandfather Kwong continued: "To know why Tai Ming wore a queue we must go back in Chinese history, to the time when the Mongol Emperor Kublai Khan and his successors ruled China for nearly a century in the Yuan Dynasty from the year 1230 until 1368 A.D., when they were driven out of power by the Chinese."

Virginia Lee is the victim, so completely brainwashed that she sees no discrepancy between an old man from China talking about China in reference to the white Christian calendar. Yet she would be the first to protest if John Wayne were to speak about Abraham Lincoln freeing the slaves in the Year of the Pig. In the early novels, confirming the education of the white reading audience became an obsession, to the point where writers such as Virginia Lee obviously had to do a lot of research into such things as Chinese history, Chinese-American history, Chinese art, and Chinese opera—all from the white point of view. And the white point of view was that Chinese were "culturally superior." That the cultural superiority of the Chinese served white supremacy by keeping Chinese in their place is clear in the work of Jade Snow Wong and Virginia Lee. They both respond to racism silently and privately, not with action but with an attitude of a noncommunicative cultural superiority that as a response is ineffectual. Virginia Lee in *The House that Tai Ming Built* illustrates this concept:

The first thing Lin noticed as she stepped into the house of Mrs. Hayes was the wallpaper in the foyer. It was a lovely medallion design in pale yellow. She wondered if Mrs. Hayes knew that the ancient Chinese had invented wallpaper and that it was not until the fourteenth century that wallpaper was introduced into Europe.

This was not a firsthand knowledge of Chinese culture, but it was being passed off as such. Virginia Lee paraphrases Chinese history as written by white and Chinese scholars.

Kai-yu Hsu correctly states that "These largely autobiographical works tend to present the stereotype of Chinese culture as described in the connoisseur's manual of Chinese jade or oolong tea, and the stereotype of the Chinese immigrant who is, or should be, either withdrawn and stays totally Chinese, or quietly assimilated and has become unobtrusively American, exhibiting a model of the American ideal of the melting pot process."

An American-born Asian, writing from the world as Asian-American who does not reverberate to gongs struck hundreds of years ago or snuggle into the doughy clutches of an America hot to coddle something ching chong, is looked upon as a freak, an imitator, a liar. The myth is that Asian-Americans have maintained cultural integrity as Asians, that there is some strange continuity between the great high culture of a China that hasn't existed for five hundred years and the American-born Asian. Gerald Haslam in *Forgotten Pages of American Literature* perpetuates this idea:

> . . . the average Chinese-American at least knows that China has produced "great philosophies," and with that knowledge has come a greater sense of ethnic pride. Contrasted, for example, with the abject cultural deprivation long foisted upon Afro-Americans, Asian-Americans have an inner resource: The knowledge that their ancestors had created a great and complex civilization when the inhabitants of the British Isles still painted their fannies blue.

Thus, fourth-, fifth-, and sixth-generation Asian-Americans are still looked upon as foreigners because of this dual heritage, or the concept of dual personality which suggests that the Asian-

American can be broken down into his American part and his Asian part. This view explains Asian assimilation, adaptability, and lack of presence in American culture. This sustaining inner resource keeps the Asian-American a stranger in the country in which he was born. He is supposed to feel better off than the blacks, whose American achievement is the invention of their own American culture. American language, fashions, music, literature, cuisine, graphics, body language, morals, and politics have been strongly influenced by Black culture. They have been cultural achievers, in spite of white supremacist culture, whereas Asian America's reputation is an achievement of that white culture—a work of racist art.

The overthrow of the Manchus, the Sino-Japanese War, World War II, the success of the Communist Revolution, and the Cultural Revolution are five major events resulting in a China the Chinese of a hundred years ago, the ancestors of fourth-, fifth-, and sixth-generation Chinese-Americans, never saw and wouldn't understand. These new Chinese are emigrating to America. The assertion of distinctions between Chinese and Chinese-Americans is neither a rejection of Chinese culture nor an expression of contempt for things Chinese, as the whites and the Chinatown Establishment would make them out to be. It is calling things by their right names. Change has taken place in China, in American Chinatowns, and in the world generally—changes that have been ignored and suppressed to preserve the popular racist "truths" that make up the Oriental stereotype.

It is the racist truth that some nonwhite minorities, notably the Asians, have suffered less and are better off than the other colored minorities. It is generally accepted as fact that Asians are well liked and accepted in American society, that they have been assimilated and acculturated and have contributed to the mainstream of American culture. There is racist hate and racist love. That is, if the system works, the stereotypes assigned to the various races are accepted by the races themselves as reality, as fact, and racist love reigns. The minority's reaction to racist policy is acceptance and apparent satisfaction. Order is kept, the world turns without a peep from any nonwhite. One measure of the success of white racism is the silence of the minority race and the amount of white energy necessary to maintain or increase that silence. The Chinese-American is told that it is not a matter of being ignored and excluded but of being quiet and foreign. It is only recently that we have come to appreciate the consequences of that awful quiet and set out collecting Chinese-American oral history on tape. There is no recorded Chinese-American history from the Chinese-American point of view. Silence has been a part of the price of the Chinese-American's survival in a country that hated him. That was the trouble with the language. It was full of hate. Silence was love.

The failure of white racism can be measured by the amount and kind of noise of resistance generated by the race. The truth is that all of the country's attention has been drawn to white racism's failures. Everything that has been done by whites in politics, government, and education in response to the failure of white racism, while supposedly antiracist, can be seen as an effort to correct the flaws, redesign the instruments, and make racism work. White racism has failed to convince the blacks that they are animals and failed to convince the Indians that they are living fossils. Nightriders, soldier boys on horseback, fat sheriffs, and all the clowns of racism did destroy a lot of bodies, and leave among these minorities a legacy of suffering that continues to this day. But they did not destroy their impulse to cultural integrity, stamp out their literary sensibility, and produce races of people who would work to enforce white supremacy without having to be supervised or watchdogged.

In terms of the utter lack of cultural distinction in America, the destruction of an organic sense of identity, the complete psychological and cultural subjugation of the Asian-American, the people of Chinese and Japanese ancestry stands out as white racism's only success. The secret lies in the construction of the modern stereotype and the development of new policies of white racism.

The general function of any racial stereotype is to establish and preserve order between different elements of society, maintain the continuity and growth of Western civilization, and enforce white supremacy with a minimum of effort, attention, and expense. The ideal racial stereotype is a low-maintenance engine of white supremacy whose efficiency increases with age, as it becomes authenticated and historically verified. The stereotype operates as a model of behavior. It conditions the mass society's perceptions and expectations. Society is conditioned to accept the given minority only within the bounds of the stereotype. The subject minority is conditioned to reciprocate by becoming the stereotype, live it, talk it, believe it, and measure group and individual worth in its terms. The stereotype operates most efficiently and economically when the vehicle of the stereotype, the medium of its perpetuation, and the subject race to be controlled are all one. When the operation of the stereotype has reached this point, at which the subject race itself embodies and perpetuates the white supremacist vision of reality, indifference to the subject race sets in among mass society. The successful operation of the stereotype results in the neutralization of the subject race as a social, creative, and cultural force. The race poses no threat to white supremacy. It is now a guardian of white supremacy, dependent on it and grateful to it. In Monica Sone's *Nisei Daughter* the operation of the stereotype in the Japanese-American is clearly evident:

> Although I had opinions, I was so overcome with self-consciousness I could not bring myself to speak. Some people would have explained this as an acute case of adolescence, but I knew it was also because I was Japanese. Almost all the students of Japanese blood sat like rocks during discussion period. Something compellingly Japanese made us feel it was better to seem stupid in a quiet way rather than to make a boner out loud. I began to think of the Japanese as the Silent People, and I envied my fellow students who clamored to be heard. What they said was not always profound or even relevant, but they didn't seem worried about it. Only after a long, agonizing struggle was I able to deliver the simplest statement in class without flaming like a red tomato.

For the subject to operate efficiently as an instrument of white supremacy, he is conditioned to accept and live in a state of euphemized self-contempt. This self-contempt itself is nothing more than the subject's acceptance of white standards of objectivity, beauty, behavior, and achievement as being morally absolute, and his acknowledgement that, because he is not white, he can never fully measure up to white standards. In *American in Disguise* (1971), this self-contempt is implicit in Daniel K. Okimoto's assessment of Japanese-American literary potential:

> . . . it appears unlikely that literary figures of comparable stature to those minorities like the Jews and Blacks will emerge to articulate the nisei soul. Japanese-Americans will be forced to borrow the voices of James Michener, Jerome Charyn, and other sympathetic novelists to distill their own experience. Even if a nisei of Bernard Malamud's or James Baldwin's talent did appear, he would no doubt have little to say that John O'Hara has not already said.

The stereotype within the minority group itself, then, is enforced by individual and collective self-contempt. This gesture of self-contempt and self-destruction, in terms of the stereotype, is euphemized as being successful assimilation, adaptation, and acculturation.

If the source of this self-contempt is obviously generated from outside the minority, interracial hostility will inevitably result, as history has shown us in the cases of the blacks, Indians, and Chicanos. The best self-contempt has its sources seemingly within the minority group itself. The vehicles of this illusion are education and the publishing establishment. Only five American-born Chinese have published what can be called serious attempts at literature. We have already mentioned Pardee Lowe, Jade Snow Wong, Virginia Lee, and Betty Lee Sung. The fifth, Diana Chang, is the only Chinese-American writer to publish more than one book-length creative work to date. She has published four novels and is a well-known poetess. Of these five, Pardee Lowe, Jade Snow Wong, Virginia Lee, and Betty Lee Sung believe the popular stereotypes of Chinese-Americans to be true and find Chinese America repulsive and do not identify with it. They are "exceptions that prove the rule." In an interview taped by Frank Chin in 1970, Virginia Lee said, "so in other words, you want the white population to start thinking of Chinese other than being quiet, unassuming, passive, et cetera, right? That's what you want, huh?"

"I don't want to be measured against the stereotype anymore," answered Frank Chin.

"But," she said, "you've got to admit that what you call the stereotype does make up for the larger majority of Chinese-Americans, now I've seen that in school. [Virginia Lee is a schoolteacher.] I think it behooves all minorities, Blacks, Chinese, what not, not to feel so insulted so fast. It's almost a reflex action."

Frank asked her if she would continue to write about Chinese America. She said, "I wouldn't want to go on a Chinese, you know, American conflict like that again. I don't want to do another one."

"Why?" he asked. "Was it difficult?"

"It wasn't difficult," she said, "but very candidly now, this might not even . . . " She took a deep breath. "I just don't think it's that interesting."

And Jade Snow Wong on Chinese America as it exists here: "The American-Chinese I grew up with, in high school, out of forty or fifty . . . none of them went to college. We're not friends now." Jade Snow Wong, Virginia Lee, Pardee Lowe, and Betty Lee Sung are all of the first generation to go completely through the public school system. The preceding generations were barred, by law, from attending public schools. Their parents went to segregated mission schools if they went to school at all. Diana Chang lived from infancy to her early twenties in China.

Of these five, four were obviously manipulated by white publishers to write to and from the stereotype. Of these four, three do not consider themselves to be serious writers and welcomed the aid of editors, as Jade Snow Wong describes in this interview:

"Elizabeth Lawrence was the one who asked me to write it. And the other one was Alice Cooper, who's dead now. She was my English teacher at City College."

Frank Chin asked her, "What did their help consist of?"

"Oh, Elizabeth Lawrence, you know, she said, 'I want a

story,' or something. Then I wrote up maybe three times as
long as what finally came out in the book. I sent it to her and
she went through it and said, 'ten, twenty, thirty pages, this
may be necessary for the writer to write, but it's not necessary
for the reader to read.' So then she took parts out. And then I
took what was left of the manuscript and went to Los Angeles
to see Alice Cooper who helped me bind it together again."

"You think this is right? Are you happy with the book?"

"I finally got to read it the second time about two or three
years ago. It reads all right. Some of the things are missing
that I would have wanted in, then, you know, it's like selling
to Gumps or sending to a museum. Everybody has a purpose
in mind, in what they're carrying out. So, you know, you kind
of have to work with them. If this is what they want to print,
and it's the real thing. I mean they didn't fabricate anything
that wasn't so."

This was the talk of a good businesswoman, not a serious or
very sensitive writer. Chin asked, "But you feel things were left
out?"

She matter of factly expressed an acceptance of her inferior
status as if it were a virtue. "Oh, maybe they were too personal,
you see. I was what? Twenty-six then. And, you know, it takes
maturity to be objective about one's self."

The construction of the stereotype began long before Jade
Snow Wong, Pardee Lowe, Virginia Lee, and Betty Lee Sung
were born within it and educated to fulfill it. It began with a
basic difference between it and the stereotypes of other races.
The white stereotype of the acceptable and unacceptable Asian
is utterly without manhood. Good or bad, the stereotypical
Asian is nothing as a man. At worst, the Asian-American is contemptible because he is womanly, effeminate, devoid of all the
traditionally masculine qualities of originality, daring, physical
courage, and creativity. The mere fact that four out of five
American-born Chinese-American writers are women reinforces
this aspect of the stereotype, as does the fact that four of these
writers, the four autobiographers, completely submerge and all
but eradicate all traces of their characters in their books. Sung,
by writing almost exclusively about "cases I heard of" and what
happened to "an acquaintance of mine," and Wong by writing

about herself in the third person, further reinforce the stereotypical unmanly nature of Chinese-Americans. Virginia Lee's novel *The House that Tai Ming Built* depicts a Chinese-American girl, for instance, who is just too much for the wishy-washy boys of Chinatown and falls in love with an "American," meaning "white," man.

The Chinatowns of Jade Snow Wong and Virginia Lee and Pardee Lowe differ starkly from the drab, even boring Chinatown described in Louis Chu's novel *Eat a Bowl of Tea*. In *Eat a Bowl of Tea* you have the first Chinese-American novel set against an unexoticized Chinatown—the kind of Chinatown that has been duplicated wherever large numbers of Chinese emigrants settle. It was basically a bachelor society, replete with prostitutes and gambling, existing as a foreign enclave where the white world stands at an officially described distance, where Chinatown and its inhabitants are tributaries to a faceless and apathetic authority. Published in 1961, one can imagine the reception of such a work by a public so fully grounded in the machinations of family associations, picture brides, and a reminiscence for a China that no longer exists. From Lin Yutang's euphemized portrait of Chinatown to C. Y. Lee's imported apothecary of ginseng and tuberculosis, the white reading audience has been steeped in the saccharine patronage of Chinatown culture.

Chu's portrayal of Chinatown is an irritating one for white audiences. The characters in this book are not reassured by the pervasive influence of the kind of Chinatown that we see in the autobiographies and pseudo-novellas of Wong, Lee, and Lin. The kind of Chinatown that the characters are secure in is a Chinatown devoid of whites. It is a Chinatown that we are familiar with—filled with vulgarity and white whores, who make up for the scarcity of Chinese women. In the same way that Chu's Chinatown holds the white reader at a distance, his characters speak a language that is offendingly neither English nor the idealized conception that whites have of a "Chinaman's tongue"—the pseudo-poetry of a Master Wang in *Flower Drum Song* or a Charlie Chan. Witness:

> "Go sell your ass, you stinky dead snake," Chong Loo tore into the barber furiously. "Don't say anything like that! If you want

to make laughs, talk about something else, you troublemaker.
You many-mouthed bird."

The manner and ritual of address and repartee is authentic
Chinatown. Chu translates idioms from the Sze Yup dialect,
and the effect of such expressions on his Chinese-American
readers is delight and recognition. Chu's unerring eye and ear
avoids the cliché, the superficial veneer and curio-shop expressions. He knows Chinatown people, their foibles and anxieties,
and at once can capture their insularity as well as their human-
ity.

This picture of a predominately male Chinatown is not
unique in Chinese-American literature. As early as 1896, Sui Sin
Fah wrote about the Chinese on the Pacific Coast. Like Louis
Chu, she accurately portrayed Chinatown's bachelor society.
In the story "A Chinese Feud," she wrote:

> He saw therein the most beautiful little woman in the world
> moving about his home, pouring out his tea and preparing his
> rice. He saw a cot; and kicking and crowing therein a baby—a
> boy baby with a round, shaven head and Fantze's eyes. He saw
> himself receiving the congratulations of all the wifeless, mother-
> less, sisterless, childless American Chinamen.

Historically, Chinatowns were predominately male. Chinese
families like those described in Jade Snow Wong, Virginia Lee,
and Pardee Lowe's books were rare. In these better known
works, the frustrated bachelors of Chinatown, making up the
majority of the Chinatown population, are symbolically rejected or totally ignored.

Unlike Chinese-American literature, Japanese-American
writing has only recently accepted the concept of the dual personality. Daniel Okimoto's *American in Disguise,* of all the
Japanese-American book length works, unquestioningly accepts
the concept of the dual personality and makes it central to the
work. Significantly, though Lawson Inada, who ignores the concept, also published a book in 1971, Okimoto's book has been
favorably reviewed by the nation's press, while Inada's book of
poetry *Before The War,* the first book of poetry published by
an American-born Japanese-American, has been ignored, as is
most poetry, and the reviews of his work submitted to metro-

politan newspapers have been rejected. The works of Japanese-American writers Toshio Mori (1949), John Okada (1957), Mine Okubo (1946), and Lawson Inada (1971) all see through the phoniness of the concept of the dual personality and reject it. Even Monica Sone's *Nisei Daughter* (1953) rejects this concept in spite of the publisher's blatant attempt to emulate Jade Snow Wong's *Fifth Chinese Daughter* (1950) and capitalize on that book's success.

"Although a 'first person singular' book, this story is written in the third person from Chinese habit." Thus Jade Snow Wong, in her author's note, immediately gives herself to the concept of the dual personality. George Sessions Perry, on the book's dust jacket, both accepts the concept of the dual personality and accidentally hints at its debilitating effect on the individual, if not its phoniness:

> Here is the curious dissonance of a largely Americanized young lady seeing her purely Chinese family life from both her and their points of view.

The suggestion is that the "dissonance" arises from her being a "largely" but not completely Americanized "young Chinese girl." The "dissonance" that thrills, bewilders, and charms Perry is built into the concept of the dual personality that controls his perception of Asian America. That the concept does not arise naturally from the Asian-American experience is dramatized clearly in Monica Sone's account of attending public school in the daytime and Japanese school (Nihon Gakko) in the afternoon:

> Gradually I yielded to my double dose of schooling. Nihon Gakko was so different from grammar school I found myself switching my personality back and forth daily like a chameleon. At Bailey Gatzert School I was a jumping, screaming, roustabout Yankee, but at the stroke of three when the school bell rang and the doors burst open everywhere, spewing out pupils like jelly beans from a broken bag, I suddenly became a modest, faltering, earnest little Japanese girl with a small, timid voice.

This concept of the dual personality was forced on her from without. Social pressure and education make her both Japanese and American. From her own experience, she is neither:

> Mr. Ohashi and Mrs. Matsui thought they could work on me
> and gradually mold me into an ideal Japanese ojoh-san, a re-
> fined young maiden who is quiet, pure in thought, polite,
> serene, self-controlled. They made little headway, for I was too
> much the child of Skidrow.

She declares herself a "child of Skidrow" and a "blending of
East and West." For the Nisei authoress this was a fatal mistake,
in terms of sales and popularity. The concept of the dual personality and conflict between the two incompatible parts are
central to Wong's work, as it is with the work of all Chinese-
Americans except Diana Chang. *Fifth Chinese Daughter* has
gone through several paperback editions in the United States
and England. It has been published in several languages and is
critically and financially the most successful book ever produced
by a Chinese-American.

Unlike Chinese America, Japanese America produced serious
writers who came together to form literary-intellectual communities. As early as the twenties, Japanese-American writers
were rejecting the concept of the dual identity and asserting a
Nisei identity that was neither Japanese nor white European
American (according to a 1934 essay by Toyo Suyemoto in
"Hokubei Asahi").

Through the thirties and forties Japanese-American writers
produced their own literary magazines. Even in the internment
period, Japanese-American literary journals sprang up in the
relocation centers. During this, one of the most trying and
confusing periods of Japanese-American history, their writing
flourished. In the pages of *Trek* and *All Aboard* and the magazines and newspapers of camps around the country, Japanese-
American English was developed and the symbols of the Japanese-American experience codified by writers like Toshio
Mori, Globularius Schraubi, poet Toyo Suyemoto, artist Mine
Okubo, and Asian-America's most accomplished short story
writer, as of this writing, Hisaye Yamamoto. In spite of the
more highly developed literary skills of Japanese-American pub-
lications, much of it commissioned by Japanese-American community organizations, more books by Chinese-Americans have
been published than by Japanese-Americans.

No-No Boy (1957) is the first and, unfortunately, the last novel by John Okada. At the time of his death in 1971, he was planning a new novel on the Issei and their immigration from Japan to America. As it stands, this novel is the first Japanese-American novel in the history of American letters and the second book to be produced by a Seattle Nisei in the fifties (the other was Monica Sone's *Nisei Daughter*). Some scholars of Asian-American literature have said that *No-No Boy* has no literary value, but is worth reading as a fairly accurate representation of the emotional and psychological climate of Japanese-Americans at a certain period in history. Okada is worth reading as a social history, not as literature, these critics say. The distinction between social history and literature is a tricky one, especially when dealing with the literature of an emerging sensibility. The subject matter of minority literature is social history, not necessarily by design but by definition. There is no reference, no standard of measure, no criterion. So, by its own terms, Okada's novel invented Japanese-American fiction full-blown, was self-begotten, arrogantly inventing its own criteria.

The minority writer works in a literary environment of which the white writer has no knowledge or understanding. The white writer can get away with writing for himself, knowing full well he lives in a world run by people like himself. At some point the minority writer is asked for whom he is writing, and in answering that question must decide who he is. In Okada's case, being Japanese or American would seem the only options, but he rejects both and works on defining Nisei in terms of an experience that is neither Japanese nor American. Okada's hero, embodying his vision of the Japanese-American, cannot be defined by the concept of the dual personality that would make a whole from two incompatible parts. The hero of the double and hyphenated "No" is both a restatement of and a rejection of the term "Japanese-American"—"No" to Japanese and "No" to American.

The question of point of view is only partially stylistic in the case of minority writing. It has immediate and dramatic social and moral implications. As social history, the mere gesture of Japanese-American writing is significant. Then the question of control follows, that is, what forces are operating and influencing the writer and how aware of them is he?

Specifically, how does he cope with and reflect prevalent white and nonwhite attitudes of the period? How is he affected by the concept of the dual personality? By Christianity? How does he define the relationship between his own race, the other minorities, and the white race? How seriously committed to writing and his point of view is this writer? And if, as is too often the case, the writer is no writer at all, by his own admission, the question of white publisher and editor manipulation is raised, usually after the answer has become obvious.

So the serious Asian-American writer, like any other minority writer, who works with the imperatives and universals of minority experience and applies them to his work, is treated as a quack, a witch doctor, a bughouse prophet, an entertaining fellow, dancing the heebie-jeebies in the street for dimes. Okada wrote his novel in a period all but devoid of a Japanese-American literary tradition above ground. There were only three predecessors, a book of short stories, Toshio Mori's *Yokohama, California,* an autobiography, *Nisei Daughter,* and the short stories of Hisaye Yamamoto. Okada's novel was an act of immaculate conception, it seemed, producing from nowhere a novel that was by any known criterion of literature so bad that Japanese-American literary critics ignored the book or dumped heavily on it, loaded up again and dumped on it again. *No-No Boy* became an instantly forgotten work, evidenced by the fact that fifteen years after its publication the first edition of 1,500 copies had not sold out.

The critics have forgotten that the vitality of literature stems from its ability to codify and legitimize common experience in the terms of that experience and to celebrate life as it is lived. In reading Okada or any other Asian-American writer, the literary establishment has never considered the fact that a new folk in a strange land would experience the land and develop new language out of old words. Strangely, the critics accept this change in science-fiction stories of new planets in the future. Even the notion that the cultural clash produced by future overdoses of mass media will make new folks and new languages is accepted, as shown by the critical success of Anthony Burgess' *A Clockwork Orange* in the sixties, funny-talking Flash Gordon in the fifties, Buck Rogers and *The Wizard of Oz* in the thirties.

The critics were wrong in calling Toshio Mori's language "bad English," as William Saroyan did in his introduction to Mori's book *Yokohama, California:*

> Of the thousands of unpublished writers in America there are probably no more than three who cannot write better English than Toshio Mori. His stories are full of grammatical errors. His use of English, especially when he is most eager to say something very good, is very bad. Any high school teacher of English would flunk him in grammar and punctuation.

The critics were also wrong in ignoring or being too embarrassed by Okada's use of language and punctuation to deal with his book at all. The assumption that an ethnic minority writer thinks in, believes he writes in, or has ambitions toward writing beautiful, correct, and well-punctuated English sentences is an expression of white supremacy. The universality of the belief that correct English is the only language of American truth has made language an instrument of cultural imperialism. The minority experience does not yield itself to accurate or complete expression in the white man's language. Yet, the minority writer, specifically the Asian-American writer, is made to feel morally obligated to write in a language produced by an alien and hostile sensibility. His task, in terms of language alone, is to legitimize his, and by implication his people's, orientation as white, to codify his experience in the form of prior symbols, clichés, linguistic mannerisms, and a sense of humor that appeals to whites because it celebrates Asian-American self-contempt. Or his task is the opposite—to legitimize the language, style, and syntax of his people's experience, to codify the experiences common to his people into symbols, clichés, linguistic mannerisms, and a sense of humor that emerges from an organic familiarity with the experience.

The tyranny of language continues even in the instruments designed to inject the minority into the mainstream. Virtually every anthology of Third World writing containing Asian-American sections confuses Chinese from China with Chinese-Americans, conveniently ignoring the obvious cultural differences. C. Y. Lee and Lin Yutang, born and raised in China, are secure in their Chinese culture, and unlike Chinese-Americans, are Chinese who have merely adapted to American ways and write about Chinese America as foreigners. Their work inevitably authenticates the concept of the dual personality. However, their being Chinese precludes their ability to communicate the Chinese-American sensibility. The other Chinese-American writers collected in this new splash of anthologies most often include Jade Snow Wong and Pardee Lowe, who also reinforce the stereotype. Lowe's book, *Father and Glorious Descendant,* came out in 1943. The dust jacket revealed the racist function of the book, saying that *Father and Glorious Descendant* "is a timely document at a moment when America must learn how to assimilate its loyal minorities."

The deprivation of language in a verbal society like this country's has contributed to the lack of a recognized Asian-American cultural integrity (at most, native-born Asian-Americans are "Americanized" Chinese or Japanese) and the lack of a recognized style of Asian-American manhood. These two conditions have produced "the house nigger mentality," under which Chinese- and Japanese-Americans accept responsibility for, rather than authority over the language and accept dependency. A state of dependency is encouraged by the teaching of English and the publishing establishment. This state of dependency characterizes the self-consciously grammatical language of Jon Shirota's first two novels, *Lucky Come Hawaii* (1966) and *Pineapple White* (1970). Shirota's communication of his Nisei orientation is handicapped by a language he seems to feel is not his own, unlike Toshio Mori and John Okada, who write strong in a language that comes from home. Mori and Okada demonstrate, as did Claude McKay, Mark Twain, and N. Scott Momaday, that new experience breeds new language.

John Okada writes from an oral tradition he hears all the time, and talks his writing onto the page. To judge Okada's writing by the white criterion of silent reading of the printed word is wrong. Listen as you read Okada or any other Asian-American writer. Okada changes voices and characters inside his sentences, running off free form but shaping all the time. These voice changes grate against the white tradition of tonal uniformity and character consistency, but more accurately duplicate the way people talk: "a bunch of Negroes were horsing around raucously in front of a pool parlor." There is a quick-change act here among "horsing around" and "raucously" and "pool parlor." The style itself is an expression of the multivoiced schizophrenia of the Japanese-American compressed into an organic whole. It's crazy, but it's not madness.

John Okada's work is new only because whites aren't literate in the Japanese-American experience, not because Okada has been up late nights inventing Japanese-American culture in his dark laboratory. And though he presents an ugly vision of America in which Japanese-Americans wander stupified with self-contempt, then overcompensate with despairing wails of superpatriotism, his book cannot honestly be dismissed as an operatic cry of self-pity or a blast of polemic. Yet the book has been ignored, if not by whites, then by Japanese-Americans fearful of being identified with Okada's work. Charles Tuttle, the publisher of *No-No Boy,* writes in a letter, "At the time we published it, the very people whom we thought would be enthusiastic about it, mainly the Japanese-American community in the United States, were not only disinterested but actually rejected the book."

Depression, despair, death, suicide, listless anger, and a general tone of low-key hysteria closed inside the gray of a constantly overcast and drizzling Seattle pervade the book. Definitely not the stuff of a musical. There is at the same time something genuinely uplifting and inspiring about this book—at least for Asian-American readers. The book makes a narrative style of the Japanese-American talk, gives the talk the status of a language, makes it work and styles it, deftly and crudely, and uses it to bring the unglamorous but more commonly lived aspects of Japanese-American experience into the celebration of life. The style and structure of the book alone suggest the Japanese-American way of life of a specific period in history. All in all, there is nothing arcane or mysterious about why this book satisfies and, through all its melodramatic gloom, cheers the blood to running warm. This is new literature, one for which the experience and the people have already been tried and want nothing but the writing and the reading. This isn't an attempt to appeal to old values, translate life into a dead language, or drive whites into paroxysms of limpid guilt, or an effort to destroy the English language.

Ichiro, the *No-No Boy* of the title, is a Nisei who refused to be inducted into the armed forces during the war and chose prison instead. The novel opens with Ichiro's arrival in Seattle, home from two years in prison. He has come home to a mother who is so convinced that Japan has won the war that she refuses to send money or goods from the family store to relatives writing from Japan, begging for help. Ichiro's father is an alcoholic; his younger brother, Taro, drops out of high school to join the army to make up for the shame of Ichiro's being a "no-no boy." Other "no-no boys" fade into easy booze and easy women and out of Ichiro's life. His best friend turns out to be Kenji, a war hero with a medal and without a leg, whose heroism has cost him his leg, and by the end of the book his life. Kenji, the admirable war hero, dying of a progressive creeping crud that repeated amputations of his leg have failed to check, seems to have the divinity of the suffering. He gives Ichiro an understanding woman, an abandoned wife whose husband, rather than coming home, re-enlists and stays in Europe. Kenji makes Ichiro himself a symbol of goodness and strength.

Ichiro has come home to a world in which everything he touches and loves dies, is killed, or goes mad. All offers of life, the love of a woman, a job by an understanding Mr. Carrick, are refused because he is unworthy, because he must somehow prove himself worthy by himself. He has been spat on, rejected by his brother, lost his good and his bad friends and his parents. Ichiro seems to be a pathological loser. What he does is wrong, and what he doesn't do is wrong. He is full of self-contempt, self-pity, and yet is governed by an innate sense of dignity, if not a coherent sense of humor. He is not Stephen Dedalus out to "forge the unformed conscience of his race in the smithy of his soul," but he is searching for something more than his identity. It is the nature of the language itself, this embryonic Japanese-American English language that can only define the Japanese-American who is neither Japanese nor American, in anything but negative terms, that makes every attempt at positive expression an exercise in futility and despair. "Think more deeply and your doubts will disappear," Ichiro's mother says. "You are my son," she says, triggering a spinning, running internal monologue and one of the most powerfully moving passages in the book:

> No, he said to himself as he watched her part the curtains and start into the store. There was a time when I was your son. There was a time that I no longer remember when you used to smile a mother's smile and tell me stories about gallant and fierce warriors who protected their lords with blades of shining steel and about the old woman who found a peach in the stream and took it home, and, when her husband split it in half, a husky little boy tumbled out to fill their hearts with boundless joy. I was that lad in the peach and you were the old woman and we were Japanese with Japanese feelings and Japanese pride and Japanese thoughts because it was all right then to be Japanese and feel and think all the things that Japanese do even if we lived in America. Then there came a time when I was only half Japanese because one is not born in America and raised in America and taught in America and one does not speak and swear and drink and smoke and play and fight and see and hear in America among Americans in American streets and houses without becoming American and loving it. But I did not love enough for you were still half my mother and I was thereby still half Japanese and when the war came and they told me to fight for America, I was not strong enough to fight you and I was not strong enough to fight the bitterness which made the half of me which was bigger than the half of me which was America and really the whole of me that I could not see or feel. Now that I know the truth when it is late and the half of me and the half that remains is enough to know why it was that I could not fight for America and did not strip me of my birthright. But it is not enough to be only half an American and know that it is an empty half. I am not your son and I am not Japanese and I am not American. I can go someplace and tell people that I've got an inverted stomach and that I am an American, true and blue and Hail Columbia, but the army wouldn't have me because of the stomach. That's easy and I would do it, only I've got to convince myself first and that I cannot do. I wish with all my heart that I were Japanese or that I

were American. I am neither and I blame you and I blame myself and I blame the world which is made up of many countries
which fight with each other and kill and hate and destroy again
and again and again. It is so easy and simple that I cannot
understand it at all. And the reason I do not understand it is
because I do not understand you who were the half of me that
is no more and because I do not understand what it was about
the half of me which was American and the half which might
have become the whole of me if I had said yes I will go and
fight in your army because that is what I believe and want and
cherish and love.

This passage is central to the book in suggesting the wholeness
that Ichiro contains and is searching for. His whole life is contained in the paragraph, beginning with childhood and Japan
in the form of his family moving from the first "no" through
the samurai defending their lords to Ichiro refusing to defend
America and ending on a hypothetical positive chord ringing
with "yes" and "cherish and love."

A sign of Ichiro's strength, and his sense of despair, and the
truth of his being neither Japanese nor American is the fluid
movement into the sick joke about the inverted stomach that
simultaneously recalls the stereotype of Japanese being slant-
eyed, sideways, doing things backwards, and draft-dodger humor. His being not Japanese is subtly underscored by his avoid-
ance of Japanese terms: "gallant and fierce warriors" instead of
"samurai."

Okada's *No-No Boy* is an exploration of the universe of racial
self-contempt. At one point, through Ichiro, Okada suggests
that self-contempt based on your physical and cultural difference from other more favored races produces a contempt for
all who are like you:

> . . . I got to thinking that the Japs were wising up, that they
> had learned that living in big bunches and talking Jap and
> feeling Jap and doing Jap was just inviting trouble, but my
> dad came back . . . I hear there's almost as many in Seattle
> now as there were before the war. It's a shame, a dirty rotten
> shame. Pretty soon it'll be just like it was before the war. A
> bunch of Japs with a fence around them, not the kind you can
> see, but it'll hurt them just as much. They bitched and hol-

lered when the government put them in camps and put real
fences around them, but now they're doing the same damn
thing to themselves. They screamed because the government
said they were Japs and when they finally got out, they couldn't
wait to rush together and prove that they were.

The literature of Japanese America flourished through the
thirties, into the war years and the camp experience. These
were years of tremendous literary and journalistic output. The
question of Japanese-American identity, the conflicts between
Issei and Nisei, yellow and white relations, black, white, and
yellow relations, and the war were all examined and re-ex-
amined in camp newspapers, literary magazines, diaries, and
journals. The result of the camp experience was a literate Japanese America that had encompassed broad areas of American
experience. Highly skilled writers came from camps, like Bill
Hosokawa and Larry Tajiri who became editors of the Denver
Post, and fiction writers and poets like Iwao Kawakami, Hiroshi Kashiwagi, Paul Itaya, Jack Matsuye, Toshio Mori, Toyo
Suyemoto, and Hisaye Yamamoto. The journalists got recognition, but the writers of fiction and poetry, all native to their
brand of English, with rare exceptions remain confined to the
pages of the Japanese-American Citizens League paper, the
Pacific Citizen. To preserve the illusion of our absence, many
Asian-American writers have been asked to write under white
pseudonyms. C. Y. Lee was told a white pseudonym would en-
hance his chances for publication. To his credit, he kept his
name.

The first novel published about the camp experience was
predictably written by a white, non-Japanese woman, Karen
Kehoe. The appearance of *City in the Sun* in 1947 led the
Pacific Citizen to wonder why a Japanese-American had not
written a work of fiction or nonfiction about the camp experience. The editors then went on to speculate that perhaps the
experience had been too traumatic. The truth is that the camp
experience stimulated rather than depressed artistic output.
The Japanese-Americans did write of the camp experience, but
were not published outside the confines.

Blacks and Chicanos often write in unconventional English.
Their particular vernacular is recognized as being their own

legitimate mother tongue. Only Asian-Americans are driven out of their tongues and expected to be at home in a language they never use and a culture they encounter only in books written in English. This piracy of our native tongues by white culture amounts to the eradication of a recognizable Asian-American culture here. It is ridiculous that a non-Japanese woman should be the one and only novelist of the Japanese-American camp experience. And it is a lie.

As in the work of John Okada, there is nothing quaint about Lawson Inada's poetry, no phony continuity between sign-inspiring Oriental art and his tough, sometimes vicious language. No one, not even William Saroyan trying hard, can make Inada out to be quaint or treat his work as a high-school English paper. "Inada's poem is lean, hard, muscular, and yet for all that it has gentility, humor and love," Saroyan says on the jacket of Inada's first book, *Before the War*. Inada is a monster poet from the multiracial ghetto of West Fresno, California, where he ran with blacks, grew up speaking their language, playing their music. But his voice is his own, a Japanese-American, Sansei voice afraid of nothing. It is as distinct from the blacks now as country-western is from soul.

In an anthology of Fresno poets, *Down at the Santa Fe Depot*, Inada wrote of hatreds and fears no Asian-American ever wrote of before. Inada is tough enough to write about self-contempt. He took the names white folks called Chinese and Japanese and used them to violate the holy word of the English language. The result is not death but magic and a new American truth:

CHINKS

Ching Chong Chinaman
   sitting on a fence
trying to make a dollar
chop-chop all day.

"Eju-kei-shung! Eju-kei-shung!"
that's what they say.

When the War came
they said, "We Chinese!"

When we went away,

> they made sukiyaki,
> saying, "Yellow all same."
>
> When the war closed,
> they stoned the Jap's homes.
>
> Grandma would say:
> "Marry a Mexican,
> a Nigger, just don't
> marry no Chinese."

The Chinese were contemptible for being actively "not Japanese." In *No-No Boy*, Kenji tells Ichiro, essentially, to be not Japanese. "Go someplace where there isn't another Jap within a thousand miles. Marry a white girl or a Negro or an Italian or even a Chinese. Anything but a Japanese. After a few generations of that, you've got the thing beat."

Inada echoes *No-No Boy*. The similarity is and is not accidental. Inada is bound to Okada by a common sensibility and not by any real knowledge of his predecessor. Inada did not learn of the existence of Okada's work until ten years after he had written "West Side Songs." Both articulated the belief common among Japanese-Americans that one remedy for being a contemptible, self-hating Japanese-American is to leave that society, associate oneself with whiteness of some kind and rise in the world.

As in "Chinks," "Japs" ends with the formal name of the race, and it, not Chinks or Japs, is the dirty word.

JAPS

> are great imitators
> they stole
> the Greek's
> skewers,
> used them
> on themselves.
> Their sutras
> are Face
> and Hide.
> They hate
> everyone else
> on the sly.

They play
Dr. Charley's
games—bowling,
raking,
growing forks
on lapels.
Their tongues
are yellow
with "r's"
with "l's."
They hate
themselves
on the sly. I
used to be
Japanese.

Inada confronts his own experience. Everything in his life is in his deceptively simple and humorous poems that have the feel of having been written in the guts of a juke box. He tears himself apart exposing all the symbols of Asian assimilation—education, the preservation of Oriental culture—as acts of desperation, terrific efforts to buy a little place in the country. It is the fear of America that causes this, not assimilation.

A constant theme in Asian-American literature, from Pardee Lowe's *Father and Glorious Descendant* through *No-No Boy* to Frank Chin's play *The Chickencoop Chinaman* (1972), is the failure of Asian-American manhood to express itself in its simplest form: fathers and sons.

"There is nothing good about being a son," says the unnamed narrator in Wallace Lin's "Rough Notes For Mantos." "I know; I am a son. When you have to admit that you have a father, allowing people to think that you are a father and son, as if any relation existed between those two terms, when there is really nothing to say."

What exists in these works is that mutual self-contempt. In Pardee Lowe's *Father and Glorious Descendant*, Father names his "Glorious Descendant" after Governor Pardee of California not to inspire his son with an American identity but to offer his son up as a sacrifice to white supremacy. Inspired by his American name, young Pardee has childhood visions of becoming the first Chinese-American President of the United States. The true meaning of his name comes home when his father tells him to forget his dream, not only because it is impossible, but because it is, by implication, immoral. The book seems to celebrate a healthy relationship between father and son. Set in the context of Asian-American literature and history, this relationship is thinly disguised mutual contempt. In *No-No Boy,* the most sympathetic emotion Ichiro can muster for his father is pity. The dominant emotion is contempt. The perpetuation of self-contempt between father and son is an underlying current in virtually every Asian-American work. "Chinamans do make lousey fathers. I know. I have one," says Tam Lum, the main character of *The Chickencoop Chinaman.* He suggests that he is "a lousey father" himself when he says, "I want my kids to forget me." As the comic embodiment of Asian-American man-hood, rooted in neither Asia nor white America, Tam is forced to invent a past, mythology, and traditions from the antiques and curios of his immediate experience. In an effort to link himself with the first known Chinese-Americans, he states, "Chi-namen are made, not born, my dear. Out of junk-imports, lies, railroad scrap iron, dirty jokes, broken bottles, cigar smoke, Cosquilla Indian blood, wino spit, and lots of milk of amnesia."

In white writing there is a tradition of communication break-ing down between father and son. The son rebels against the accepted past, strikes out for the future to dare the unknown. In *The Chickencoop Chinaman* the past is the unknown. Tam breaks with the past by trying to find it, define it, and identify with it. At the end of the play he links himself with the rail-road, Chinese restaurants, and the future:

> Now and then, I feel them old days, children, the way I feel the prowl of the dogs in the night and the bugs in the leaves and the thunder in the Sierra Nevadas however far they are. The way my grandmother had an ear for trains. Listen, children. I gotta go. Ride Buck Buck Bagaw with me . . . Listen in the kitchen for the Chickencoop Chinaman slowin on home.

Chin, if not Tam Lum, is saying that an Asian-American sensi-bility is not a recent invention.

Language is the medium of culture and the people's sensibility, including the style of manhood. Language coheres the people into a community by organizing and codifying the symbols of the people's common experience. Stunt the tongue and you have lopped off the culture and sensibility. On the simplest level, a man in any culture speaks for himself. Without a language of his own, he no longer is a man. The concept of the dual personality deprives the Chinese-American and Japanese-American of the means to develop their own terms. The tyranny of language has been used by white culture to suppress Asian-American culture and exclude it from operating in the mainstream of American consciousness. The first Asian-American writers worked alone within a sense of rejection and isolation to the extent that it encouraged Asian America to reject its own literature. John Okada and Louis Chu died in obscurity, and Toshio Mori lives in obscurity. In the past, being an Asian-American writer meant that you did not associate with other Asian-American writers. Emulating the whites, we ignored ourselves. Now we seek each other out.

Recently in San Francisco twenty Asian-American writers, representing three generations of writers, gathered together for the first time as Asian-American writers. Attending were Kai-yu Hsu, editor of the first Asian-American anthology of writing, Toshio Mori, one of the first Asian-Americans to publish a book-length creative work, Lawson Inada, the first Asian-American to publish a book of poetry, Frank Chin, author of the first Asian-American play produced in the history of the American legitimate theater, Victor and Brett Nee, authors of the first Chinese-American history from the Chinese-American point of view, and young Asian-American writers, many of whom are included in this book and who represent the first generation of Asian-Americans to be aware of writing within an Asian-American tradition. We know each other now. It should never have been otherwise.

Frank Chin
Jeffery Chan
Lawson Inada
Shawn Wong

An Introduction
to Filipino-American
Literature

WE WILL MAKE the strongest case for the urgency and necessity
of the following works, a case that no other Asian-American can
have: that is, the total absence of published Filipino-American
writers in the United States today. We were asked to write a
literary background of Filipino-American works, to make sure
that the publishers would say, "Yes, let's help them, it's unjust,
they need to be exposed." Here is our stand. We cannot write
any literary background because there isn't any. No history. No
published literature. No nothing. Just "Flips" all over the
place. The only published writing we can speak of that is
worthy of note are those writings of Filipinos in the Philippines
about the Philippines.

About five authors left the Philippines (already mature men
whose psychology and sensibilities were Filipino) and wrote
about Filipinos in America. Two such men were Santos and
Bulosan. No Filipino-American ("Flip"-born and/or raised in
America) has ever published anything about the Filipino-
American experience or any aspects of it. That is about two
generations of an ethnic group wiped out; simply literary geno-
cide. In those "lost generations," there are good, maybe great
writers. We think that Filipinos in America can no longer
afford to ignore these potentially great writers. They have a lot

to say that has never been heard before, and in the end America will be the inevitable loser, not them.

One frightening thing about Philippine literature today is not so much that it is rarely read but that when it is read, it is read out of context. Readers come prepared with a vision; they come prepared to read something in English or American. Thus they approach the literature with the cultural expectations that they have acquired from years of familiarity with Longfellow and Tennyson, Eliot and Lawrence, Faulkner and Hemingway. When the reader comes to Philippine literature in English, he recognizes the English words for English words. But the reader's *sensibility* is all wrong—it does not yield something comfortably recognizable, so he complains that Philippine literature will never make it.

In the past hundred years the Filipinos had four traumatic literary experiences. Three countries misunderstood and underestimated the Filipinos artistically and spiritually as a race and a people. The first came on the eve of the Philippine revolution against Spain. Propaganda and protest were being tried desperately by the leaders of the people in order to bring about drastic reforms. Out of this turmoil emerged a genius, José Rizal, who, when he wrote propaganda, could not quite wrench the art from it. Two novels from him are worth mentioning, *Noli me Tangere* (*Do Not Touch Me,* 1886) and *El Filibusterismo* (*The Subversive,* 1891), both written with a Victorian point of view. These two works, despite the author's vehement objections against an armed rebellion, were, ironically enough, the only sparks strong enough to touch off the long-time-coming cry of *Pugad Lauin.* There was a third spark, an even stronger one —that of Rizal's execution. Much loved by the masses and the *illustrados,* he was shot by an all-Filipino firing squad framed in the gunsights of an all-Spanish firing squad (should any of the Filipinos fail to fire) on Sunday morning, December 13, 1896. Two years later, however, the Spanish government was driven off the land forever.

Then it became America's turn to interfere with the Filipinos. The Filipinos found a new ally in the United States because of the Spanish-American War, which began in Cuba. Emilio Aguinaldo ("The Man"), the leader of the revolution against Spain in the Philippines, readily embraced this opportunity to crush the Spanish ruling system for good and to befriend a model nation, powerful and moral, the likes of which neither Aguinaldo nor any other Filipino leader had ever seen before.

But it was too good to be true. The first incident that aroused "The Man's" mind (already made overcautious by the innumerable treacheries in the history of his ever-vanquished people) was that the Americans would not allow the Filipinos, who had struggled so long, to march in the streets of Manila to taste victory—their victory. Furthermore, the Americans under Arthur MacArthur, Elwell Otis, and Frederick Funston told the Filipinos to disperse their troops to the outskirts of Manila until they were sent for. And Aguinaldo's emissaries were not permitted to be present at the Treaty of Paris when the spoils were being divided by the victors.

The spoils, of course, were the Philippines; and the victors, of course, were the Americans. Being divided meant buying or paying off Spain for $20,000,000. Aguinaldo rapidly changed tactics and constructed another revolutionary government deep in the hills with a new enemy in pursuit—this time the Americans. Bitterly disappointed, heartbroken, and mentally tortured by the conflict between pride and survival of a suffering, dying, and embattled people, Emilio Aguinaldo turned away from the horrors of bloodshed and surrendered to the Americans in 1901. He would not have completed peace until sixty-three years later, when he died of natural causes in his home in Cavite at the age of ninety-five.

Less than three weeks after Manila's capitulation to the American forces, the U.S. military government was set up and seven city schools were reopened. The work in these schools was mainly a continuation of the Spanish system, with English as the only additional subject. General MacArthur considered the establishment of schools the best tool toward the complete pacification of the Philippines. He had no idea of the true weight his statement would carry. Schools not only succeeded in pacifying the Filipinos, but English became the greatest agent in westernizing and modernizing the Philippines.

In April, 1900, English became the official language of instruction in public schools. The early teachers were taken directly from the army. To augment the small number of American teachers, the Philippine Normal School was founded in 1901. Shortly afterward, on July 1, 1901, six hundred American teachers, deaf to Mark Twain's prophecy that imperialism curses the colony as well as the colonizer, sailed from San Francisco on the transport ship *Thomas* with two thousand tons of leftover American and British books. The six hundred were the advance guard of a strong civilian army that was to follow in yearly waves of varying numbers until 1933.

These teachers introduced to the Filipinos many American writers and thinkers—Franklin, Washington, Jefferson, Irving, Bryant, Poe, Hawthorne, Emerson, Thoreau, Longfellow, and Holmes. A lot of other white writers still quicken the heart of and direct the minds of the Filipinos.

A new language is not merely new letters that form new words. It brings with it a brand-new and surprisingly fresh way of looking at things around you, a new childhood, a rebirth whether you like it or not, a new pair of eyes.

In 1908 the University of the Philippines was founded and became the center of literary effort. The *U.P. Folio* was begun in 1910 by liberal Dean D. S. Fansler and Harriott Ely Fansler. According to Leopoldo Y. Yabes in his essay "Filipino Literature in English" (*Herald Midweek Magazine,* May 15, 1940), they were the moving spirits behind "the first responsible and scholarly literary organ of the Filipino writers in English to appear in the Philippines. They inspired [their students] to look at their own people with pride, with unprejudiced eyes, to study their native customs, to applaud their own folk wisdom unashamed, to collect and record basic materials as a store for future historians, anthropologists, and writers. They cautioned them not to ape indiscriminately the English and American writers that they were studying and counselled them to write of their people truthfully and sincerely."

A careful examination of the creative effort of the Filipino writers during this period (1898–1925) shows a lack of artistic discipline and a tendency to wordiness and painful sentimentality. Writers were also too blindly imitative of American and English writers. In 1926, however, a highly original and honest poet and short-story writer, José Garcia Villa, came into the foreground and started his controversial and influential yearly rolls of literary honors, from the Philippines to the United States to Great Britain and Europe.

Filipino writers became conscious of their new freedom. They went deep into literature to seek other freedoms. They experimented with many literary forms, subjects, techniques, and moods. They revolted against literary conventions. Villa, the leader of the new movement, sounded the call to arms when he published his unconventional poem "Man Songs" (*Herald Midweek Magazine,* 1929). For doing this, he was expelled from the University of the Philippines in 1929. In that same year he won the $1,000 *Free Press* Award for the best short story of the year. With this money he left for the United States, where he has since roamed in self-exile. Scribner and Sons published his *Footnote to Youth: Tales of the Philippines and Others* in 1933. Edward O'Brian published one of his stories in *The Best Short Stories of 1932* and dedicated the volume to Villa.

Two periodicals, both owned by foreigners, were the first to give money to Filipino writers. *The Free Press* was the first local publication for short stories and the *Philippine Magazine* was the first for poems. It is strange that in our own country foreigners have shown more interest in our literary development than have our own people or government.

Then, the Japanese invaded the Philippines in 1941 and once again the psyche of the Filipino people was disrupted. War, hate, poverty, and corruption permeated the land. A sense of bitterness, sarcasm, and irony prevailed throughout the literature of that period and exists even now. Most representative of the literature of that era was Stevan Javellana's *Without Seeing the Dawn* (1947). After the war years, the contemporary writers of fiction emerged.

There is, however, a category of Filipino writers that we deliberately by-passed. This category will be dealt with in the second section of this introduction. We are speaking, of course, of the writers who went abroad (primarily to the United States) —why they left home, what they did abroad, what they saw and wrote there, why some stayed, why some went home, why some keep going back and forth. We will speak of a vital part of Filipino literature, that being written today by Filipino-Americans, the children of a dream, the fruits of illusion vs. reality in this land of milk and honey.

The average American, if he thinks of the Filipino at all, is likely to picture him as someone rescued in 1898 from deprivation and perhaps from depravities both indigenous and induced, and nourished sacrificially ever since, until he has become indistinguishable from the creditor whose goods he imports so lavishly. In self-defense and under the influence of postwar partisan nationalism, a Filipino may be compelled to assert so vehemently that he is not American that, at times, he may be considered anti-American. Yet, he is gradually forced to realize that although he may properly reject histories written for him by others, he cannot escape history itself. He cannot refrain from choosing among actualities which of his many inherited tracks of experience he will follow.

From his literature emerges a constant, if often unself-conscious, image of the Filipino as a stranger in his own country and an alien to much of his past. This recurring image compels an urgency to account for what he is rather than for what he is not. The increasingly clear impulse among Filipino writers is to struggle toward a national self-knowledge that is positive without being false and that, through its art, is particularized and harmonized enough to avoid being fantasy or formula (Leonard Casper's paraphrase of Carlos P. Romulo's *Identity and Change,* 1965).

Considered to be the first Filipino novel in English, *A Child of Sorrow* by Zoilo M. Galang was published in 1921 (contained in the *Encyclopedia of the Philippines* XX, pp. 1–108). It contains these lines:

> It was April in the Fertile Valley, the month when the sampaguitas began to open its petals to receive the soothing dew of the starry evening hour, when the rose, lovely and tender, gave its best and lured countless butterflies; when the *dama de noche* fragrantly suffused the atmosphere at the magic touch of the night which gave it vitality.

The Peninsulars by Linda Ty Casper, a novel published in 1965, begins like this:

In the early morning sun, the Mexican creoles standing guard on the forty-foot limestone walls appeared like bleached shadows above the weather-splintered drawbridges, through bastion towers, past bronzed and iron cannons named after a company of saints, they walked sleepily twenty feet above the sea and the river. Black coarse sand held down the stricken reflections of the July sun. Upon the moat scum multiplied like a centipede. The most loyal and royal city, the very noble city of Manila stood in the accumulated silence of the 1750's.

Forty-three years separated *A Child of Sorrow* from *The Peninsulars.* However, the lines quoted seem to indicate that much more than mere calendar years actually set apart these first and latest Filipino novels in English. The adjective-studded lines are still there, but the flowers and butterflies and starry April evening have given way to "bleached shadows" and "stricken reflections of the July sun."

Nearly forty years after the publication of Galang's *A Child of Sorrow,* a love story by Emigdio Enrique Alvarez was published by Hill and Wang of New York. The novel, entitled *The Desert Flower,* has for its principle character another child of sorrow named Ercelia who, unlike Rosa, the original child of sorrow, suffered more ills of the mind and the spirit. Unlike Rosa, who kept wearing the Filipino dress to the end—or so it must be assumed—Ercelia at twenty-one changed from the Philippine dress to the Western *vestido,* a symbolic change indeed of the Eastern and Western influences on the Filipino character. *The Desert Flower* did not enjoy relative popularity. Its audience was American, and in the 1950's it had no shock value at all compared to the erotic novels of the time.

The author's emphasis on the male anatomy is matched in a Freudian degree by St. Elena's celebration of the female parts. Beside these two novelists, Galang is a pimply adolescent pining at the moon, wondering whether his beloved was at that hour doing the same. *The Desert Flower* suffered from one other flaw that seems to be characteristic of novels intended for an American audience. The author stops in the middle of the narrative to explain things essentially Philippine, such as the *mestiza* dress and what a *juramentado* is, and *carromatas* and our beliefs in witches, the *waling waling,* the *cala churchis,* the *balintawak,* and the *rigodan de honor.* There is a detailed explanation of the *gayuna* and weddings and fiestas.

Like A Big Brave Man, a novel by Celso Carunungan, is also an "explaining novel." Published in New York in 1960, it is flawed by an abundance of explanations in the narration. As early as page 2, the author explains that people in the Philippines use coconut husks for polishing their wooden floors. When he is not explaining, he is showing off something genuinely Philippine as though it were an article on exhibit at a World's Fair. In one or two ways, reading Carunungan's novel brings Carlos Bulosan to mind, particularly in Bulosan's caricatures of the Filipinos, his innocents abroad, lost in the big cities of America and wondering why there is no place to urinate during cold wintry days. But Bulosan's characters at their funniest compel a sort of compassion for their plight and are somehow touched with disaster. There is one other point of comparison between *Like A Big Brave Man* and Bulosan's *America is in the Heart.* Directly and indirectly each sings the praises of America and the American. Each has the common refrain "America Hallelujah!" Carlos P. Romulo, who has also written a novel, *The United,* used this theme in his speeches during the war and in his earlier works. A striking resemblance exists in some books published abroad and written by Filipinos.

There is the love element, though not necessarily present as a theme, in practically every Filipino novel in English. It is present in N. V. M. Gonzalez's *The Winds of April* and *A Season of Grace* (1956). The love in *The Bamboo Dancers* is more sophisticated, but not, unfortunately, more successfully told than in Gonzalez' earlier novels.

The country's history as a background for novels has a scope that some novelists mistake for grandeur. Some optimistically hope it may be epic. It seems inevitable that the Filipino novel should touch on the country's history, its past, its present, and perhaps its future. Sometimes the result makes for fascinating history, but at other times it is merely dull fiction. Fortunately, there are Filipino novelists who have been more concerned with the country of the heart, setting their stories against the changing times and the nature of man.

There was a news item in the papers some time ago about a number of Filipinos in America who have lived there for many years and who have since become American citizens. Now they want to return to the Philippines and are encountering difficulties because they are no longer Filipinos in the legal sense. Most of them have families and grown-up children who have never seen the country of their fathers. This little news item, lost among the seemingly bigger news of the day, is mentioned because it seems pertinent to the condition of all those exiled "Flips," and it looms heavily on their children, that is, today's Filipino-Americans. There are aspects in our lives as a people, in the States or in the Philippines—such as the continuing flight and return of men and women who break their roots from the native soil—that make up the form and substance of Filipino literature. Somehow, after more than half a century, the movement comes full circle.

Juan C. Laya's prize-winning novel in the 1940 Philippine Commonwealth Literary Contest, *His Native Soil,* opens with Martin, a "Flip" old-timer in the States, returning to the Philippines after many years of absence. He stands on the deck of the ship and watches the shore away from which he has lived for so long. He has money and hopes. After a series of frustrations in the Philippines, he loses both. He realizes that he has stayed away too long; he is as much a stranger in his homeland as he is in the States. He decides that being a stranger in a foreign land is more bearable. The novel ends with Martin on board a ship bound for America. He stands on the deck and watches the shoreline of his native country grow dimmer.

If the main character in a Filipino novel leaves his native country, he always seems to return, except in Bulosan's stories, in which the Filipino character finds life in America a challenge and, in spite of prejudice and violence, washes away his bitterness with a lyrical apostrophe to the real America, which is in the heart.

Says Ben Santos, a foremost Filipino writer in English: "The future of Filipino literature, I am convinced, is in the hands of those who would be bold enough and capable enough to strike new paths away from the roads that have already been long taken, who constantly live, even if in imagination, only with true tragedy, who would dedicate their life exclusively to the writing of it. In this sense, the future of the novel by Filipinos (at home and in the States) belongs to all those who write in English, both the old and the new, the young who have the power of words and the daring of those who have nothing to lose except time of which they have plenty."

Surely, we cannot exclude this burden, this duty, from those "Flips" here in the United States. This is indeed the child of sorrow who has grown up since the twenties into a woman capable of keeping her grief to herself or finding ways and means out in the latest psychology and science. The peasants from the clearings and the coconut lands have gone up in the world and traveled by various means. Those who have turned rebels grieve over their wounds if they have not yet met their ends through violence, wars, or unsettled times. The men with the roving eyes and hands are guilt-ridden and punish themselves with continuing exile far away from their native soil and now drink in private and join communal piety.

In 1973, the Filipino still asks, What is love? What is liberty? Who am I? What am I doing here? He asked the same questions in 1921, only now he blushes with the answer he is often forced to give.

Today's Filipino-American writer, unlike earlier Filipino writers in America, is faced with the problem of distinguishing his Filipino uniqueness from his Americanization. It is a harder problem than that faced by his predecessors, because his uniqueness is not in being a Filipino writer but in being a Filipino-American writer.

Two published postwar Filipino writers, Bienvenido V. Santos (b. 1911) and Carlos Bulosan (1914–1956) wrote books concerning the life of the Filipino in America. Bulosan's autobiography, *America is in the Heart* (1946), deals with his struggles in the city and labor camps of America at a time when Filipinos were being put down by Americans as being nothing more than menial servants and laborers. It is the story of every Filipino who went to America expecting the pot of gold and discovered a pile of dung instead. Santos' book, a series of short stories forming a novel entitled *You Lovely People,* also relates Filipino life in America. As Father Miguel

Bernad says in *Pathways to Philippine Literature in English:* "*You Lovely People* is almost a total picture of Filipino life in America, of dislocation, of emotional and cultural starvation compensated for by reckless poker games or visits to unwholesome night clubs or going about with women of dubious character."

Filipino-American writing since Bulosan and Santos has been confined mostly to poetry. No major publisher has published an exclusively Filipino-American work. A few isolated works have been published or are being published in Asian-American and other ethnic anthologies or newspapers. The Filipino-American writer's slow emergence in the American literary scene has been stifled mainly by the fact that it is only now that the Filipino writer is beginning to recognize his Filipino-American experience.

Being born or reared in America is like being put into a kettle with other ethnic groups, simmered by years of racism, identity crises, and subsequent ethnic rejection, and then coming out with a blend of the many influences from that environment. Thus, we have Filipinos who are more versed in other ethnic cultures and who talk, act, and actually believe themselves to be white.

One of the problems the Filipino-American writer faces is in maintaining ethnic awareness amid the bombardment of other influences. Sam Tagatac, a Filipino writer and film-maker, tells of his early writing experience: "I would complete a short story and discover that the character was either Mexican or Spanish, almost any other ethnic group but Filipino. There was just nothing Filipino to identify with at that time, I thought then."

Other Filipino-American writers experience this same ethnic neglect. There are exceptions, however, and more often than not age is the major factor. "I lived half my life in the Philippines, came here when I was twelve and feel more Filipino than American," comments Oscar Peñaranda, writer and teacher of Philippine literature at San Francisco State.

Santos and Bulosan, being born and spending most of their childhood in the Philippines, have Filipino-oriented minds. The Filipino born and reared in America writes from an American perspective. The age at which a person comes to America is a crucial factor in determining what type of writing he does. Although a few of the Filipino writers in San Francisco still speak fluent Philipino, their heads are American. Like Sam Tagatac, who used Chicano characters in his stories, many of today's Filipino-American writers are becoming aware of an ethnic surge developing in Asian-American writing. They can't help but be affected by it.

Being brown in a white society holds traumas that are reflected by the fact that many Filipino-Americans lose their taste in *adobo,* their tongues tangled in Filipino. Many Filipino-American writers have been so assimilated into the American way that there are little, if any, ties left with their being Filipino, except maybe in the recognition of a few Filipino words.

Unlike Santos and Bulosan, who wrote about the American experience through Philippine heads, today's Filipino-American writer is an American grasping to trace his nebulous heritage. One outlook on this is expressed by Bayani Mariano, a Filipino-American writer by way of Mindanao, Philippines, and San Francisco, California:

> The artist asks of the audience that he be considered not apart from his work, but as a totality in relation to it. The motivation to create something artistically is dependent upon one's own personality and all the necessary experiences that impinge or that have impinged upon it. A realization effects a change in one's outlook. And to realize one's own identity in terms of commonality, a specific commonality, is to realize the tension present between cultures and subcultures. Art then not only becomes a means of communication, but is also a means in effecting a change upon the situations that exist in the society and between societies.

In the realization of one's own identity, most Filipino-American writers go through an early stage of rhetorical "brown is beautiful," angry poetry that releases a flood of proud statements concerning ethnocentrism suppressed by years of miseducation and whitewashing. As the Filipino-American poet goes through this cathartic stage of ethnic consciousness, he becomes more aware of Philippine literature and its lack of "soul." According to the noted Filipino novelist, N. V. M. Gonzalez, currently teaching at California State College at Hayward, the Filipino "body" is traveling much too fast for its "soul":

> The artist in our society is our soul and we (the non-artists) are the body (or travelers). The main problem in Philippine art today is that the two have yet to get together because the Philippine nation rejects or denies the influences of such inherent contributors as the Chinese and the Igorots but instead gives priority to the European and American influences in Philippine culture.
>
> We cannot accept that our culture is mainly borrowed from regional cultures to begin with.

The Filipino-American writer is faced with a similar dilemma. He must accept the fact that his uniqueness is that he has a different "soul" from his brother writers in the Philippines. He must accept the fact that the inherent contributors to *his* literature can range from the Last Poets to Rod McKuen; from the civil-rights issue in America to his own local community problems.

"We must establish an integrity with the material that we have before we can begin to solve our cultural problems. Let the body do its thing, but leave the soul alone." Gonzalez' comments on the state of Philippine art reflect certain aspects similarly faced by today's Filipino-American writer. Before he can develop his ethnic writing, he must be aware of the past experiences of Filipinos living in America. What kind of poetic response can he give then when he reads:

> . . . the prejudice against them [Filipinos] may be measured by the statement by a San Francisco judge that they are "scarcely more than savages" and the denunciation of an official of the Los Angeles Chamber of Commerce that they are "the most worthless, unscrupulous, shiftless, diseased semi-barbarians that ever came to our shores." [Carey McWilliams, *Brothers Under the Skin,* p. 238]

Carey McWilliams' book has a chapter devoted to the Filipino experience in American history entitled "Little Brown

Brother," giving a background of how the first Filipinos brought to America were done so for the purpose of cheap labor.

"Where is the heart of America?" asks Manuel Buaken. "I am one of many thousands of young men born under the American flag, raised as loyal, idealistic Americans under your promises of equality for all, and enticed by glowing tales of educational opportunities. Once here we are met by exploiters, shunted into slums, greeted only by gamblers and prostitutes, winged promises of liberty, equality, fraternity. What has become of them?" (*New Republic*, September 30, 1940, from *Brothers Under the Skin*, p. 248).

Today, "where is the heart of America?" is just as good a question to the Filipino in the Philippines as it is to the Filipino-American.

After such re-education, the angry response becomes more understandable. The following is a poem by Sam Tagatac and is a particular response:

STARFIGHTER

I see your riding
the yellow sun out here
in the Asian copra

because you've brought rocks
from the moon
told how green
blue the earth's seas
how Vietnam
and Southeast Asia fell
under a cloud

out of sight
a okay you say
you've knocked hell
in five blows
a golf ball through the universe
with a folded six iron

i know better
i know better i
see the horses of
your plains
no more

The Filipino-American poets see America through the proxy eyes of lonely old men living in drab hotel rooms. There is emerging a recognition of the lonely bravery endured by first-generation Pinoys. There is that growing awareness that writing about the Chicano or the Chinese experience should be left to writers in those respective groups. Only a Filipino-American can write adequately about the Filipino-American experience.

Unlike the Chinese- and Japanese-Americans, whose cultural presence in America is visible both economically and geographically, the Filipino-American community is less visible. "To be a Filipino in California is to belong to a blood brotherhood, a free masonry of the ostracized. Since most Filipinos, in Hawaii and the mainland, have married out of the group, the minority seems destined to disappear or vanish into larger minority clusters. Here, again, the lack of an integrated native culture facilitates the adoption of the ways and customs of other groups." (*Brothers Under the Skin*, p. 141)

"The linguistic homogeneity that had been incorporated in the Spanish language," writes Carlos Bulosan, "was uprooted by the English language and the weaker dialects of the people succumbed one after the other without any favorable effects upon either invading or invaded culture."

Although geographically and racially he is Oriental, the Filipino is so influenced by Western ways that many adopt and imitate anything American. The Filipino-American, aware of the contradictions in American society, is thus confused and dismayed when he visits the Philippines and finds brown faces with white minds. It is easier to judge someone who is looking at you from a distorted mirror. The Filipino-American writer is seeing and writing about the myth of the American dream, while the Filipino is drawn by the dream that is perpetuated by the heavy American influences in his country.

Oscar Peñaranda
Serafin Syquia
Sam Tagatac

ASIAN-AMERICAN
WRITERS

We Are Not New Here

CARLOS BULOSAN
(1914-1956)

Carlos Bulosan was born in the Philippine village of Mangusmana. He left the Philippines in 1931 and came to California where he worked as a fruit picker. He traveled on freight trains throughout America and returned to California where he became a labor leader. He is the author of several collections of poetry and short stories, *Letter From America* (1942), *The Voice of Bataan* (1943), and *The Laughter of My Father* (1944). His autobiography, *America is in the Heart,* was published in 1946. Four years after Bulosan died of tuberculosis his letters were published under the title *Sound of Falling Light: Letters in Exile.*

From
AMERICA IS IN THE HEART

I TRIED HARD to remain aloof from the destruction and decay around me. I wanted to remain pure within myself. But in Pismo Beach, where I found Mariano, I could not fight any more. He and I slept on the floor of a small cottage, where two others were living. It was used by prostitutes when summer came and the farm workers were in town with money. When our companions woke up in the morning, Mariano and I rushed to the small bed and slept all day, waking up only at night when the gambling houses opened. I would walk among the gamblers hoping they would give me a few coins when they won.

Throughout the winter and far into spring, I lived in this cabin with my companions. When I was hungry I went to the chop suey house in our block. I would sit with gamblers and when the waiter came with a pot of hot tea and rice cakes, I would drink four or five cups and put the cakes in my pockets. Then my hunger was appeased, and I could talk again. I almost lost my power of speech, because when I was hungry the words would not come; when I tried to speak only tears flowed from my eyes.

One night, when the Korean woman who owned the restaurant saw me looking hungrily at some half-emptied plates left by white customers, she said: "When you are hungry, come here and eat. This is your home."

When I went to the kitchen to wash dishes to pay for my food, the woman threw her hands up and said: "That is enough! Go home! Come again!"

I went again and again. But I had no home that winter. One of my companions died of tuberculosis, so Mariano burned the cabin and left town. The nights were cold. Once in a while I could hear church bells ringing, and I would say to myself: "If you can listen long enough to those bells you will be safe. Try to listen again and be patient." They were my only consolation, those bells. And I listened patiently, and that spring came with a green hope.

I went to Seattle to wait for the fishing season in Alaska. There seemed no other place in this wide land to go; there seemed to be tragedy and horror everywhere I went. Where would I go from here? What year was it when I had landed in Seattle with a bright dream? I was walking on Jackson Street when I suddenly came upon Julio, who had disappeared in Sunnyside after the riot in Moxee City.

I went with Julio to a Japanese gambling house on King Street, where he taught me how to play a game called Pi-Q. I watched him play, learning his tricks. Before the gambling houses opened, we sat in his room for hours playing Pi-Q. Julio was very patient and kind.

"Gambling is an art," he said to me. "Some people gamble because they think there is money in it. Yes, there is money in it when you are lucky. But then the meaning of gambling is distorted, no longer an art. You could win ten dollars a day all your life, and make an art of gambling, if you would only try. I am an artist."

When Julio had perfected the art of gambling, he turned to picking pockets. I watched him practicing for hours. He would put a silver dollar on the edge of the table and walk toward it, snatching the dollar swiftly as he passed. Then he would use a fifty-cent piece, a quarter, and finally a dime. When he could snatch a ten-cent piece without dropping it, he mingled among the people in the streets and practiced a new art.

I followed him. How swift and nimble he was! Once, in a department store, he was almost caught. I hurried past him whispering in my dialect that he was being watched. His room was filled with inexpensive trinkets.

"Why don't you sell it and use the money for something good?" I said.

"You are distorting the art of picking pockets again," he said. "My 'pickings' are works of art. I use them for artistic expression only."

His "pickings" were neatly arranged on the table, on the floor; and some of the cheap wrist watches were hanging on the bed posts. I thought I had understood Julio when we walked across the Rattlesnake Mountains. But I was wrong. He was again a new personality, shaped by a new environment. I felt that I should leave him. I was angry that the old Julio was lost, for he had given me something, a kind of philosophy, which had sustained me for a long time."

"I'm going away," I said. "I want to work—anything but gambling. Or picking pockets."

"You are a damn fool!" he shouted. Then suddenly, realizing that he had made a mistake, he said: "There is no work anywhere. Why don't you go to the gambling houses and wait for the hop-picking in Spokane?"

It seemed a good idea. I went to a Chinese gambling house and started playing at a Pi-Q table. At night, when the place was crowded, I stopped playing and sat by a table. I noticed a Filipino farm worker, an elderly man, who was playing heavily at one of the tables. He left when he had lost all his money. Then he came back with a gun and began shooting at the Chinese dealers.

There was a general scramble, and I ducked behind a table that had fallen on the floor. I was terrified but managed to gather a handful of bills, crept to the back door, and rolled down the stairs. I ran frantically to the street, in front of the gambling house.

The Filipino had gone completely crazy. He was running up and down the sidewalk with a long knife, stabbing everyone in his way. The people ran for their lives. But for some it was too late. He had killed eight and wounded sixteen before the policemen caught him.

I lost track of Julio. But I was glad, when I took the freight train for Portland, of the things he had taught me before he disappeared. Word of the incident in Seattle had reached Portland before I arrived, and all the gambling houses were closed. I took another train to Sacramento where a Filipino mass meeting was being held. I skirted the crowd and took a bus for San Bernardino, where Chinese gambling houses were open to Filipinos.

I lost almost all my money. I stayed on for another day, but on the fourth day I gave up hope. I had only fifteen cents left. At night, when the gambling houses closed, I went to a Filipino poolroom and slept on a pool table, which was warmer and softer than the hard benches along the walls. But it was not the first time, for I had slept on pool tables in Santa Barbara, before Alfredo had appeared with plenty of money.

The next morning, desperate and hungry, I sat in front of a gambling house hoping to try my luck with my fifteen cents when the place opened. I did not go in right away, but killed time talking to the other gamblers. Three hours before closing time, I started playing and went on until the place was closed. I was jubilant. I had won nearly five hundred dollars!

"*Now,*" I said to myself, "this is the life for me in America."

I took the bus for Los Angeles. No more freight trains for me. They were only for hoboes. I called up my brother Macario from the station, but he had left his job. I did not know where Amado lived, so I took a train for San Diego hoping to gamble there for a week.

It was twilight when I arrived in San Diego. I rented a room at the U. S. Grant Hotel. It was a new life. No more sleeping in poolrooms and going hungry. No more fear of want.

It was Sunday and the gambling houses were closed until Monday. I took a ferry boat to Coronado, a small island off the bay. When I returned to the ferry station the boats had stopped running for the night. I walked back to town and tried to get a room, but all the hotels refused me.

I went to the ferry station and slept on a bench. The following morning I took a streetcar to Coronado where, in a drugstore fountain, I was refused service. One young girl, who was a student, told me that there was a Filipino clubhouse on the island.

I went to the clubhouse. Frank opened the door, and it was

a happy reunion. I thought that he had gone to Chicago when we parted in Utah. He was now a photographer. He was living with fifteen other Filipinos, mostly hotel and restaurant helpers. He took me to the kitchen where some of the men were playing Pi-Q.

I took my place by the table, pulling my hat down over my face. I wanted to win their money: it did not matter to me whether they were laboring men or not. I had to play with them, and cheat them, when I had the chance. Cheating was an imperative of the game.

The men went to work reluctantly, one at a time, and came hurrying back to the table, throwing their wages on it. I cheated them flagrantly because they were poor players, laughing aloud and kidding them while I won. But I was afraid of this bunch of work-worn, fear-stricken men. I knew that they were capable of violence, unlike professional gamblers who, upon discovering that you are one of them, lose a few more dollars and leave the table. I had discovered that there was fraternity among professional gamblers; when one was destitute, others are ready to give him a hand.

In the afternoon, when all the men came back, I won all their money. They became quarrelsome. Frank told me that one of the men had a wife who was in a hospital. But the man was shy and full of pride, and I knew I could not do anything for him. Why did he gamble his money when his wife needed it? Did he think he had the right to marry when he was scrubbing floors for thirty-five dollars a month? To hell with him!

So I was becoming hard, and brutal too: and careless with my talk. I went to San Diego and played in Chinatown. But I could not forget the man whose wife was in a hospital. I kept seeing his face on the gaming table, forlorn and pitiful. I played without direction, angry with myself. And I began to lose.

The next morning I went to Coronado. On my way to the Filipino clubhouse, I bought fifty dollars' worth of groceries for the men. They were all in when I arrived; some were dancing with their girls, and a man was playing a guitar. I gave the groceries to Frank and went out to buy some whisky. When I returned Frank was cooking a meal.

The men started playing Pi-Q in the kitchen. I sat at the

table and purposely lost one hundred dollars, the remainder of
the money I had won from them. I stopped playing and joined
the dancers in the living room. A young Mexican girl dragged
me to the floor. I began dancing with her, feeling the warmth
of her body close to mine.

"My name is Carmen," she said. "What is yours?"

I told her.

"Let's go to my room," she whispered.

"All right." The blood was pounding in my temple. "I will
follow you."

Her lips were hot upon mine when Frank came into the
room, stopped at the door, then sat weakly on the bed.

"This is my room," he said. "We have very little memories in
America," he said, looking at the girl with sad eyes. He crossed
the room and opened a drawer, bringing out a girl's diaphanous
gown. "I got this for a girl years ago. I promised to keep it for
her always. But she said that if I ever found one I could like—"
he looked at Carmen sadly—"it would be all right with her.
Will you try it on, Carmen?"

Gentle and loving he was, helping Carmen on with the gown,
kneeling on the floor around her and smoothing it to her body.
Then it came to me that I would never again hurt Frank, or
Carmen; that if I felt like hurting someone, it would be those
men and women who had driven Frank to the floor, kneeling
by an unfaithful girl.

I left the room quietly. I stayed on in San Diego and gam-
bled. When I had a stroke of luck, I transferred to the El Cortes
Hotel. I sent a postal money order to myself and went to San
Francisco, but the city was dead. The gambling houses were
closed. I stayed in Chinatown, and walked up and down Market Street. Once, in a cheap rooming house, I met a Filipino
who was struggling to become an artist. I gave him some money,
and left for Stockton.

It was again the asparagus season and the farm workers were
itching to lose their money. But I hated to gamble in the Chinese houses. I went to Walnut Grove, thirty miles away, where
the Japanese controlled the gambling. I stopped playing when I
had only five dollars left.

At noon the following day, I played again and made twenty-five dollars. I went to Stockton hoping to find Claro, but his restaurant was closed. I became restless and went to the bus station and bought a ticket to San Luis Obispo.

I felt that it was the end of another period of my life. I could see it in my reaction to the passing landscape, in my compassion for the workers in the fields. It was the end of a strange flight.

I bought a bottle of wine when I arrived in San Luis Obispo. I rented a room in a Japanese hotel and started a letter to my brother Macario, whose address had been given to me by a friend. Then it came to me, like a revelation, that I could actually write understandable English. I was seized with happiness. I wrote slowly and boldly, drinking the wine when I stopped, laughing silently and crying. When the long letter was finished, a letter which was actually a story of my life, I jumped to my feet and shouted through my tears:

"They can't silence me any more! I'll tell the world what they have done to me!"

JEFFERY PAUL CHAN
(1942-   )

Born in Stockton, California, Jeffery Chan is the former chairman of Asian-American Studies at California State University at San Francisco. His works have appeared in *West* magazine, *Asian-American Authors, Seeing Through Shuck,* the *Bulletin of Concerned Asian Scholars,* and the *Yardbird Reader.* He is the founding director of the Combined Asian-American Resources Project, Inc. He is known for championing the inclusion of Asian-American literature in the study of American literature. He was a member of the National Council of the Teachers of English, Task Force on Racism and Bias, Textbook Review Committee. He was also Asian-American consultant to Harcourt Brace Jovanovich. He lives in the San Francisco Bay area with his wife, Janis, and his children, Jennifer and Aaron Bear.

THE CHINESE IN HAIFA

BILL DREAMED he heard the cry of starving children in Asia bundled together in a strangely familiar school yard. They pressed up tightly against a Cyclone fence and they were dressed in quilted black uniforms that reached down to the ground with wide sleeves they used for handkerchiefs dabbling at their flat brown noses, a mosaic of fingers and faces reaching toward him through the squares of wire. Their gaping figures settled into the grain of the vestibule door of his grandfather's house. It was solid oak with cleverly fashioned brass mullions molded to the likeness of Taoist household deities, blending wheat chaff and shoots of new rice into the bodies of farm animals, with the toothless smile of Hotai and a border of tiny lion dogs snatching at tails and paws or locked jaw to jaw in a faceless struggle. The frieze was grimy with age and a narrow green cuticle outlined the hole where the brass met the wood and where the clear lacquer had begun to flake and crack. The door swung back and instead of his children he saw what might have been the fleeting figure of his wife driving a line of coolies down a dark hallway. Take everything, take everything, she screamed. Then his father appeared, oversized on a stretch of bright green fairway. He was wearing his powder blue slacks and his favorite alpaca sweater, white with dark blue piping up the sleeves. Bill caught sight of a golf ball nestled in a clump of dandelions. His father was intent on the ball, lining up a second shot to the green. Bill felt apprehension tighten his throat. His hands trembled as his father suddenly relaxed his pose. He looked over his shoulder, straight into Bill's eyes. He winked and casually pushed the ball clear of the weeds. The ball exposed was incandescent, each dimple seemed to catch fire until it shone brilliant white and the glare made Bill turn away but he could not escape it because he was not there.

The movers finally managed to wedge their van under the carport roof. At first Bill Wong kept to his study. He heard his wife out on the driveway and avoided her, avoided the squabble she'd promised when she phoned the night before from "The Chickencoop," his name for his sister-in-law's duplex in Chinatown. Last night on the phone he heard the television hissing the news and there was the brittle sizzling of a wok in the kitchen. His wife was calling from the living room. He suspected the conversation was being overheard. He pictured his sister-in-law, her husband, the oldest daughter with her hand over her mouth, all perched around the extension, three monkeys listening intently. He politely inquired about the children who now lived in Hong Kong with their grandmother. They were happy. "Of course they're happy," she snapped. "They like their grandma." Her sister was happy to get the furniture, the linen, the dishes. Bill resisted the urge to ask where in the hell she would put it. But she read his mind. "You got the house. I get everything else tomorrow, Bill, everything." The emphasis was like everything else in their marriage, awkward, unnecessary. Would the kids drop him a postcard? There was a pause, then his sister-in-law answered from the kitchen.

"Bill? This is Mamie," she said abruptly. Now Bill was sure her husband was listening, too. His wife fumbled with the receiver in the living room, then hung up.

"Goddamn it, put Alice back on the phone." He tried to sound testy, but it came out like a whine. All of Alice's family could read his mind.

"I'm still here," Mamie said.

"That's swell."

"Now, Bill. Alice and us think it's better if the kids don't think about you for a while," she began.

"Mamie, this is none of your goddamned . . . oh, shit . . ."
How in the hell would they accomplish that? Horrible Chinese tortures? A water cure? Prefrontal lobotomy?

"You know they're learning to write Chinese? By Christmas, they can write to you in Chinese."

Her twisted optimism and the smell of bait rising from her unctuous tones made him sick. "Gee, that's terrific, Mamie. How am I supposed to read it?"

"Now don't you be selfish, Bill. You let your own ignorance rob your kids of their heritage. That's your way."

"Terrific, Mamie," he said, letting his voice drop to a whisper.

"What did you say? What, Bill?" he heard as he slammed the receiver against the wall. It had bounced on the linoleum twice, then swung by the cord, emitting shrill angry squeals.

There was nothing left to hear. The following day he sat in the shade by the side of the house sipping from the hose and smelling bay leaves. He watched his wife with the toaster under her arm struggle down the steep driveway to her car. She had come in the company of the moving men. Mamie had her kids to look after.

Her atrocious green knit dress was tight around the sleeves and her arms looked creased and damp with sweat. She'd gained some weight in the few months since the divorce. She looked vulnerable. She avoided seeing him, and she left before the van finally rolled down the hill at dusk, followed by a pack of neighborhood dogs that barked and snapped. The engine exploded as the muffler tore against the pavement. He watched the truck make its way down the narrow road. Then there was nothing left to see.

The lights of his neighbor's garage beamed through the tangle of ivy that had begun to climb the window of his study. He smiled at his reflection. "Let's get stoned," he invited himself. He yanked his desk drawer open, found the dope, and rolled a joint. Without thinking, he looked over his shoulder, then examined his reflection again. Paranoia, he thought. No one here to tell him not to smoke, no children around to be corrupted. He studied himself, one eyebrow raised, peering out from a frame of ivy. He swept the stray crumbs of pot from his desk blotter into a plastic bag, then tucked the cigarette papers and bag into a manila envelope marked "interdepartmental mail," snapped a rubber band around it, and set the package into his filing cabinet under "D" for dope. He ignored the papers he was supposed to correct, neatly stacked on his desk. The top page was stained red where he had spilled wine the night before.

Alice had thrown everything that was his into the long narrow corridor behind the laundry room. She'd stuck it all into paper cartons, filled boxes with his books and clothes and jumbled them on top of one another, a precarious pile threatened with momentary collapse. But there was nothing unusual about the room's disorder. The cold and damp creeping through the unheated walls had already warped the unpainted pine bookshelf he had built after the collapse of his marriage. Overdue notices from the school library were sandwiched between pictures drawn by his daughter that curled out from his bulletin board with her name and date of execution. They were nearly a year old.

He clenched the joint tightly between his teeth, touched a match to the end without inhaling the flame, then filled his lungs with smoke. He felt petulant and self-indulgent. It was all clear. His wife was a vampire, and now she watched him from every dark window in the empty house. Soy sauce dribbled down her jaws. Now that he was starting to relax, settled down with his smoke, she wanted to make love. Afraid? There was nothing to be afraid of.

In the kitchen someone had taken a chicken pie out of the refrigerator and left it to thaw on the counter top. He pulled a chair from the study and sat at the back door, listening to the chicken pie drip into the sink and the sounds of the neighborhood settling into evening. He could still hear birds slapping against the curtain of eucalyptus trees in the grove at the bottom of the driveway. The night had turned cold and a thick cloud cover erased the last lights in the sky. He finished his smoke, pinched the last ember between his fingers, then swallowed the roach. Supper. The taste of ash and paper, the alfalfa smell of it all, shut his lips against a mouthful of saliva he could feel welling up from his throat. But there was no place to spit. He stripped his shirt off and washed and drank from the garden hose. "God in heaven, I'm free," he said. His voice was tentative and hoarse. He went back in the house and fell asleep on the carpet in the empty living room.

The morning sun had just broken over the ridge of hills, burning away the fog trapped in the crown of redwood trees behind the house. Bill finished his shower, then dripped water down the hall to the linen closet where he discovered she had taken every towel from the shelves. He remembered her words. "Everything. Everything." He rubbed himself dry with an old sweatshirt he found in a bag of garbage in the kitchen that smelled of rotting chicken pie. Peering out the window at the trees, he wondered what time it was. She had taken the clock radio that always rested on the kitchen table. The table was gone, for that matter. He walked into the living room and kicked the front door open. The warm, steamy air began to condense on the windows near the floor, and he drew a stick figure with his big toe on a frosted pane of glass. He heard someone crunching up the path. The hair on his legs rose in the chill and he remembered he was naked. He wrapped the still damp sweatshirt around his waist.

Herb Greenberg carried a thermos bottle in his hand and the morning paper tucked under his arm. The sleeves of his old work shirt were wet from the heavy dew on the shrubs and his hands and fingers were white with cold. He had a transistor radio stuck in his shirt pocket with the earphone plugged into his ear so that he looked like he was wearing a hearing aid. He clumped heavily up the stairs, slapped the paper and thermos down on the porch rail, and pulled two coffee mugs from his back pockets. They looked at one another for a moment before Herb broke into an embarrassed grin, his wide walrus mustache twitching with what looked like dried toothpaste at the ends.

"Listen," he said. "My mother started at five-thirty this morning making blintzes 'cause she's flying to Haifa today, the Japs just bombed an Israeli airliner in Rome, and I just left the kids at the Hauptmanns. Let's get the hell out of here and go fishing." He walked past Bill to eye the empty living room. "Oh, man," he shouted. "Alice took everything, huh?"

"Morning, Herb." Bill opened the thermos and filled both cups. "Hey, the coffee smells fine. Thanks."

"That, my friend, is genuine Kenya Blue. Real coffee! None of this MJB crap. Ethel was in the city yesterday picking up my mom at the airport." Herb stepped out on the porch and took his mug in both hands, blowing a cloud of steam. "She saw Alice and the moving van yesterday afternoon and she guessed you didn't have a coffeepot anymore."

"Listen, I had to towel off with a roll of toilet paper!" Bill laughed and ran his hand through his hair, rubbing his damp scalp. "What time is it anyway? It must be early because I'm still out of my mind. Kenya Blue sounds like something I smoked last night."

Herb held his hand up, signaling Bill to be quiet. "Goddamn Japs," he whispered. "Good God in heaven, did you hear that?"

Bill put one finger in his ear. "No."

"I been following it on the news," he said. "Three Japanese terrorists opened up on passengers getting on an Israeli jetliner in Rome. Machine guns and hand grenades. Can you imagine that! And here my mother's going to Israel today. Christ on his everlovin' crutch! What in the hell do the Japs have against us?"

Bill was confused. "Japanese disguised as Arab guerrillas?" He tried not to smile. "To do in your mother?"

"No, no. They were Japs, dressed like Japs," Herb said bitterly.

Bill wanted nothing to do with the conversation they were having. If Herb wanted to rage about Japs, that was his business. "Listen, thank Ethel for me. The coffee and all, that's very thoughtful."

Herb removed the plug from his ear and coiled the wire into his pocket. "Thank her yourself. I think she's all hot to find you a nice Jewish girl."

"What, are you inviting me home to meet your sister?"

Herb waggled a finger in his face. "My *mother,*" he said. Bill sat back on an aluminum garden chair and stuck his feet out over the railing. The coffee cut through the hangover and he squinted in the sunlight, looking over the wet trees and the ribbon of road that led out of the canyon to the town that sat by the freeway that went to the city where his wife, his children, and the Chinese were forever distant strangers. His feet were cold, his toes were numb. He pushed the chair back, tipping.

Herb grabbed his naked shoulder from behind and Bill nearly
fell over backward.

"Yeah, Wong, I'm inviting you to lunch if you can catch it.
There's a low tide at nine we can make." He caught the chair
and held it, threatening Bill.

"How can I refuse?"

Herb set him upright. "All right. You see? I saved your life
again. I should adopt you since you obviously don't know how
to take care of yourself." He laughed, pointing into the empty
house. "Today's agenda calls for rock fishing till noon."

"You sure you want me in the house with your mother
around? I don't want her to get the idea that I might be a terrorist in disguise." The sweatshirt had slipped off, and he hoped
Ethel wasn't looking out from the garage.

"Nahh. You're no Jap." Herb grinned. "You're a Chinaman.
I explained that all to you already. Go on now and get your
pants."

Bill dressed quickly, and together they walked across the hill
to Herb's house. He saw Ethel peering from the kitchen window
and he waved. Herb continued to rave about the Japs as they
tied his long bamboo fishing poles to the side of the car. Ethel
appeared, wiping her hands on her apron.

"Good morning, Bill."

"Morning, Ethel."

"Herb," she said.

Herb answered, "Good morning, Ethel."

"Please take out the garbage before you leave."

"Where's Mama?" he said, turning toward the kitchen.

"She went back to bed. Don't make so much noise." She
turned to look at Bill as he wrapped twine around the aerial
to hold the fishing poles. "Did you hear what time we had to
get up this morning?"

"Yes, I heard." Bill looked at her face. She wasn't wearing any
make-up. She had that clean, well-scrubbed, early in the morning look she wore after the kids had gone to school when the
three of them would have coffee in their kitchen before he
drove Herb to the bus stop on his way to class. "I am a Japanese terrorist this morning. I fell asleep on the rug last night
and my back hurts. It's awful. I want to shoot up an airport
and scream at people in Japanese."

"Well, you do look a little awful," she offered, teasing.

"Just put your finger there." He indicated a knot he wanted held down.

"Catch something we can eat for lunch and we'll cook it Chinese style."

She stood next to him, her finger on the twine. With her other hand she massaged his back. "Sure. Ahhh. Sure." Bill tensed and glanced back at her. She smiled coyly.

"Does the little terrorist want me to walk on his back?"

A short blast from the horn startled him, and he saw Herb behind the wheel. He leaned over and remonstrated, "She's too small, Wong. Throw her back and we'll catch a bigger one."

"Yes, boss," he said.

Bill stood up on the gray knuckle of rock. His tennis shoes were frictionless along the face of the tide pool. He stepped where the water was shallowest and barely touched the green slime of algae surrounding every foothold. Tiny crabs skipped and fell before him off the rocks and skittered like gravel into the water before his feet slipped past them. Every rock seemed to be covered with crabs. The sound of the breakers steadied in his ears like his own breathing, like meditation. He lit a cigarette while his hands were still dry enough to strike a match. The imperceptible movement of the tide washed over the rock he stood on and he could feel water seep into his shoes. His feet felt warm and scummy. He slipped along a carpet of purple seaweed knee deep into the water and made his way along a submerged granite shelf, groping with the tip of his pole behind a ribbon of kelp into a long, deep fissure. He pulled back a fraction to let the hook dangle without getting tangled around the pole. Something nibbled at his bait, a slight bump and a nudge. It reminded him of his wife making love. "Come out, Alice," he crooned.

And whether it was the excitement of the catch or the weary energy he drew from the roach digesting in his stomach from the night before, he knew for certain it was his wife tucked warily in the dark crack, guarding his children from him, her arms and legs wedged against the tight walls of her watery cave. Come out, Alice, he sang, come on out of there. He eased the tip of his pole in another inch.

Why do you waste your time fishing for that stuff, she used
to say. I can buy it for you cheap. For a dollar in Chinatown,
she used to say.

He shortened his grip and with both hands set the hook with
a quick jerk, and he had her, he had this fish passing for his
wife. He felt a violent current of energy running the length of
the fishing pole. Whatever it was, it was big. He looked behind
him, judging the distance to the beach. The water was too deep
to wade straight across, so he edged around the pool to the last
visible foothold and stood out of the water. He jammed both
feet tight against a clump of mussel shell, trying to steady himself. His pants pockets poured sea water down his legs. He
braced himself, then pulled hard, wrenching the fish from its
hiding place. She pushed off from the shallow bottom, nearly
jerking the pole out of his hand. The weight of her snapped at
the short line, snapped the tip of his pole back and forth, and
he felt his shoes scrape against the sharp edges of the shells,
then pull away. He landed on both feet in water up to his waist.
Now the violence was real for him. Too real. The fish pushed
off from the shallow bottom and jumped clear of the water.
The pole slipped from his hands and hit him. He stepped backward, green water and kelp and foam splashing in his face, his
feet slipping on the rocky bottom. His feet came out from
under him and he landed hard on the dry gravel. The pole lay
between his legs. The fish on the end of it panted in the brack-
ish puddle.

To hell with her, he didn't want her any more. The hook
must have passed through the roof of her mouth. Blood flooded
the white of one bulging eyeball. He stood up and kicked the
pole into the water. "Hey, that's my pole!" Herb shouted from
behind him. "And that's our lunch!" His soaking pants had
nearly fallen off, and sea water stung the cuts on his hands and
arms. He sat on a piece of driftwood and watched the fish twist
over slowly, propped up by a hard ridge of bone on the top of
its head, and he could see the flesh on its belly was a bright
blue. Die, Alice, he thought to himself. The tail swept back
and forth in a mimickry of agony, its gill plates snapped open
and shut forcing air through its lungs and strangling it. Red
fiddler crabs scurried around the fish, plucking delicately at the

fins. Again it rolled over, its face impaled on the hook, the barb gleaming out of its one bloodshot eye. There was an impish expression on its face. A smile suggested by its thick purple lips, the fishing line pulling up against the mouth, became a sneer that belonged to his wife, his ex-wife. She seemed pleased. Why not? She'd just eaten.

Herb appeared on the bluff directly behind him and he laughed with excitement. "That damn thing must weigh ten pounds! Man, it sure is ugly, Wong!" Bill looked up at him and waved. He remembered now that the fish was for Ethel. They would cook it, Chinese style. He laughed to himself.

"That's my wife you're talking about."

Herb came leaping down from the rocks. "What did you say?"

"That's a capizone. Not known for their beauty." Bill took the end of the pole and heaved it out of the water, letting the fish roll in the dirt.

Herb was out on the patio picking coriander for the fish and Bill and Ethel were cooking in the kitchen. Bill watched him wander past the straw flowers Ethel had gathered on the windowsill just over the sink, pinpoints of startling amethyst and ruby in smoke glass bottles. Tiny ceramic miniatures of farm animals Ethel bought in Chinatown pastured around a can of cleanser. Ethel padded barefoot across the kitchen floor and dipped hot oil over the fish laid on a bed of bean cake. "I hope I'm doing this right," she said.

"What we need is a piece of window screen stretched across some sort of frame. That way you wouldn't waste so much oil." He took the spoon from her hand.

"Did you cook for Alice?"

"Sure. I cooked. I even made a screen for frying the fish."

"But she took it." Ethel cocked her head, catching his words as they fell. "Everything," they said simultaneously. "Alice took everything!" They laughed.

The kitchen was redolent of garlic and ginger. The fish sent up clouds of thick steam as the oil crisped its flesh, drawing blisters of juice where the body had split apart.

"Careful!" Bill caught her by the shoulder as the oil ex-

ploded, sending a hot shower down around her legs. She danced
back a pace from the stove.

"Ooh, I think I got the oil too hot."

"That's all right, but you better stand out of the way." Her
eyes are positively green, he thought, they seem to change
color in the sunlight coming through the open door.

"I saw the moving people yesterday. Was that the refrigerator
going down the driveway?" She balanced her head against her
hand, a finger stuck in her mouth, gnawing on her wedding
ring.

"I went into the kitchen after everybody was gone," Bill
said, "and found my frozen dinner in the sink. It was so sad,
my dinner, all thawed out and starting to smell."

"Poor baby. You can put all the frozen dinners you want in
our freezer, and we'll even give you a key for your very own."
She heaped green onions and tomatoes on a chopping board.
As she brushed past him he caught the aroma of lilac and garlic
and something else like home permanent solution in her hair,
her tight blonde curls turning limp and feathery in the humid
kitchen. She wore one of Herb's old shirts with the tails
wrapped around her waist. When she held herself to attention
slicing tomatoes at the counter, he marveled at her legs, tanned
to the ankles. Her faded denims were cut off and rolled up to
where the pockets stuck out around her thighs like the un-
creased tabs on a paper doll. Her toenails were brushed with
blue polish.

Herb appeared at the kitchen door just as a covey of jets
from the Naval Air Station laid a vapor trail across the sky. A
clap of thunder rattled the dishes and silverware on the table.
He stood there clutching the coriander wetly in one hand and
watched the planes disappear.

"Leave the door open, Herbie. I don't want the smoke to settle into the walls." She smiled warmly at Bill, a guileless and
direct smile that made him conscious of his eyes lowering to
her knees, to her bare brown feet. "You must be starving to
death," still a lax affectionate smile, a lopsided complexity as
she rubbed the corners of her eyes tearing in the clouds of oily
smoke.

He looked at Herb. "I think it's done."

Herb settled into his chair. "Where's Mama? Still asleep?"

He put a stalk of green onion in his mouth and clipped the stems from the coriander with a pair of scissors. Bill swung the plate to the table with a flourish of Ethel's pot holder. Herb deliberately sprinkled the leaves of coriander over the steaming fish, and they all sat back in their chairs. It was a moment of respect reserved for some unspoken grace. Ethel whispered, "I think she's still asleep."

"Let her sleep then. Look," he said with mock awe. "Look at it." All three groaned loudly, Herb beating on the table with his fork. "Let's eat it!"

Ethel started spooning fish onto Bill's plate. "Herbie, are you sure you want to drive her to the airport? You know you're going to hit all that weekend traffic."

"Sure, sure. It's me or you, and I'd rather it be me. You're the mommy. You can have the kids when they get home. That's why we have a successful marriage, Bill. Sharing and caring."

Bill waited until Ethel was settled into her chair. Then he said, "You can't sit down yet. Give me a fish eye."

Herb looked around the table, then went to the refrigerator for horseradish. Ethel leaned back and maneuvered a gallon of wine over her head from the counter to the table and filled their glasses, spilling as much as she poured. "No, no," she said. "The eyes are for Mama Goldberg."

Their knees touched under the table. Bill was sure it was an accident, as sure as he knew there were bony ridges just beneath her kneecaps. He could almost feel them. He finished his wine. "More, please," he said, holding out his glass.

"I think all this hijacking nonsense is ridiculous. You know your sister had her handbag searched in Los Angeles when she took Mama to the airport." She bit into a tomato wedge and the juice ran down her chin.

Herb spooned horseradish over his fish. "It wasn't a hijacking. They didn't even ask for anything, no demands, nothing, just opened up with their Soviet," stressing the word *Soviet,* "machine guns, and blasted away. One's still alive. I hope they castrate the bastard so he doesn't breed any more like him. Fire with fire."

Ethel brought her eyebrows together and took a sip of wine. "That would be a bucket of cold water."

Bill stood up as Herb's mother suddenly appeared in the

kitchen. She was tall like her son, the same dark brown hair and dark eyes, slightly puffed with sleep, glazed, framed with waxy mascara. "So. When do we leave?" she said excitedly.

"Mama, you should have slept longer," Herb said as he leaned across the table to kiss her cheek.

"I can sleep on the plane." She turned her head to accept the kiss, reaching at the same time to take Bill's hand. "You must be Bill. My son and daughter say nice things about you."

"How do you do," Bill began, but her smile suddenly vanished. She stood awkwardly over the table, Bill's hand in her own, and sniffed at what she saw in front of her. She completed the smile, let go of his hand, and picked at the fish with a teaspoon. "Very tasty, dear, but you know it's not nice to look at the whole thing. It looks right up at you."

They all stared down at it. The eyes were a solid milky white. A clove of garlic protruded from its mouth and Ethel pushed it back, giggling.

"Is it fresh?" she demanded.

"Bill caught it this morning, Mama," Herb told her.

"Where?" she inquired suspiciously.

"In the ocean, Mama, in the ocean. We went fishing this morning, after you went back to sleep."

She prowled around the kitchen replacing dishes. She snatched a dishtowel from the back of Herb's chair and put it through the handle of the dishwasher, then took a sponge and wiped up spilled oil from the counter top. "Where are the children now, Ethel?"

"Mrs. Hauptmann's got them, Mama. She gives them their lunch today." Ethel delicately removed a bone from between her lips. "They don't like fish either."

"So who can blame them?" She began laughing at herself, caught Bill's eye and stopped. "All right, food is food. Is this the way the Chinese cook fish, Bill?" He nodded. She heaved a sigh. "Bill, you just have to put up with me. I have to know everything, don't I, Herbie?"

"Herb said you made blintzes this morning, Mrs. Goldberg."

"You like blintzes? Ethel, you give Bill some blintzes from out of the freezer."

"I love blintzes," Bill said.

She sat down between Herb and Ethel and motioned to Bill. "Eat." She was too excited to eat. "You have that house with the steep driveway right next door? You must get a lot of sun up there. You have a garden?"

Bill nodded through an exchange of questions and a barrage of small talk. Now and again he caught Ethel smiling. She began to imitate his every nod. When he folded his arms, she folded hers. Mrs. Goldberg explained that she would fly to Tel Aviv, then to Haifa. Her niece had married an Israeli engineer. Bill poured wine for her, and she allowed for a second glass, then a third. She described an enormous family as she talked, and she reached out with her hands to touch her son. She held his hand to her cheek, and rapped the knuckles of her other hand on the table for luck. "We have big families," she said with a great deal of satisfaction. She reached for Ethel and patted her on the arm. "You must know about big families, Bill. The Chinese always have big families, like Jews. Herbie and Ethel are waiting for what I don't know. Two beautiful children, but just two. Did you come from a big family, Bill?"

"No," Bill said. "I was an only child."

"You know, I can tell. You don't know how to talk through an old lady. You're too quiet. That's a good thing sometimes, but sometimes a good thing is too much."

"My mother had a large family."

"Yes?" she said. "How many?"

"Nine."

"Nine? Nine is a good size. We had eleven, but one died."

"Who, Mama?" Herb carried his plate to the sink.

"I had a sister and she died of pneumonia when she was four. She was Miriam. I was only five, but I remember her."

"My mother had a sister who died when she was young," Bill confided.

"Yes?" She beamed across the remains of the fish. "There, you see?"

Bill thought it was a strange issue to make an alliance from. But he was drawn to her, hostile, then open, testy like a peacock and at once glorious. "But I never heard them speak of her," he offered. "I saw her picture once in a photo album my uncle kept."

"But that's the way. They had nine to take care of, your grandparents."

"Yes," he said.

"That's what families are for," she said.

"What are they for?"

"So when you lose one, you have more."

"Wouldn't it be the same if you never had one, never started?"

"Started what? Everybody's got a family. What do you mean? You come from one family, you make another."

Bill didn't know whether to laugh or not. He was confused. Maybe she was drunk.

"Now you, Bill, you're not young but you're not old, either. When you're as old as me, maybe you want to sit in one place. Stand still, maybe. Maybe. Me, I don't want to wait around to die."

Ethel was at the sink listening to them talk. "Mama's got one foot in the grave."

"No! That's a bad joke! I'm not dying, not yet! I'm only being practical. Who wants me to die on them? Who wants to walk into my room and find me home, but not home. It would kill my friends, I mean, they're not chickens. So I keep moving. Maybe I'll go in the airplane or someplace maybe where they can send a body home, but they pack me up. It's easier. I fall down and maybe I won't scare somebody to death. I don't know. Maybe you're right. If you never start—how can that be? Everybody has family." She stopped abruptly. Finishing the rest of her wine, she started to laugh. "You made me talk and I don't even know what I'm talking about, Bill."

Herb roused himself from the half-sleep he had fallen into while his mother was talking, and got up from the table. "It's about time. Let's get your luggage, Mama."

Bill rose, smiling. He steadied himself on the table. He began, "I'm glad we got drunk together."

But she put her hands to his lips. She leaned across the table and whispered in his ear. "Who would have me," she hissed, "who wants an old lady around the house after a few days?"

"Come live with me, Mama," Bill said softly.

She stood back and smiled at him. "You should have children, Bill."

And before he could reply, Herb lied. "Bill's a confirmed bachelor, Mama."

"Well, not confirmed," Bill said.

She nodded as if she understood. She straightened herself up and began to talk energetically. "I stick my nose into everybody's business. But I'm a great-grandmother once over so it's forgivable. You'll pardon me, but I'm sure your mama would say the same thing. You should marry, have children." She indicated Herb and Ethel with a wave of her hand. "Have a big family. My speech is over." She laughed, and Bill heard a faint edge of contempt in her laughter.

Ethel winked at Bill from over her shoulder. "Maybe you can find Bill a nice Jewish girl, Mama, in Haifa."

"Are there Chinese in Haifa?" Herb asked.

"The Jews and the Chinese," she said, standing in the middle of the room and weaving her eyes back and forth from her son to his wife, "they're the same." She walked to the door and Herb followed. "You know there are Jews in China, there must be Chinese in Haifa. It's all the same, even in Los Angeles." She went out the door.

They stood in the garage together while Herb put her suitcases in the trunk and started the car. Mrs. Goldberg gave Ethel a long hug, then walked up to Bill. "You have a safe journey Mrs. Goldberg. I'm glad to have met you."

"So polite you are." She shook his hand. "I was glad to meet you, too. You're too quiet, though." Then, loudly, over the noise of the car, she said, "Ethel, you get him married. You get married before I come back."

He nodded.

"Drive carefully, Herbie," Ethel shouted as the car backed slowly out of the garage. She waved as the station wagon turned the corner and disappeared.

Ethel breathed a sigh of relief. They stood together in the driveway. A riot of fuchsias hung from the redwood baskets suspended over their heads. The sound of bees flew around their ears. "Thank you, Ethel. Lunch was fine."

"Oh, Bill." She stretched her arms and yawned deliberately in his face. "Mama's right, you're so polite." She crossed over the driveway, tracing little dance steps on the concrete. Then, setting her foot on a tricycle, she pushed off up the path lit-

tered with empty paint cans and discarded lumber that con-
nected their houses, coasting to a stop against some loose cinder
blocks scattered in the weeds. She looked over her shoulder at
him. "Bet you can't catch me," she shouted.

Bill felt such irony in the confession he made to himself as
he slowly followed her through the trees. He probably couldn't
catch her. His feet struck the hard pan and he nearly stumbled
over the exposed roots of creosote bushes that held the hill
together during the long wet winters he would spend in his
empty house, alone with his neighbor's wife. He found his footing in the eroded path the rain cut in the earth. He gathered
his energies together and took the hill at a jog. He could see
Ethel's head, just visible beyond his driveway. He followed her
path, marked by a cloud of fine yellow dust that hung in his
face and caught in his nose and throat.

She was standing on the porch pouring herself a cup of
coffee from the thermos he'd forgotten to return. He stood for
a moment at the bottom of the stairs, catching his breath. She
saw him, smiled, then wandered uncertainly through the open
doorway. He found her in the living room, her back to him,
staring at the blank walls. She refused to turn around even
as he wrapped his arms around her from behind.

"Got ya!" he said, his tone a shade too jovial. Herb's shirt
was already unbuttoned. He untied the shirt tails and gently
kissed the nape of her neck.

"You didn't chase me," she complained in a whisper as his
hands covered both of her breasts.

Bill spent the rest of the evening in his study. He had thrown
the window open to let the stale air escape, and he heard the
Greenberg children's noisy return just before nightfall. He
watched the lights of Herb's station wagon as it pulled up the
road a few minutes later, saw the momentary red afterglow of
the brake lights, heard the engine sputter to a stop and the
garage door slide shut. His hands went searching through his
desk drawer and found a nail clipper. He pared methodically
at his fingernails, scraping bits of dry fish scale from under the
cuticles. He licked his thumb and tasted the salty wrinkles that
lined the back of his hands. Tiny cracks appeared where he'd

cut himself on the rocks, and they stung as he scratched away the dried skin.

It was cold now, and he closed the window. A few shreds of ivy caught in it and hung inside the frame. He could see fog gathering along the lowest ridges of the hillside, caught in the brittle blue glare of a street lamp. He pulled the filing cabinet open, shook out some dope and rolled a joint, carefully brushing the stems and seeds into an ashtray. He snapped his desk light on and lit the joint, the smoke easing down his throat and filling his lungs. He held his breath for a moment, then blew a white cloud billowing around the lamp. There was an initial disappointment, a change that he could taste as chemistry blunting his mind, the acrid combustion of cigarette paper and spit. But suddenly the taste was gone. His mouth was dry. A premonition that Ethel was looking over his shoulder made him glance into the darkened window to catch her reflection behind him. But he was alone. His hand held the burning joint in front of his mouth, the smoke curling undisturbed across his face. A vague collection of swarthy Japanese in mufti crowding around Herb's station wagon at the airport grew in his mind's eye.

DIANA CHANG
(1934-   )

Diana Chang was born in New York City, but spent her childhood in China raised by her Eurasian mother. She graduated from Barnard College in 1949. She was the recipient of a John Hay Whitney Foundation Fellowship and is the author of four novels. Chang has published poetry in numerous magazines, quarterlies, and anthologies and is an editor of *The American Pen*.

From
THE FRONTIERS OF LOVE

THE NIGHT BEFORE, Sylvia Chen had dreamed heavily, and awakened reluctantly in the morning. Later that day, she thought, she would probably have proof again that her dreams were often reversed in time—they did not always come after the event which might have caused them but often before, as though they were forecasts of the weather ahead.

"Come in," Sylvia said a few hours after waking and, as she said it, it sounded familiar, a cue that would lead her forward into that Saturday, and illuminate what she had dreamed. Though she had not heard a sound, she knew her father was standing by the door of her room. His hesitancy could reach her no matter how occupied she was; it traveled along her nerves and stammered in her senses.

"Come in, do," she insisted, but ungenerously did not turn around from her book.

The afternoon had just begun, taking the city in its lap. Her father now stood at her window, looking over the wall that hedged in the open garden of their neighbor's property. He cleared his throat, and she could see him leaning on the sill, turning his head to the right where another apartment house, a duplicate of their own, stood casting its shadow into their courtyard. The Chinese families who lived there took long siestas on the narrow balconies. Only the servants moved around below, soundlessly, in white jackets and black trousers, straightening the wash or taking in the deliveries. To Sylvia the after-lunch quiet seemed to give the scene the quality of a fable. Beyond, on the near horizon, the intersection of streets was quiet. Bicycles, rickshaws and pedestrians moved slowly in the simmering heat.

She could feel her father struggling within himself to speak, to appeal to her. Stubbornly, she did not want to help him.

"Sylvia," he brought out at last, almost plaintively and without looking at her, "your mother is mad at me."

She turned to stare at the back of his head, forcing her eyes to be noncommittal. It always shocked her to hear him utter in his Chinese accent such colloquial phrases as "mad at me" or "sore at them." He had a long face for a Chinese and a high, receding forehead; these expressions were wholly out of keeping with this fine and tailored face, and his rather remote air.

"But that's not so serious, is it?" Sylvia asked, and regretted her tone immediately. He had often confessed to her that before his children he felt half-relic, half-contemporary. Of course, he often pointed out, children were one's equals in modern China, but today she felt he was prepared to reverse that— he was almost equal to his daughter.

"Couldn't you—couldn't you just go in and say a word to her?" he asked. He turned around, smiling; his smile always grew in proportion to his distress. "It's so much easier for you, you see."

She knew he would let himself say no more. His strict code of dignity would not allow it, and already she was beginning to yield, to do his bidding, as she always did, for no one but her mother could stand up to his soft insistence. Because he so feared direct encounters, Sylvia had never dared to question anything he did or said. Even to have remarked, "But I think it is wrong for me to arbitrate every time," would have seemed a frontal attack on his delicate ego. They were prisoners of their shyness with each other.

But Sylvia couldn't resist saying in a grudging tone. "But of course, for this is the land of the go-between," and as an unwilling one, got up and walked into the living room. A barricade of static hung between it and the bedroom where Helen, her mother, was sitting. She was probably traveling around the world on the impetus of her anger.

"Mother," Sylvia ordered, as soon as she reached the bedroom door. "Mother, stop sulking at once!"

Helen looked up from her nails, which she was filing by the open window. Sylvia could see her blue-eyed stare in the mirror. Her back was turned to her, like a cat's, deaf to everything except her own willfulness.

"Helen Ames Chen," she cajoled, for with her mother Sylvia was not at all shy. "Mother," she said again, but only half-heartedly. Her parents' quarrels were like beds that had to be made up every morning, only to be disordered again. In the end, Liyi would come into the bedroom, feeling that the situation had been changed by his daughter's ineffectual words, and Helen would shed a few tears and they would seem to rediscover each other. They would seem bride and groom again. Helen might go into peals of senseless laughter and Liyi would stand beside her, plaiting her long blond hair, proud and pleased as a new husband.

"Oh, for pity's sake, Mother!" Sylvia said, for Helen refused to respond. Her mock wail made her sound adolescent to herself. At home, she thought, as she stood in the doorway, not knowing what to do next, you had to discount five years from your age. At home, no child could act adult without feeling he was disinheriting his parents. They made you feel guilty that years affected you at all. Relationships were like pressures that pushed you in thirty-six directions of the compass. But, as in a crowded streetcar, if you learned how to maintain your balance against all the weights, you might arrive at yourself.

"Mother," Sylvia said with a sigh, feeling her father moving nervously in the living room. "Let's go for a walk, Mother. Just you and I, and we'll splurge and have ice cream somewhere. Just like sisters."

Helen stirred at that, as easily mollified and distracted as a child, and before she could make a show of reluctance, Sylvia continued, "I'll get dressed and be right back," and left. Out of the corner of her eye, she caught her father's delighted wink. But she did not acknowledge it. Each of her parents had a way of wanting to make her an accomplice.

"You look pretty, my dear," Helen said a little later, "all

dressed up to go out with me. And I shall get dressed up to go out with my daughter," and she came up and kissed Sylvia behind her ear, "my one and only daughter." And then Helen was off, tossing her dress and bag and slip and hat and veil on the bed. One by one she put them on, her gaiety contagious, and patted herself and Sylvia with *eau de cologne,* spanking fresh as a morning at the beach. The spontaneity felt familiar, like a phrase of music that cannot be placed, but which recurs at different times until several moods have accrued to it. Such good spirits could not last, Sylvia knew, but put her doubts away. After all, nothing lasted, but no one was insecure about the ephemeralness that was a part of misery, too.

"Where shall we go?" Sylvia asked, when they were at the gate downstairs, and it seemed to her they had the vistas of all the summer resorts they had ever been to, the boulevards of Tsingtao, looking naval and Mediterranean on Sunday, the bright, bleak edges of Hulutao, the terraces and hotels of Chefoo and Hongkong on the bay—all the vistas seemed laid before them again.

"Let's be really crazy," Helen said, emphasizing the word "crazy," as though putting it within inverted commas, for unless she was beside herself with anger, she rarely stooped to expressions that might be considered colloquial. "Let's be really mad and—and go to Bubbling Well Road."

They laughed and practically skipped down the street arm in arm.

Walk, turn left; walk and walk, turn right. More walking. And still Sylvia did not feel tired, for the air was fresh after the morning storm, the trees stirred, sprinkling them with rain; all the trees and all the houses, and all the little people on all the little streets—everything was small and clear and manageable. She could be happy because she was small, too; her life was little, complete, defined. In a sudden, brief glimpse she saw what life was—quite beautiful and quite manageable. The storm had left, and now they seemed to be going up some steps leading into the afternoon.

No one, Sylvia thought, could do anything more outrageous in Shanghai than take a walk on Bubbling Well Road in the International Settlement and have ice cream. The ice cream was an anachronism in the mouth, sliding down like a memory from her tongue to her stomach, as she let the cream and the luxury absorb her. There wasn't much ice cream in Shanghai these days; only infants and the very ill were able to get rations of milk, for the Japanese had killed most of the cows at the beginning of the war. Sylvia could see rows of brown, white and speckled cows standing in the fields and dairies, standing at ease on three legs and munching, waiting to be machine-gunned by the conquerors to provide meat for their troops.

Sylvia looked at her mother now with new eyes—familiarity had an unfortunate way of breeding a perspicacity which almost denied a mother an independent identity. As though the sparkling light of the afternoon illuminated Helen, Sylvia had a strange sense of "remembering" her against the background of Shanghai, a city barricaded for so long. Americans like her mother had been allowed to stay out of the internment camps because of their Chinese husbands; instead they were required to wear red arm bands with numbers printed on them. She was conspicuous—as Sylvia had always found her mother conspicuous—and to any Japanese gendarme who wanted to stop her and inspect her identity card, Helen was number 123.

They continued down the avenue, while Helen said, "Now if we were back in New York," but Sylvia was not listening. She had caught sight of *Yiao ching*, the schizophrenic Chinese girl who had bleached her hair platinum. *Yiao ching* had turned the corner with the air of someone avoiding an unwanted admirer, vulnerable, petulant and egocentric, but she could not avoid the eyes that followed her strange figure. Sylvia wondered how anyone so brainless could be so neurotic, how so much mental aberration was linked to so little gray matter.

But Miss Chu is most consistent, Sylvia said to herself—this girl who always matched her Hollywood coiffure to wedge shoes, and used hatboxes for handbags, slung a trophy of dead fur around her neck. Sylvia had run into her innumerable times and knew the small, bewildered Chinese face, the leaf-shaped eyes which peered from under the platinum mop, as she sidled in and out of shops, signing checks with her Parker 51 pen.

That Parker pen saved her, as did her Ronson lighter, these American gadgets that every Chinese who called himself mod-

ern coveted and obtained by illegal means, on the black market,
if the proper channels did not yield their precious cargoes. By
owning these, Sylvia thought, *Yiao ching* still operated as a
Chinese, a Lana Turner whose real image, if only she would
probe deep enough, would always be Yang Kwei-fei, the Tang
Dynasty beauty.

"Now if we were back in New York," Helen repeated and
went on, "we could take in a Broadway show or spend a weekend in Connecticut. We could go up to the Cloisters, or the
Frick Museum, have dinner in the Tavern on the Green, and
then take a long, long drive on those highways they have in
America. You remember them, dear. You must remember the
traffic and the signs everywhere, the small towns and wayside
places, busy gas stations and certified rest rooms." Sylvia's
breath caught slightly as she looked at her mother striding pur-
posefully down the sidewalk, making a bit of Philadelphia
here in Shanghai because of her sturdy oxfords and the aggres-
sive swing of her legs. Mother was homesick. Helen was homesick for America, and Sylvia felt green and tender for her.

"I'm so sorry," Sylvia said, for her mother was very far from
home.

"Are you really?" Helen asked sharply, for she could not
sustain dreaminess for long. "Sorry because we ever came back?
But you wanted to." It was true; Sylvia had hated America
that year. "Sorry because out here we're just decaying, out
here in the middle of nowhere." "Out here" was the vocabulary
of extraterritoriality and colonialism, and Helen meant it
literally, in the Rudyard Kipling sense, white man's burden
and all. Out here in the jungle, out here in the desert, out here
among the savages, out here in the leper colony. And the
Chinese to her were part savage, part leprous and totally mysterious.

But it's natural for her to think this way, Sylvia reminded
herself, tamping down the pulse that had begun to beat too
fast. So many things could set off this sensation of wanting to
run, or wanting to stay and fight it out until the true meaning
behind everyone's words could be determined. But this was her
own mother, this woman was part of her, and surely her mother
had the right to be terribly homesick.

"And you and Paul had wanted so much to go to America. Do you remember? You were practically babies then and you wanted so much to go to America because I had told you about the hot cross buns, and shopping in Rogers Peet, and sodas and sundaes in Schrafft's, and putting nickels in the Automat slots, and the sightseeing tours everywhere, and New Year's Eve in Chinatown.

"You were so eager to leave China that year—of course, there were the air raids—that you even said (and the young can be so hard)—that you even said it was all right to leave Daddy in Shanghai, that you simply must go to America. Paul, you and I must go to America, just until the 'incident,' the war, blew over. And on the *Empress of Japan* you didn't seem to miss your Daddy at all, but ate everything on that menu, and it was quite a menu.

"I don't understand you," her mother continued. "First you wanted to go so badly, then you hated it, and now I just don't know what you feel. I just couldn't venture a guess at all."

She stopped suddenly in exclamation over a cart of flowers that had spilled half its load on the sidewalk. She must buy some from the poor vendor, and she set to picking, comparing and bargaining.

It was all wrong. But it was her mother's truth, and maybe her mother was right. Her mother at least had a point of view, and Sylvia had only an undependable pulse, racing over nothing at all, quibbling over such unspecific things. But she couldn't, she couldn't accept her mother's version of things. Sylvia felt threatened, afraid, as though Helen could rob her of herself—as though Helen, in her vigor, could obliterate Sylvia's very existence.

Sylvia and her brother Paul had not been babies in 1937, but they had been young, only twelve and seven, and of course they had thought it was a great lark to go to America, the America Helen had told them about for all of their lives. Maybe it was because the trip coincided with the beginning of Sylvia's adolescence, but everything was less wonderful than expected; everything was a disappointment. The hot cross buns were bought in a crowded Hanscom's bakery, not (as it had been in Helen's childhood) in a dimly lit, romantic little store.

And the hot cross buns were bought in the glare of daylight and on aluminum counters (America's face was aluminum as China's was ceramic), and not after the opera, as Sylvia had somehow imagined it, the satin and cloaked night people pouring out of the Alhambra of music and song, each clutching sweet hot cross buns in their gloved hands. And Rogers Peet was only a store for men's furnishings. When the carton boxes arrived in Nanking with Rogers Peet written on them, it seemed that the store was a combination of bazaar and treasure house, something foreign and mysterious as a hoard in Egypt. And Schrafft's was a pretension for the dull-minded, and the Automat was a mess hall for prisoners of desolation and loneliness. And as for Chinatown, Sylvia could not even bear to think of it to this day, that ghetto begging tourists to inspect its shame. And, of course, there were other things, bigger things, more important things that unhinged her, because she had walked out of her childhood the same year she discovered that her mother's America was an illusion and was, for her at least, untrue. How terrible it was that she had given the first twelve years of her imagination to such a lie.

She would walk down Third Avenue and stare unseeing at all the antique stores, just to be near something ancient—a small ruin of candelabra, a small heap of moldering beauty, something old and patina-ed to remind her of China, something old and intimate and taking up room for no other reason than for its own inefficient self.

She had been homesick then, but she had also been an adolescent, and thought not always of home, but also of the air, or the thing that could not be seen, touched or found on land or sea. She wanted the day to be special, not only for herself, but for everyone, and she wanted this thing, this thing that no one had ever seen, heard of or dreamed of before, to be waiting for her as she left the front stoop. It must behave in a way true to itself, but it must behave magnificently. And the thing and she would know, would simply recognize each other, and there! she and the thing—which was air, man, earth and idea, all wrapped up into one unity—would recognize each other, and that would be the beginning, the end and the middle of her life. Of course, needless to say, it never happened; nothing was waiting at the front stoop, and her disappointment, the name she gave to her disappointment was America.

Sylvia laughed at herself, laughed at the memory of herself as a twelve-year-old who was now, after all, only wrapped up in eight more years of foolishness. But this foolishness was called growing up. No wonder her poor mother did not understand her. Who would (for Sylvia thought of adolescence as a somewhat psychotic period of one's life), and who wanted to achieve perfect understanding with insanity?

Her mother now laughed, too, echoing Sylvia, and handed her a bunch of roses and some young bulbs. "Aren't they exquisite, my darling? They're American Beauty roses; they look just like the ones I had in the garden in Nanking. And the bulbs. You know how your father loves narcissi. They are so delicate and Chinese. And I'll carry these," and the vendor filled her arms with two dozen gladioli of assorted colors. They were still stiff with freshness, hard flowers unfurling from the ungiving stems. They stood away from each other, even wrapped in the funnel-shaped paper, and as a bunch they had to be held like a brittle package.

I'm like those gladioli, Sylvia thought, young, hard and ungiving still. I must learn to relax, to resist less. My mother shouldn't threaten my existence; she doesn't mean to; it all lies in me. And the tether seemed to give way, and even the leavings of their conversation did not disturb her on the rest of the way home, not even when her mother said, "It was the biggest mistake of my life, returning to China in thirty-eight." And Sylvia knew she didn't mean that the mistake had anything to do with Liyi. Helen loved Liyi and would always love him. But she didn't love China (why should she?), and she did not recognize the conflict, an inheritance she did not even know that she had given her children.

But the afternoon's aura seemed to have been left at the front gate as they climbed the stairs.

"Those bulbs," Helen said, as she tossed her hat on the bed. "Give me those bulbs right away. No, no, not like that; you'll hurt them, silly. There, now, you take care of these gladioli

and I'll pop these roses in here." The roses were for her bedroom, hers and Liyi's; the gladioli Sylvia arranged in two
cut-glass vases (purchased one extravagant day at Jensen's) in
the living room. Helen moved in quick, energetic strides up
and back, left and right, the bulbs held in one hand, and soon
the flowers were arranged with the greatest efficiency, while
Sylvia held her breath.

Her father had been reading in the living room, waiting for
his girls to return, and now rose, standing in absent-minded
admiration of the surfeit of flowers. In China, flowers were
not purchased only at the florist, but even at market places,
next to garlic and pigs' feet, at corners and bazaars, and they
seemed to flourish in dirt and manure, in flood and drought.

"Oh." He suddenly recovered his senses. "Let me take care
of the bulbs. I know just what to do with them."

"Certainly not," Helen flashed. "I'm taking care of them. I
bought them, didn't I? For you. But I bought them and I'm
taking care of them and you keep out of this!"

"Yes, yes, yes," and he smiled at Sylvia. "Yes, Helen, yes."
Her father knew when to shunt onto a sidetrack, to bide his
time. For when Helen got charged up, she was dangerous,
ready to plow down anything that stood in the way of her goal.

"But," he ventured placatingly, "may I bring you a dish to
put them in? Allow me to do just that much for my wife."

"Allow you nothing," Helen retorted. "I'm doing this. Stop
interfering, for heaven's sake. Can't you see I'm thinking!"

There was no doubt that she was thinking, Sylvia thought,
watching her eyes roam the room under the pleated brows.
Until she had discharged this energy, completed the task, they
would have to try not to exist, try to be invisible. If anything
lay on her track before she slowed down, the accident would
tear a rent in their lives.

"Out of my way," she said to Sylvia, who stood transfixed
before the cabinet. "Can't you see your mother wants to get
something," and she gave her a jab with her elbow. "What is
the matter with you, can't you move?" She rattled the door
of the cabinet, which she had locked with housewifely posses-
siveness just the day before.

"Get the key! Get the key!" She stamped her foot. "Do you

hear me, get the key!" And Sylvia resisted an involuntary desire to jump, to run, to oblige—anything but to stand there, grinding down her nerves.

"What key?" Sylvia asked slowly, deliberately. "And where is it?"

"In the bedroom, naturally. On the bureau, with that other bunch. Hurry, my hand is getting into a cramp, holding these fool bulbs." Helen was practicing forbearance, marking time and controlling her temper with great effort.

There were seven keys entangled in paper clips and rubber bands. Sylvia told her so, raising her voice a little so it would carry into the living room. "Shall I bring them all?"

"Oh, for heaven's sake. Bring the whole bureau, but bring something quick. I can't stand here forever because of you!"

Sylvia spread the keys out on her palm and held up the palm for her mother's inspection. Helen picked one and tried to jam it into the cabinet, but it wouldn't go in. Besides, she had to use her left hand, since her right was tightly clasped about the bulbs, dripping mud and threadlike roots.

Her mouth clenched tight, she tried another and a third. "Why don't you," she cried, glaring at Sylvia, "know which key it is? You take no interest in your own home." Her vengeance reached out into the future. "You'll be sorry one day. You'll be very sorry." She turned on her heel and collided with Liyi, who held a plate in his hand. She recovered very quickly, very angrily, and said, "Give it to me quick, and don't try to be funny," snatching the dish out of his hand and clapping the bulbs onto it. Sylvia stood like a camera, receptive but incapable of moving.

Then she could see that Helen was thinking again, her eyes darting; she strode away, staring furiously at her right hand, so soiled and uncomfortable with dirt. Her whole body was contorted with rage. She strode into Paul's room—he was out riding his bicycle after the morning of rain—to put the dish on the window sill, as they always did, for Paul's room was the sunniest, his window lined with cacti and flowerpots.

Sylvia heard a strange noise, a moan perhaps, a tortured sound, and Helen stepped back into the living room. Her task had not been completed, for the dish was still in her hands. Her eyes were filmed over and fixed in anger, frustration and confusion. Her mouth still hung open after uttering the ugly cry.

"He's sleeping in there!" she said. "Sleeping, sleeping in my house!" She flung the dish and the bulbs at Liyi. They crashed messily at his feet. "Your stupid nephew sleeping in my house. Oh, I tell you I can't stand it. I can't stand it another second." So Peiyuan, Sylvia thought, Peiyuan who now shared her brother's room, had been sleeping after his day of job-hunting. And Helen had not been able to reach the window sill beyond his bed.

"I can't stand him," she said on the point of tears, "sleeping with his big teeth showing! My house isn't my own, with him around!"

And there was Peiyuan now—not quite fully awake, standing in the doorway, understanding every word of it. He was a rustic with an uncanny capacity for understanding anything in English that referred to him. What would her father do about this? Sylvia was afraid for him.

She was afraid, and although she knew it was a craven thing to do, she left the room and slammed her bedroom door behind her. The scene outside her window had changed. It was dusk now, but she did not notice. She was breathing in long, controlled gasps, angrily and despairingly.

Helen's explosion would resolve itself, Sylvia knew. But the thought brought her no comfort. She felt shattered, both agitated and enervated. Her mind was frozen on a single incident.

The day Peiyuan had arrived, Helen had come into the living room and stood apart. Then she had acted as though she had to invite herself to sit down. Sylvia and her brother Paul had not been able to look at her staring at Peiyuan. They knew what she saw, and knowing had made them Judases. She stared at an intruder, an unhandsome Chinese boy, disheveled from his journey, a bumpkin. Wait till she sees his bed roll, Sylvia had thought. He wasn't a city boy, and so he had worn a coarse and faded long gown, and a pair of denims under it. His feet had been dusty in canvas crepe-rubber shoes, and his cheap watch was as large as a clock on his wrist. He had the features that Helen found so antagonizing on some Chinese. Such small eyes (What's the matter with you Chinese, having such small black eyes?), the kind of Chinese nose that looked stuffed and adenoidal, and such large, uneven white teeth. The cowlick made him look unkempt, indolent, unmannered as only the Chinese could be, what with their spitting out of tramcars, picking their ears at movies, belching at meals. His whole appearance was slack, except for the activity of his eyes, bright and eager (but they were small, tight-lidded, like Korean eyes), and the mobility of his mouth (hardly ever closing upon those teeth).

Sylvia had not had to give Paul a sign to know. Their hearts had contracted slowly, and they breathed as though in secret. They could never explain their cousin Peiyuan to Helen. Even in a starched shirt and tie, he would not be transformed. He was not an idealized Chinese whom Helen might approach understanding, accepting. He was real and their apartment had suddenly become too small.

Helen made Sylvia defensive about China. Now Sylvia re-membered—in her dream last night she had been haunted by her father's eyes. They seemed to whisper as he carefully stared, carefully examined nothing at the middle distance; he was Chinese, so Chinese, she often envied him; he could afford to forget that he was. Emotions had spoken across her dream as though she were a telephone exchange; emotions turned into faces. She had been an umbrella under which they stood: Liyi and Helen. But the umbrella of herself closed in slow motion. She had then stood between Liyi and Peiyuan. She grew specific and plain. She had felt rather than seen danger among them. Morning came, and she had awakened reluctantly.

Her concern for the country reiterated itself in the daylight, a concern that was simple, feminine, specifically organic to her experience. Memory was a miniature locomotive, making a small intimate trail into the lamenting Chinese landscape. The land she had seen as a child was populated with the resigned living and the limitless dead; the mud houses of the peasants and the dirt mounds of the buried; the farmer looking up as the train passed like a slow planet through his fields; the village folk crowding against the train windows, offering wares and services, hot tea and steamed cakes, roast ducks, eggs, bird cages, cricket crockery, toys made of glass, paper, split bamboo. But her mother never bought anything, except tangerines perhaps, for they had had their picnic box packed at home with sandwiches and fried chicken, enough to last a day and a night, if the journey was to be a long one. Only Yennai, the *amah*, sometimes leaned out of the window and argued with the vendors, bargaining with dignity and shrewdness and retiring to her corner of the compartment with triumph and a pot of tea.

It could not be that summers in Peitaiho had really existed, that Chefoo and Tsingtao were not figments of an imagination that had stepped out of its healthy limits. Where were those whitewashed stones which guided one's way in the moonlight to a house by the sea, trickling in finger-high waves at Baby Beach? She was six, clutching the reins of a donkey, her straw coolie hat trailing on the sand, while behind the hedge her brother sat sucking his thumb in a bed of flaming marigolds.

All things were blue and white, the sea and the sails, the sky and the sheets blowing on the clothesline. Where were the Bartlett kids now, those blond children who stole an ear of corn in the field one day and ran and ran and ran, certain they were pursued by the police, and hid with her in the stone jar half filled with rain water? Then there was Johnny who gave her a flower and was a true lover at seven. He was American, too, and even in her memory their blondness made her uneasy. It was as though a bird repeated his call, reminding her and making it overcast in the weather of her reminiscences. And she could still taste Chefoo and smell the raw silk they brought in bolts to the hotel, letting the yards fall in wide folds on the terrace amid their tea and butter creams. There was refuse floating in the harbor and great American Navy ships anchored in the distance and a feeling of rain and geese coming down from the north. When she was ten, they spent three months in Tsingtao, clopping down the drives in carriages, eating succulent noodles out of a bowl in the restaurant on the beach, tracing the formality of the pebbled walk around the Aquarium. In Laoshan behind the bay, topsy-turvy Chinese tea houses were perched over waterfalls and her mother was caught bathing nude by a sedan-carrier, and screamed and ran out of sight. Sylvia wondered if any of this had really existed at all, had any of it really been?

Those were the yellow days of childhood, and white and blue seemed always to be the colors of discovery. She slid back several years, looking for herself in another city, the incantations of longing making her thoughts as large and formal as prayers. . . .

Peiping, the old walled city, was her first home. Sylvia remembered a medieval incandescence flaring in all its seasons. Life there, between walls that divided and secluded and marked off in patterns of regular and irregular squares, was as fully *now* as the warm grasp of a hand, as quilts tucked thickly under the chin, as minutes spent coin by coin by an old man in the sun. She remembered childhood and hot cereal and soft-boiled eggs. She thought, tasting these again, that one's first memories should be of loving and that these should be under the Peiping sky; that one's early eyes should grow deep with looking upon that northern largeness; that one's proportions might embrace both the utter intricacy of the new moon—the thinnest shining lunar prophecy of a crescent suspended over the spring mud—and the boldness, the lustiness, the full-blown wonder of solid sunlight and blackest artesian depths—that these should be and remain and live at the young core of every adult, be the solid unwavering pivot of the unchanging child in every grown person, the point of eternal return, the memory which is the person, beyond which no history can recede!

In the northern spring, the New Year began with celebrations and red lace paper pasted on doorways and clanging of gongs, a chilly beginning in loud noises and bright colors, then warming, softening, destroying the winter stoniness of earth with March dust from the Gobi. Sand-blinded, the rickshaws wore khaki hoods buttoned like upright sleeping bags, and the rain fell from heaven straight down into the foot-thick dust like closely packed nails of liquid under the hammering of thunder.

Then, the kites! Offerings to wind and sky! Octagonal or triangular, airy as a skeleton with feathery fins, or fancy as a fiery dragon with scarflike tails undulating in the wind. Fish swimming sturdily, star shapes, circles linked with tinkling wires, humble homemade rag and sticks, an unsteady clown climbing, a disembodied strip of brilliance wriggling up the sky, a shape, a form, a color—all looked into the stratosphere. When still earthbound, they were awkward, stumbling across the walls amid shouts and laughter. Then they gathered strength, pulling, tugging to be free, bursting into the upper sunshine, high above the city wall, floating, sliding, resting on a shadowless reef, anchored to a small boy, an animated dot below, or an aspiring blue-trousered man sprinting across a square, or an old pipe-smoker squatting on his haunches; they linked—by a thin disappearing line of silver, an intangible linear thought, a wire shimmering between the infinite and a dark head in an encamped town—a kite, a thread, a spool, a hand.

In summer, the trees bloomed, acacias, lilacs, mimosas, and the bushes producing giant peonies bent over with their burdens. The house was cool, green, with shades letting in only a fragrance as distracting as a stealthy kiss. Mornings were lemon-colored, afternoons gold, the heat dry and virile, hitting one at the front door like the sound of drums. Down the streets, people hugged the shade, as though the sunlight might efface them, so deep and intensely it shone. The imperial parks and lakes were busy with families in rowboats, arrested in jungles of lotus plants; students found love in small pergolas, tourists examined the white ballustrades, the marble and tile, the walls encrusted with dragons, the windows cut out like peaches and pears. Cameras snapped their eyelids, making a harvest of permanent reflections, to be leafed through in other times, in other worlds.

If she had been a good girl all month, one night Sylvia would be taken to the Tsengs', to a garden party in a huge palace-like home. Evenings were uncharted continents for grownups only. The lanterns glowed mysteriously both indoors and out, the house sprawled like a large latticelike cage, gleaming with dark Chinese furniture and porous places where the porch seemed to hang askew from the left wing. Musicians squeaked away on instruments, emitting a tart sound, sliding off into tones both raw and sweet. Then a crashing of cymbals and the shadow play was on, the white cloth screen flickering with the colored puppets jigging around like noisy little deities. Much running back and forth with dishes and cups, the grownups chattering in shrill voices. There were hectic exclamations when a gust of wind almost blew down the screen and the lanterns shuddered and tore loose, to be pursued in the rock garden. A prelude of autumn chilled the party, and the ladies were estranged in their flimsy dresses and thin jade bracelets. "Indoors, indoors," someone ordered with hospitable truculence, "and more wine before midnight!" The musicians shrugged and the puppeteers took advantage of the commotion to test their chopsticks in the forty dishes on the lawn.

The autumn moon was the most glorious, predicting desolation, leading as it did into the dark of the year. October lingered, clear as the blue-white of a child's eye; it rested in an open movement, flowing over and above the walls. The rancid human smell of the alleyways was washed clean, and heaven blew cool, agate colors into the leaves. The heart was released and longed for a mooring, for the sun of the year was leaving on a tide of time, and winter was wide spaces between the northern cities.

Snow on Peiping! In her thoughts, object and emotion melted into each other—the dusty plodding of camels' feet felt like the cushioning of fatigue against the long winter night. Her bedroom was a nest at the end of the long corridor of home. The Chinese seemed to have learned the art of quilt-making from the falling seams of snow blanketing a familiar nature. Hush, there was no sharpness here! Whiteness was a presence like large words written in the sky: purchase spring with minted snow! The child-in-her had thought this must be God descending in myriad white miracles. Oh, dream me, dream me, Sylvia raved as a talisman against the present. Let there be silence; the dazzling shadow of the infinite fell on those pines, those tiled roofs, that rocky earth, winter hardening, selfishly unyielding, turning its back upon the chilly human orphans and hungry dogs trotting quickly on icy feet. In wintry aspirations the spirit strengthened, under sterile moonlight were human intimacies born. So went Peiping into spring, breaking fearfully like girlhood into love, so went hamlet, village, town, city, all the explored and seminal land, peopled for so long by so many dark heads. . . .

Sylvia did not know how long she had been standing before her bedroom window. It was almost completely dark outside. The apartment was quiet, another Shanghai evening rubbing warmly against its walls.

FRANK CHIN
(1940-   )

Born in Berkeley, California, Frank Chin was spirited off to Oakland to realize big ideas. He claims to be the first Chinese-American brakeman on the Southern Pacific Railroad and still sports an old railroad standard his grandfather carried in the S.P. steward service. Chin's fiction has appeared in little magazines and anthologies. His play *The Chickencoop Chinaman* was produced at the American Place Theater in New York in 1972 and became the first Asian-American play in New York stage history. At this writing, he is finishing a novel, *Charlie Chan on Maui*, for Harper and Row and is working on a new play, tentatively entitled *The Year of the Dragon*.

THE CHICKENCOOP CHINAMAN

THE CHARACTERS

TAM LUM: A Chinese-American writer and film-maker with the gift of gab and an open mouth. A multi-tongued word magician losing his way to the spell who trips to Pittsburgh to conjure with his childhood friend and research a figure in his documentary movie.

HONG KONG
DREAM GIRL: A dream monster from a popular American song of the twenties.

KENJI: A research dentist. Japanese-American born and raised. Tam's childhood friend. Sullen, brooding. A zombie with taps on his shoes.

LEE: Possible Eurasian or Chinese-American passing for white. She's borne several kids in several racial combinations, but mothers only one, Robbie, her weird son.

ROBBIE: Lee's weird son.

THE PLACE

The Oakland district of Pittsburgh, Pennsylvania.

THE TIME

The present.

ACT I

Scene 1

ON RISE: *Curtain rises to limbo stage. Black.*
The sound of a screaming jet in flight runs for several seconds. In the dark a chuckle is heard, a mischievous but not sinister little laugh from TAM LUM. *Overriding his chuckle, the voice of* HONG KONG DREAM GIRL *as the stewardess and in-flight presence.*

HONG KONG DREAM GIRL (*as Stewardess*) (*VO in limbo*). Ladies and Gentlemen, we are preparing to land in Pittsburgh. Please see that your seatbelts are securely fastened and your seat backs in the upright raised position and observe the no-smoking sign. For your comfort and safety, we ask that you remain seated and keep your seatbelts fastened until the plane has come to complete stop. Thank you.
Overhead spot comes on. Upstage and high on a platform, TAM *stands in a shaft of light. The rest of the stage is dark.*

TAM. She asked me if I thought she looked like she was born in Hong Kong. She looked all right to me except that I thought she was maybe fresh in from drill team practice.
Enter GIRL *dressed as* TAM *describes. She struts and turns across the stage to the rhythm of brush and drums, from one pool of light to the next. She is Asian, beautiful, grinning, doll-like and mechanical. A wind-up dream girl steppin' out.*
. . . because she was wearing high white boots with tassels and a satin dress that had epaulets on it. And underneath one of them super no-knock, rust-proof, titstiffening bras, with the seams and rivets and buckles showing through. And she walked like she was on parade. And had a drill team Jackie Kennedy, non-descript bouffant hairdo. And hands! Hands just made to hold, not to speak of twirl a baton. Yessir, hands like greased smoothbore cannons. So

(5 *1*)

she asked if I thought she looked like she was born in Hong Kong.

GIRL. Do you think I look like I was born in Hong Kong?

TAM. "Sure you do, Honey," I said, thinking back to the days of high school assemblies and the girl with medals jingling on her satin and sequin chest. Twirling her baton! I especially remember her flaming baton number done in black light to the Ritual Fire Dance. She said, "You . . ."

GIRL. You can tell I was born in Hong Kong, even though I've been here for six years?

TAM. . . . She asked. And I replied, "And there's a whole lot more where that came from!"

GIRL. Where were you born?

TAM. Chinamen are made, not born, my dear. Out of junk-imports, lies, railroad scrap iron, dirty jokes, broken bottles, cigar smoke, Cosquilla Indian blood, wino spit, and lots of milk amnesia.

GIRL. You sure have a way with the word, but I wish you'd do more than pay lip service to your Canton heritage.

TAM.

Through the rest of the speech in this segment, TAM *goes through voice and accent changes. From W. C. Fields to American Midwest, Bible Belt Holy Roller, etc. His own "normal" speech jumps between black and white rhythms and accents.*

My dear in the beginning there was the Word! Then there was me! And the Word was CHINAMAN. And there was me. I lipped the word as if it had little lips of its own. "Chinaman" said on a little kiss. I lived the Word! The Word is my heritage. Ah, but, it has been many a teacake moon, many thousands of pardons for a dirty picture snapped in my raw youth now, that these lips have had a hankering for servicing some of my Canton heritage in the flesh. But I've never been able to get close enough. Now you, my Hong Kong flower, my sweet sloe-eyed beauty from the mysterious East, I can tell that your little fingers have twiddled many a chopstick. Your smoothbore hands have the memory of gunpowder's invention in them and know how to shape a blast and I dare say, tickle out a shot. Let me lead your hands.

GIRL. I can tell you are really Longtime Californ', and kind of slick too, but you were telling me of what you were made.

TAM. I am the natural born ragmouth speaking the motherless bloody tongue. No real language of my own to make sense with, so out comes everybody else's trash that don't conceive. But the sound truth is that I AM THE NOTORIOUS ONE AND ONLY CHICKENCOOP CHINAMAN HIMSELF that talks in the dark heavy Midnight, the secret Chinatown Buck Buck Bagaw. I am the result of a pile of pork chop suey thrown up into the chickencoop in the dead of night and the riot of dark birds, night cocks and insomniac nympho hens running after strange food that followed. There was Mother Red built like a fighting cock and running like one too. Hellbent for feather, cocksure, running for pork chop suey in the dead of night. And DESTINY.

GIRL. And then you were born?

TAM. No, lass. Moonlight shone through the chinks of the coop. And seabreezes from the West brought the smell of the ships and the sewers. Moonlight caught prickly in her mad hen's eye and seabreeze in her feathers as she ran a dumb cluck in a bird gallop across the great dung prairie of an Oakland Chinatown Chickencoop. Following Mother Red was her Rhode Island featherbrains. Nickel and dime birds that even after being flat on their backs in Freudian analysis couldn't grunt out an egg between them. Promiscuous and criminal birds. Too lazy even to shape up a proper pecking order, they just grooved on running their fool heads off together, making chicken poetry after Mad Mother Red.

GIRL. And then you were born?

TAM. Meanwhile, back at the doghouse was a bird of a different feather. A mean critter with Red in its eyes, seen as it heard them clucks come loco round the corner.

GIRL. And then you were born?

TAM. No. Just at this moment coming through the fence was a troup of Spanish Flamenco gypsy dwarves, Los Gitanos Cortos, taking a shortcut to their boxcar after a hard night's work dancing on the tops of Cadillacs and Lincolns in the T&D theatre parking lot. This crowd of shortstuff whiffed the pork chop suey and had visions of licking their trough clean. Like the mad dog, they ran full of wild Injuns. Blood whooping fast for to grab a quick bite.

GIRL. And then you were born?

TAM. (*As a Bible Belt Preacher*) Born? No! Crashed! Not

born. Stamped! Not born! Created! Not born. No more born
than the heaven and earth. No more born than nylon or
acrylic. For I am a Chinaman! A miracle synthetic! Drip
dry and machine washable. For now, in one point of
time and space, as never before and never after, in this one
instant of eternity, was focused that terrific, that awesome
power of the universe that marks a moment divine . . . For
Mother Red and her herd of headless wonders! One mad
hairy dog! And twelve little people in high heeled shoes,
once and for all, blind and deaf and very dumb to the per-
petration of righteous heinous love MET!
(TAM *gives razzberry.*)

GIRL. And you were born.

TAM. Born. Born to talk to Chinaman sons of Chinamans,
children of the dead. But enough of my sordid past. It's not
right for a body to know his own origins, for it leaves the
mother nothing secret to herself. I want to hear about you.

GIRL. You sure have a way with words, but I'd like it better if
you'd speak the mother tongue.

TAM. I speak nothing but the mother tongues bein' born to
none of my own, I talk the talk of orphans. But I got a
tongue for you, baby. And maybe you could handmake my
bone China.

TAM *and* GIRL *are in a single pool of light.* TAM
*moves to put her hand on his fly and stuff one of his
hands inside her shirt.* TAM *licks his lips and puckers
up for a smooch, breathing heavy. She giggles and runs
off.* BLACKOUT.

GIRL (*as Stewardess*) (*VO in black*). Ladies and Gentlemen, we
have just landed in Pittsburgh. The time is now five forty-
six, Eastern Standard Time. The temperature is forty-four
degrees. The weather is cloudy with a chance of snow.

SCENE 2

KENJI's *apartment. Night.*
*Pittsburgh's black ghetto is called "Oakland." It has
the look of having been a high class, fashionable resi-*

dential district at the turn of the Century. The build-
ings are still solid, thick-walled . . . at least they seem
that way on the outside. Inside the grand interiors
have been lost after countless remodelings.
KENJI's *apartment is high-ceilinged. New diaphragm*
walls divide what was once a big room into three. The
bathroom, complete with tub and sink, the living–
dining room and entry area, and part of the kitchen
are visible.
The apartment has the look of having been recently
moved into, while at the same time looking a long
time settled. It is on the verge of having a style. A mas-
sive round table top is set low on the floor on cinder
blocks. Wooden auditorium chairs. An overstuffed
chair. A mattress and boxspring from a double bed
serves as a couch. Tatami on the floor.
The walls are covered with posters of black country,
blues and jazz musicians that clash with the few Jap-
anese prints and art objects.
A cake with one piece cut from it is on the table. Sew-
ing paraphernalia and curtain material are on the
table.
The front door is open. Snow is seen falling outside
through a window. The crash of cars coupling up from
the railyard can be heard now and then.
TAM *and* KENJI *enter.* TAM *carries a small suitcase*
and an attaché case. KENJI *carries a travelbag of suits.*
TAM *puts his stuff down in the entryway.* KENJI *keeps*
the travelbag. TAM *flexes, shakes his legs down,*
stretches and yawns, scanning the place . . .

KENJI. Well, man, this is it. My place . . . right in the heart of
the black ghetto. Just like home.
TAM. BlackJap Kenji! Mah brother! Whew, man, I thought
for awhile you'd grownup, man. Twenty grand high class
research dentist wit' his own lab, man, his own imported
apes, twenty three hunnerd miles from the childhood.
Grownup, fat, middleclass! Ha. But here ya are, still livin
in a slum, still my blackJap Kenji.
KENJI. Who you callin "grownup"?
TAM (*Spying curtain stuff*). Yeah, Kenji's home in this Pittsburgh, with a woman and everythang. Janet?
KENJI. Naw man, that was . . . where was that?

TAM. High school. I was going to ask you . . .

KENJI. You okay?

TAM. . . . Must be me. Them hours winging here sittin on my ass broke my momentum. I feel like I lost speed . . . It's even hard for me to talk . . . and if I can't talk to you, you know I . . . and I been doing a lotta talkin, Yeah . . . Mumbo Jumbo. Dancer sends his love.

TAM flops in whatever's handy, leans back and closes his eyes . . . KENJI watches him.

LEE (*Sleepily from bedroom*). Robbie? Kenji?

KENJI responds to the voice by going to the bedroom and peeking in. He makes a quick survey of the apartment, looking into rooms, seeing who's where. He creeps up on TAM, brings his face down close and level with TAM's face and turns on Helen Keller.

KENJI (*As Helen Keller*). Moowahjeerffurher roar rungs!

TAM snaps awake, staring KENJI in the face, and deadpan says . . .

TAM (*As Helen Keller*). Moowahjeerffurher roar rungs?

KENJI (*As Helen Keller*). Moowahjeerffurher roar rungs.

TAM & KENJI (*Continuing*). My dear friends!

TAM (*Continuing*). Helen Keller! I'd know that voice anywhere!

TAM and KENJI exchange five . . .

KENJI (*As Helen Keller*). Aheeeha op eeehoooh too ooh wahyou oooh.

TAM (*As a Bible Belt preacher*). Yeah, talk to me, Helen! Hallelujah! I hear her talkin to me.

TAM jumps to his feet shuddering with fake religious fervor.

KENJI supports with Hallelujahs and repetitions.

Put you hands on the radio, children, feel the power of Helen Keller, children. Believe! And she, the Great White goddess, the mother of Charlie Chan, the Mumbler, the Squeaker, shall show you the way, children! Oh, yeah!

KENJI. Hallelujah!

TAM. Helen Keller overcame her handicaps without riot! She overcame her handicaps without looting! She overcame her handicaps without violence! And you Chinks and Japs can too. Oooh I feel the power, children. Feel so gooooood! I feeeeeel it!

Enter ROBBIE *from the kitchen. He wears a bibbed apron. A professional apron, white, no frills.*

LEE. Tom? Tom? Kenji?

TAM (*As Helen Keller*). Yarr roar heh yelp wee ooh sub coawt unh ree-ssurch llee-dung toth engd roh dove fub earthed eff fecks.

KENJI (*As Helen Keller*). Your help will help support research ending birth defects . . .

TAM. Listen to the voice of the Great White Motha, come to show you the light, Chinks and Japs, I say Listen, Children! Whooo I feel the power!

TAM and KENJI *exchange fives.* ROBBIE *is attracted to the action, comes and stands, makes himself available, grinning, looking from face to face, laughing.*

(*As Helen Keller*). nggg gah gallop nose weather bar hearth death facts sorrel lull heed new worm who whirl eye fees.

KENJI. And help those born with birth defects lead normal lives.

TAM. Believe!

KENJI. I believe!

TAM. I said, believe, children!

KENJI & ROBBIE. I believe!

TAM. AH MEAN! BELIEVE!

KENJI & ROBBIE. I believe!

TAM. Hallelujah!

TAM and KENJI *exchange five.* TAM *notices* ROBBIE, *glances at* KENJI, *grins, takes* ROBBIE'*s hand, and sets it to give him five, and gives him five.* LEE *rushes angrily into the scene, too late to stop* ROBBIE *from returning five, and grabs her son.*

LEE. Kenji!

TAM. Sister! Child!

KENJI. For the sake of tomorrow's children.

TAM & KENJI (*As Helen Keller*). Thak ahhhnggkkk are are arf rung youuuu.

KENJI. Thank you.

TAM and KENJI *strut and exchange five, laughing and sparring.*

KENJI. Remember Helen Keller's telephone?

TAM. It doesn't ring . . .

KENJI. It just gets warm!

TAM *less energetically, suddenly preoccupied, goes through the motions of exchanging five with* KENJI *who wants to snuffle and spar.* ROBBIE *gets his five from* TAM *and stuffs himself into the scene sparring with* KENJI *while* TAM *catches his breath, and rubs his face.*

LEE (*To* TAM). Leave my boy alone!

TAM. Wha . . . ? What's happening? I got nothing but out-takes in my head . . .

LEE (*To* KENJI). I'm tired of you coming in like this! I'm tired of you putting my son down! Go get your nuts off beating up your own kid! Go on! Come here, Robbie.

ROBBIE. I'm okay Lee.

TAM. How many kids you got?

LEE. . . . what's it to you?

KENJI. None.

TAM (*As Helen Keller*). Oh. Oh . . .

LEE. Oh, you . . . Think you're funny?

KENJI. Everything's cool.

LEE. I've never seen anything so . . .

KENJI. I said, everything's cool!

LEE. You never shout at me. Why're you shouting?

KENJI. Lee . . . Lee, this is my friend, Tam Lum. We used to call him "Tampax" . . .

LEE. Oh, lovely.

KENJI. . . . a long time ago. What's wrong?

LEE. I guess Kenji's told you about me. He tells all his friends.

TAM. No.

KENJI. Friends?

LEE. . . . that I'm pregnant and on my way to Africa.

TAM. No.

KENJI. How can you be pregnant? Who? What?

LEE. . . . and of course he told you the child isn't his.

TAM. No.

LEE. He didn't tell you the only reason he lets me stay here is that he thinks I'm crazy. He told you about my long distance phone calls.

TAM *moves to say "no" again but* LEE *continues*).

Robbie's waiting for you to shake his hand.

TAM. Hey, this is the wrong movie. I didn't mean to come into no situation.

LEE. That's right, run! I should've known. All afraid of the
pretty girls? But oh so anxious to do the right thing—avoid
trouble—save face. Look at you so stoic, and that dumb
little smile. Do ya talk in giggles too? Are you going to
shake my son's hand or not?

TAM. Wanna fuck?

LEE. Yeah.

TAM. Oh, wow, Kenji, you've really grown up!

KENJI. What's wrong, Lee?

LEE. I can't stand people who're rude to children.

KENJI. You're tired, babe.

LEE. I am tired.

TAM. I'm tired and dirty . . . filthy . . . hungry.

LEE. Not too tired to be polite to my son.

KENJI. Oh, hey, man, that's right. You need a bath, right?

TAM. Sure. Hey, kid . . .

LEE. His name is Robbie.

TAM. Hey, Robbie, gimme five!
    TAM *lifts his hand to slap with* ROBBIE, *but* LEE *stops
    them.*

LEE. No, not that! It's sick of you to make fun of blacks . . . the
way you walk . . . your talk . . . givin five. Who do you
think you are?
    TAM *and* ROBBIE *shake hands,* TAM *turning to* LEE
    saying,

TAM. You black?

LEE & ROBBIE. No.

TAM. I didn't think so.

LEE. I was married to a black for awhile.

TAM. You had to tell me, didn't ya? Couldn't let me guess. You
gave up Janet for this girl, eh Kenji?

LEE. No, I'm not his girl. I'm his good deed.

KENJI. Here, drop your jacket, man.

TAM. I need some coffee. Coffee. I mean coffee! Gotta be bright
for my man. Remember that night we were out with
Ovaltine the Dancer? He sends ya his love, man. Where
is that boy? he said. We're in his life story.

KENJI. Oh, hey . . . you gonna put it in the movie? I'm gonna
be on T.V.?

TAM. Movie's gonna turn on two things man, double action,
right? That title defense against Claude Dupree he did in

his forties. His greatest fight right? One. And two how his
daddy, Charley Popcorn, made him be that kind of fighter.
You should see some of the stuff we shot, man.

KENJI. Yeah. You been on the case then.

TAM. Month in Oakland, our Oakland, shooting background
and re-creating the atmosphere of the Dupree fight, after a
month with the Dancer, livin with him, man fifty hours
of him blabbing his life out on quarter inch tape. And I
got the rights to the film of that title defense against Dupree. But it's the Dancer's father, man, Charley Popcorn
that's gonna make this movie go. Remember how Ovaltine
the Dancer carried on about his mighty daddy? Well, he's
here in Pittsburgh man, and we're gonna see him!

KENJI. Yeah!

TAM *and* KENJI *exchange five.* TAM *grabs a handful of
cakecrumbs from the table during his speech.*

TAM. We'll see this Popcorn later, ya know. No equipment on
us, right? Nothin to scare him, sound him. Whoo. This
child done been hisself up two days, seein the last of the
stuff we shot through the lab, and auditioning the tapes
of his Popcorn stories. Now, I'm primed!

KENJI. Maybe you better grab some winks, man, or you won't
have no juice to run on later, you know . . .

TAM. No, no, man. If I sleep now, I won't ever wake up. No, I
came wired to meet Popcorn, just for a little bit, tonight,
check out his pornie house as a possible location, right?
And I'm gonna do it, like in that song, they say:

TAM & KENJI
Somewhere over the rainbow
Bluebirds fly
Birds fly . . .

TAM *and* KENJI *exchange five and laugh. Crumbs fall
from* TAM*'s hand.*

LEE. You're getting crumbs all over the floor. Why don't you
hang up your clothes? I was making curtains there.

KENJI. I put his . . .

TAM. Oh . . .

LEE. Where do you think you are? This place is depressing
enough without your mess . . . so dark and unhappy, and
that awful noise outside night and day. What is that noise?
It's worse today.

KENJI. Sounds like the end of World War III.

TAM. It's the railroad. They're making up a train down in the yard.

LEE. You're only saying that because you're Chinese.

TAM *turns ugly a moment, ready to mess her up, then shrugs it off.*

TAM. I'll pick up the crumbs, okay? And I'll hang up the clothes. Just show me where . . .

LEE. The closets are full.

KENJI. Just leave your stuff, man. Go take your wash and I'll talk to Lee here, okay?

TAM. Yeah.

ROBBIE *shows* TAM *the way to the bathroom.*

Yeah, kid, tasty cake.

ROBBIE. I'll have a piece cut for you when you're done.

TAM *stalls in the bathroom waiting for* ROBBIE *to leave. Instead* ROBBIE *settles himself in the doorway.* TAM *finally begins stripping down to his shorts. He wears boxer type swimming trunks.*

KENJI. Why're you acting like this?

LEE. How?

KENJI. Either be nice to my friend or shut up.

ROBBIE. You like kids. I can tell.

TAM. Kenji . . . he your dad?

ROBBIE. No. He hasn't been. You talk loud when you get mad, did you know that?

TAM. You talk funny for a kid, did you know that?

ROBBIE. I've been around. Kenji says you write movies and stuff. You don't look like you'd write kidstuff though.

TAM. Kenji say I write kidstuff? I don't think my stuff is kidstuff.

ROBBIE. That's what I mean. You don't write kidstuff. Maybe I'll be a writer and write movies . . . (TAM & ROBBIE) and stuff . . .

TAM. Why don't you talk kidstuff? A man should be a kid when he's a kid. You don't wanna be old all your life . . .

ROBBIE. Lee says a man should fight. But Lee isn't a man, is she.

TAM. Well, people said I never talked like a kid either . . . used to give me quarters for my pearl-studded palaver like I was a kind of jukebox. Take it from me, kid. Talk like a kid while you're a kid, even if you have to fake it.

ROBBIE. Kenji just tells me to shut up.

TAM. I'm sure he has his reasons. Right, kid?

ROBBIE. He doesn't like people to talk to him.

TAM. You talk too much, kid. Cool it and just ask "Why?" and "Howcome?"

ROBBIE. How come you're wearing swimming trunks?

TAM. Funny you should ask me that. This is my secret suit! Whenever I see someone in distress I strip down to my secret suit, put up my dukes, and go swimming.

ROBBIE (Laughs). Nobody tells me jokes like that.

TAM. Maybe it's because nobody likes you! No. No. Forget I said that, kid. See, you talk like a little man long enough and I talk back at you like a man. But you can take it, right? You been around.

ROBBIE. Nobody talks to me like a man. That isn't really your secret suit, is it. I mean. I'm not bothering you am I?

TAM. Naw, it's something I picked up from an old dishwasher who was afraid of white old ladies peeking at him through the keyhole. True! I swear! You see, we had the kitchen in this old folks resthome thing. He thought all them old toothless goofy white ladies was all for peeking at his bod, so he used to wear his underpants right in his bath. Crazy old dishwasher. Sometimes I'd wash his back, you know. But he was crazy about boxing.

ROBBIE. I'd help my father in his bath too.

TAM. Oh, you did? Must've been old, huh and . . . oh, I see, died and you and your mom, you came . . . Listen, I'm sorry . . .

ROBBIE. I mean, if I had a father I'd help him like you helped yours.

TAM. He wasn't my father. He was just a crazy old dishwasher.

ROBBIE. But he took care of you.

TAM. I took care of him. He couldn't get around outside of Chinatown without me. All he did for me was take me and Kenji to the fights. He'd go anywhere to catch a fight. Otherwise he was crazy. He depended on my English, my bad Chinese, was what he was doing, like when I had to take him to the police to get a form filled out for the Immigration. Nothin serious. I didn't know that. He didn't know that, Scared.

ROBBIE. You dropped your soap.

TAM. I was twelve . . . How old are you?

ROBBIE. Eleven. Twelve. Almost twelve. You okay?

TAM. When we got home he said he had to have a bath. He said I had to help him. I don't remember what kind of language he was using. I should though don't you think?

ROBBIE. I don't know.

TAM. Neither do I . . . You could see his veins like snakes swimming in rosewater.

ROBBIE. You okay?

TAM. You ever see real rosewater?

ROBBIE. No.

TAM. I helped him into his bath, and he died. It was just lights out. He finished it. Do you believe that, kid?

ROBBIE. Yes.

TAM. See what I mean? Now I tell it dry eyed, and I'm believed. I told it the same at the tub when they came, and they didn't believe me. Because I didn't cry. They got mad. They said I wouldn't get a quarter. I wasn't tellin a story . . . You know what I mean?

ROBBIE. No.

TAM. I mean, act your age, kid! Don't talk to me like a little man. I'm not your buddy. I'm an old dude who tells kids jokes, bosses 'em around gruffly, rough houses 'em, has a swell time, and forgets 'em, cuz that's what adults do. Now, do me a favor and get me my case, will ya? And tell your mother I know what trains sound like cuz I used to work on the railroad . . . No, don't. Just get my case, okay?

ROBBIE. . . . and I'll cut you some cake.

ROBBIE *goes to get case and cut a piece of cake in the kitchen.*

LEE. What were you two talking about in there?

ROBBIE. Uhh . . . somebody he knew. A Chinese dishwasher who took baths wearing a swimsuit.

LEE. Why don't you like being Chinese, Tam?

TAM. What? I'm in the bath.

KENJI. Goddammit, Lee, shut up.

LEE. I said, why don't you like being Chinese, Tam? (*To* KENJI.) I know he's your childhood friend, but you're not children anymore.

ROBBIE *returns to bathroom with* TAM's *case and cake. He sets it inside and hangs around the doorway.*

TAM. What'd you say, Lee?

KENJI *and* LEE *exchange glances.*

KENJI. Nothing, man. Be sure to wash under your arms.

ROBBIE. You're Chinese aren't you? I like Chinese people.

TAM. Me too. They're nice and quiet aren't they?

ROBBIE. One of my fathers was Chinese, like you. He was nice.
The nicest.

TAM. Fathers?

ROBBIE. A white one. A Chinese one. One was black. We talk
with them on the phone. I liked the Chinese . . . Lee says
he wasn't a man.

TAM. Whaddaya mean, Chinese like me and not a man? You
some kind of racist midget trying to ride for half fare?

ROBBIE. Should I have said that? Are you mad at me? I don't
think you should have told me about the crazy old dishwasher, but I understand. I'm not mad at you.

TAM. Listen, kid. Man to man. If I could be mad at you, I
would. I'm not mad at you. But don't talk to me. Your idea
of kid talk is just too strange for me.

ROBBIE. Why?

TAM. Ah, now! There's the kid . . . That's all, "Why?"
"Why?" Say, "Why?" kid.

ROBBIE. Why?

TAM. You got it.

LEE. What's he doing here anyway? Tell me again, please. I'm
listening carefully this time.

KENJI. Aww, Lee! I seeya. I hearya. You don't have to . . .

LEE. Well, what is he doing here?

KENJI. He's making some kind of documentary movie about
Ovaltine Jack Dancer, an ex-champion of the light heavy-
weights. The Dancer's daddy lives here, and Tam's here to
see him.

LEE. That's boxing isn't it?

KENJI. Yeah, and don't make anything of that! This could be
Tam's big chance.

LEE. Is this boxer Chinese? Of course not, he's black.

KENJI. Yeah.

LEE. I hate people making it on the backs of black people. I
don't like your friend at all.

KENJI. But you made it on your back under blacks, and that's
okay, huh?

LEE. That's not good grammar. I don't understand what you're
saying. But I think you meant to be cruel. You've never
been cruel to me before.

KENJI. Listen, Lee.

LEE. You're being cruel to me. You're going to scold me.

KENJI. No, Lee . . . I was going to say I can see what you
mean. But I think you're wrong too. About Tam, I mean.
And me faking blackness.

LEE. . . . Not you . . .

KENJI. Yeah, me. I mean, Ovaltine Jack the Dancer was our
hero, you know. We met him.

LEE. Oh, a story. That's what I need right now, a story.

KENJI. I'm explaining something. Maybe we act black, but it's
not fake. Oakland was weirdness. No seasons. No snow.
I was a kid missing the concentration camps . . . the
country with just us, you know what I mean? Now it's
blacks and Chinese all of a sudden. All changed. My folks,
everybody . . .

LEE. And you? The young prince returned from exile in the
wilderness? Turned black! Presto change-o!

KENJI. I changed! Yeah! Presto! School was all blacks and
Mexicans. We were kids in school, and you either walked
and talked right in the yard, or got the shit beat outa you
every day, ya understand? But that Tam was always what
you might say . . . "The Pacesetter." Whatever was hap-
penin with hair, or the latest color, man . . . Sometimes
he looked pretty exotic, you know, shades, high greasy hair,
spitcurls, purple shiney shirt, with skull cufflinks and Frisko
jeans worn like they was fallin off his ass. Me, I was the
black one. "BlackJap Kenji" I used to be called and hated
yellowpeople. You look around and see where I'm livin,
Lee, and it looks like I still do, Pittsburgh ain't exactly
famous for no Chinatown or Li'l Tokyo, you know.

LEE. "BlackJap"? I've always thought of you as just plain
Kenji . . . a little sullen . . . a little shy.

KENJI. I'm explaining something, okay?

LEE. I was just commenting . . .

KENJI. Okay?

LEE. Okay.

KENJI. Okay. When we were in college, we kidnapped Ovaltine.
I mean, Tam did. Tricked him out of his hotel room, and
we took him driving out of Oakland and all stood out by
the car pissing in the bushes. And I remembered I'd been
to New Orleans and, you know, stuck over on the colored
side. And I had to piss, and didn't know which way to go.
And this black dishwasher there, *saw my plight* so to speak,

and took me out to the can and we took places at urinals
right next to each other. I thought that was pretty friendly.
And I wanted to tell Ovaltine, you know, but Ovaltine
being black, might not understand a yellow man, standing
next to him, pissing in the bushes, talking about the last
memorable time he went pissing with a black man . . . He
talked about pissing with the black dishwasher in New
Orleans like it was him that did it.

LEE. Sounds just like him.

KENJI. You don't know him.

LEE. Didn't that piss you off? What'd you do?

KENJI. No, I wasn't pissed off. I was glad. I didn't have the guts
to do it, you know. He took the risks.

LEE. Ahh. But he's a charlatan, and you're for real.

TAM. No, Lass, I'm a charlatan, and he's for real.

LEE. Have you been eavesdropping?

TAM. No, I've been eavesdropping. Me and Robbie ran out of
conversation. So since Kenji was tellin all my stories.

KENJI. What's this thing of his about talkin in the bathroom
anyway? Every time I go in there here he comes to stand
in the doorway. What is that?

LEE. Didn't you do that as a boy?

TAM. Where we come from boys who hung around watchin
men in the pisser were considered a little funny that way,
you know.

LEE. It takes one to know one. *You know.*

KENJI. Lee, what is this all about? Badmouthing my friend,
someone you've never seen before, putting me down
through him . . . I explained . . . !

LEE. I never put you down!

KENJI. The hell you didn't! I'm not imitating no black people.
I'm no copycat! I know I live with 'em, I talk like 'em,
I dress . . . maybe even eat what they eat and don't mess
with, so what if I don't mess with other Orientals . . .
Asians, whatever, blah blah blah. Hell, the way you been
talkin to Tam, who's my brother, Lee, you make everything I do sound ugly, man, like I hate myself. And you got
no right to say that about me.

LEE. I never said that. I've never seen you like this before.

KENJI. I've never been like this before. I'm with my friend, and
in my house with my friend. I should be proud of my house
with my friend in here, but you're making me ashamed.

And I won't have it. You can mess around with this place anyway you want . . . put up curtains, I don't care. I like 'em. But you're just a guest here. You're not my woman or my lover or nothing but a guest. Now you act like one, you understand?

LEE. I never put you down.

KENJI. You put me down. Damn, you put me down! Bringin in this goddamn tatami grassmat Japanese bullshit and knockin the legs off the table . . .

LEE. I just thought . . .

KENJI. You just thought like some little white bitch with the artbooks. I'm not Japanese! Tam ain't no Chinese! And don't give me any of that "If-you-don't-have-that-Oriental-culture-baby-all-you've-got-is-the-color-of-your-skin" bullshit. No, I know that's not you, don't look that way. But we're not getting into no silk robes and walk around like fools for you!

LEE. You're talking an awful lot!

TAM. Oh, um . . .

KENJI. Yeah, I am, huh. I must be happy.

LEE. Tom's coming.

KENJI. Never heard of him.

LEE. My ex-husband.

KENJI. Ex-husbands and kids. You have so many. White, yellow, black. What is this Twenty Questions?

LEE. If you'd stop interrupting . . .

KENJI. I'm trying to avoid significant pauses. This conversation has got to have some flow, some pop, some rhythm, or I'm . . .

LEE. He's Chinese . . . The Chinese husband I had, and he says he's coming to take me back to San Francisco with him. He wants my baby.

KENJI. What baby? You been on the phone again with baby news?

LEE. And I'm mad and I'm scared . . . and it isn't easy for me.

TAM. Wow!

LEE. He's a writer.

TAM. What's he write, art books? Chinese cookbooks?

LEE. He's writing a book called Soul on Rice.

KENJI & TAM. SOUL ON RICE?

TAM. He thinks that title up all by himself, or did you help?

LEE. I'll tell ya how he thought it up . . .

TAM. No! Don't tell me. Just tell me, is it white rice or brown rice? Must be a cookbook.

KENJI & TAM. WILD RICE!

> TAM *and* KENJI *exchange five.* LEE *is laughing in spite of herself.*

TAM. Yeah, he didn't fulfill your lesbian fantasies. Or was it you found out you didn't like girls? So you left him for a black . . . but then, if he gave you this kid . . .

LEE. It's not his!

KENJI. It's not mine.

TAM. All right, immaculate conception. But, for him to think so, you musta given him another chance . . . Lemme see your eyes.

> LEE *turns from* TAM.

LEE. I don't like being bossed.

TAM. All these husbands and children, man. All colors and decorator combinations. A one woman minority of the Month Club. Now to Africa, wow . . .

LEE. You're supposed to be comforting me. This is serious.

TAM. Whoowhee! Chinamans do make lousey fathers. I know. I have one.

LEE. How can you laugh at a thing like that?

TAM. I reminded you of your Chinese husband!

LEE. Well, I . . .

TAM (*Teasingly*). Huh? Come on, admit it.

LEE. Tam.

TAM. Huh? Yeah?

LEE. Not exactly, maybe . . .

TAM. We all look alike.

LEE. Not exactly, but . . .

TAM. It's okay. You remind me of somebody, too. So we're even. But that's okay. This trip's going to make me well. I'm going to see again, and talk and hear . . . And I got a solution to all your problems. Don't bother with no Twenty Questions, Ouija Board, I Ching or any of that. One: I'm splitting to take care of business. And two: If you don't want to see people keep the door locked.

KENJI. We'll go see Charley Popcorn, and Lee, if you don't wanta see Tom keep the door locked. We'll be back soon, Tam's tired . . .

LEE. Why do you have to go? Let Tam go.

TAM. Yeah, I gotta see Charley Popcorn.

LEE. And you and me and Robbie can stay home with the door locked.

KENJI. But I want to see Charley Popcorn too. Father of a champion, man.

LEE. Oh, he's Ovaltine Jack Dancer's father.

TAM. The madman behind the badman! Come on, if you're gonna come on, man. Let's go someplace where we can talk and grab some eats before we see Popcorn.

LEE. Aren't you going to eat here?

TAM. I don't want to eat here!

LEE. But Robbie's been cooking for all of us . . .

TAM. Then you and him eat for all of us. I'm sorry. We hit it off wrong. Maybe under different circumstances . . . like in a dark alley.

LEE. You wouldn't joke like that if you had kids of your own.

TAM. I have two. Sarah and Jonah, named for Sarah and Jonah, remember, Kenji?

LEE. Your wife was white of course.

KENJI. What's color got to do with it? Right, Tam?

TAM. Man, you got it all down, don't ya? Yes, she was white!

LEE. I knew you hated being Chinese. You're all chicken! Not an ounce of guts in all of you put together! Instead of guts you have . . . all you have is is . . . culture! Watery paintings, silk, all that grace and beauty arts and crafts crap! You're all very pretty, and all so intelligent. And . . . you couldn't even get one of your own girls, because they know . . .

TAM. Know what?

LEE. They know all about you, mama's boys and crybabies, not a man in all your males . . . so you go take advantage of some stupid white girl who's been to a museum, some scared little ninny with visions of jade and ancient art and being gently cared for.

TAM. You're not talking about me.

KENJI. Lee, you're not talking about Tam.

LEE. I am talking about Tam. Tampax Lum, your friend. He's the worst kind. He knows he's no kind of man. Look at him, he's like those little vulnerable sea animals born with no shells of their own so he puts on the shells of the dead. You hear him when he talks? He's talking in so many goddamn dialects and accents all mixed up at the same time, cracking wisecracks, lots of oh yeah, wisecracks, you might think he was a nightclub comic. What'sa wrong with your Chinatowng acka-cent, huh?

KENJI. Lee.

TAM. I got tired of people correcting it. They were even telling me I was "mispronouncing" my name . . . kept telling me it was pronounced "Tom."

LEE. See? More wisecracks. You're just saying that.

TAM. Yeah, that's all I am. And they said I had rags in my mouth, which led to ragmouth, which ended up Tampax. But I hear something in your tongue . . . that funny red in the hair . . . You got the blood don't ya. You're Chinese, right? A breath of the blood?

LEE *turns away.*

Did your Tom know? You were giving Chinamans a chance to smack up skin to skin . . . goin home to yellowness. No, I'm not puttin you down. I'm not arguing with you one bit 'bout nothin. You're right. Everything you say is right. I'm a good loser. I give up.

LEE. Well, don't, can't you get mad? Can't you fight?

TAM. For what? My country? The Alamo? And don't say my "soul." Anyway you're the wrong woman to ask me that. I'd like to hug you for askin though.

LEE. Why don't you?

TAM *spreads his arms, rises, seems about to move to embrace* LEE, *then shakes himself and sits and holds his head. He takes on some kind of white or European accent and says . . .*

TAM. I've known many many women. But with you I'm afraid.

LEE. Come on, I'm just one of the boys.

KENJI. Good! Let's all go out by the car and piss in the bushes.

LEE. Do you see your kids?

KENJI. Well, I'm hungry . . .

TAM. Do you see yours?

KENJI. I'll give Robbie a hand.

LEE. I can't. I want to but . . .

TAM. I can't either. I don't want to. I want 'em to forget me.

LEE. You can't mean that. They're your kids! You can't turn your back on them.

TAM. My back's all that's good for them. My front's no good. Which one was Chinese? Your mother or your father? Grandmother? Grandfather? . . . Hmmm? With me in their lives, they'd grow up to be like you.

LEE. Don't you miss them? I miss my children. Robbie isn't enough. Sometimes I even miss their fathers.

TAM. I mean, we grow up bustin our asses to be white anyway . . . "don't wear green because it makes you look yellow, son," now there's Confucius in America for you. "Don't be seen with no blacks, get good grades, lay low, an apple for the teacher, be good, suck up, talk proper, and be civilized." I couldn't be friends with Kenji in the open man until . . . I mean, it took us years after the war to finally not be scared of whitefolks mixing us up with Japs . . . When I went out, I told the folks I was goin over to visit Mexicans and we didn't feature Mexicans and I was really runnin with BlackJap. BlackJap and Tampax, the Ragmouth—for my fancy yakity yak don't ya know. The Long Ranger and Tonto of all those hot empty streets that got so hot in the summer, the concrete smelled like popcorn and you could smell the tires of parked cars baking. And what made the folks happiest was for some asshole some white offthewall J. C. Penney's clerk type with his crispy suit to say I spoke English well—

LEE. You're talking too fast for me. I can't . . .

TAM (*Continuing through Lee's interruptions*). And praisin me for being "Americanized" and no juvenile delinquency. "The strong Chinese family . . . Chinese culture." And the folks just smiled. The reason there was no juvenile delinquency was because there was no kids! The laws didn't let our women in . . .

LEE. What's this got to do with anything?

TAM. . . . and our women born here lost their citizenship if they married a man from China. And all our men here, no women, stranded here burned all their diaries, their letters, everything with their names on it . . . threw the ashes into the sea . . . hopin that that much of themselves could find someplace friendly. I asked an old man if that was so. He told me it wasn't good for me to know such things, to let all that stuff die with the old.

LEE. You taking me to school?

TAM. He told me to forget it . . . to get along with "Americans." Well, they're all dead now. We laugh at 'em with the "Americans," talk about them saying "Buck buck bagaw" instead of "giddyup" to their horses and get along real nice here now, don't we?

LEE. Oh, Tam, I don't know.

TAM. I've given my folks white grandkids, right? I don't want
'em to be anything like me, or know me, or remember me.
This guy they're calling "daddy" . . . I hear he's even a
better writer than me.

KENJI. Who said that? I'll kill him.

LEE. Who said that?

TAM. My mother, tellin me I was no good, to cheer me up.
"Brabra," she said. She could never say, "Barbara." It was
always "Brabra" like . . . (TAM *hefts imaginary boobs.*)
You know there's a scientific relation between boobs and
ambition? I'm not greedy for boobs. No ambition. I'm just
gonna make this movie. Keep busy. Just do one thing
right, right? That Ovaltine-Dupree fight! Damn! He was
so happy Ovaltine the Dancer won. I bought into this movie
to do it right, with money I should be usin for the child
support. I even begged some up from the folks. Lots of
home cooking and playing a goodboy listenin to his ma, for
his "allowance."

LEE. See? You do care.

TAM. I even took a grubstake from you, eh, Kemo Sabay. You
scared?

KENJI. My silver bullets, your silver bullets, Masked Man.

TAM. My kids might see it some day, and . . . And they'll
see . . .

LEE. You see, Tam? You can't turn your back on them. You
don't mean it when you say you want them to forget you.

TAM. I mean it. I mean, in case they don't forget. I should
leave them something . . . I should have done some THING.
One thing I've done alone, with all my heart. A gift. Not
revenge. But they've already forgotten me. They got a
new, ambitious, successful, go-for-bucks, superior white
daddy.

LEE. Tam, you bastard, you make me so pissed. You could be a
wonderful father. No! No! I won't let Tom take this baby
for his rich bitch mother again.

KENJI. Huh?

LEE. You won't make me see him. Don't talk about it. Don't
even talk about it.

TAM (*Interrupting*). I was talking about ambition! They say a
man with an old lady with big tits is ambitious. The bigger
the tits on his lady, the greater the ambition. "Brabra" didn't

have any tits at all. She had depressions, like two bomb
craters in her chest. And ma said, "Brabra" . . . NO, it
was, "Son, Brabra must like writers, only Rex is successful."
I bet her tits are bigger now. But ma seemed so pleased
about it. That "I told you so" tone, as if she'd got her
revenge on me, as if she'd known all my life I was no good
and was just waiting to tell me . . . Kenji, stop me, I'm
stealing your girl with cheap woo.

KENJI. Sounds like pretty deluxe woo to me. I've been taking
notes.

LEE. I'm not his girl. I'm his guest. He says he won't touch
white girls.

KENJI. Not me, too scary.

TAM. Man, Lee's not white.

KENJI. I didn't hear it from her.

TAM. She's chicken to say it. Help her out.

KENJI. Aww, man, if I'm going to go to all the trouble of mind
to get a white girl, man, she's going to be all white. And
tall. And giant, huge tits man. And blonde. The scariest
kind of white girl there is, man, none of this workin my
way up for me. Blonde hairs all over her head. Tall . . .
and tits, man like when I walk up to her and get my little
nose stuck in her navel, man, and I look up her belly, I
feel like I'm on the road with you and see two Giant Orange
stands across the road from each other.

TAM. Yeah, do it. You got ambition. No down in the cellar for
Helen Keller for Kenji.

KENJI. I'm chicken.

TAM. If you were blonde and had these big tits, Kenji
could . . .

KENJI. No, I'd chicken out. I'm chicken.

TAM. We're all chicken.

LEE. No one here but us chickens.

TAM. It's like that inspired wino sittin on the crapper in the
T&D Theatre in old Oakland wrote on the wall:
    KENJI *listens with growing recognition.*
    "When Chickencoop Chinaman havee wetdream far from
    home, He cly Buck buck bagaw, squeezing off his bone."

TAM & KENJI. Longfellow.

LEE (*Overlapping* TAM *and* KENJI). Buck buck bagaw?
    TAM *and* KENJI *pound up a rhythm on glasses, the
    tabletop, anything handy.* LEE *stamps her feet. They*

whinney, grunt, squeak, moan, come on like a scream-
ing jungle at night full of animals.

KENJI. A firey horse with the speed of light, a cloud of dust
and a hearty

ALL. BUCK BUCK BAGAW . . . THE CHICKENCOOP
CHINAMAN!

All begin singing Buck Buck Bagaw to the William
Tell Overture and pounding on things. The tune goes
out of their voices and they're screaming noise, throw-
ing in an occasional Buck Buck Bagaw! This isn't sing-
ing but a kind of vocal athletic event.

TAM. "If you don't have Chinese culture, baby, all you've got is
the color of your skin."

ALL. BUCK BUCK BAGAW

KENJI. "How do you tell Chinks from Japs?"

ALL. BUCK BUCK BAGAW

The music becomes frantic, full of screams and whoops
and lots of beating on things. KENJI *grabs coins from*
his pocket and throws them at the wall. He stamps
empty tin cans flat. He and ROBBIE *howling and*
screaming take pots and pans out of the cupboard and
beat on them awhile, get bored and throw them across
the room, and get others. LEE *pounds on the table as*
hard as she can with her fists, beating up a rhythm,
throwing the curtain material on the floor. TAM *puts*
down the guitar and goes to the bathroom and turns
on the shower taps, making the pipes shudder . . .
and comes back to beat on cups, bottles, glasses with a
spoon. ALL *intermittently cry "Buck Buck Bagaw"*
and ALL *answer with a cry of "Buck Buck Bagaw!"*

TAM. Hey. Let's all go see Charley Popcorn at his pornie
house! Give him a family.

ALL. BUCK BUCK BAGAW

KENJI. We'll leave that Tom in the cold.

Enter ROBBIE *from the kitchen.*

ROBBIE. Dinner's ready.

ALL. BUCK BUCK BAGAW.

LOUIS CHU
(1915-1970)

Louis Chu was born near Canton, China. His family moved to Newark, New Jersey, when he was nine years old. He attended school and college in New Jersey and was graduated with a major in English and a minor in sociology from New York University. During World War II he served in the U.S. Army in Kunming, southeastern China. Chu visited China again after the war and was married there. Chu was the proprietor of a Chinatown record shop and was the only Chinese disc jockey in New York City until his death.

From
EAT A BOWL OF TEA

II

ONE SATURDAY several months before the wedding, the day had
broken humid and muggy. Heavy rains had splashed the side-
walks of New York intermittently during the night. The month
of May had just ended. Chong Loo, the rent collector, hobbled
down the flight of stairs to the Money Come club house in the
basement at 87 Mott Street in New York's Chinatown.

"No money!" Wang Wah Gay, the proprietor, greeted the
agent as he came through the door. "Wow your mother. No
money today. You come back."

"All right, uncle, all right," said Chong Loo. "I'll be back on
the fifteenth." He started to leave. Then he stopped abruptly,
with one hand on the door knob. When he turned his head, he
gave the impression of having a stiff neck; his whole body
swung with it. "Did you see the pugilist master at the Sun
Young Theater last night?" he grinned, showing his new set of
teeth. The last time he had come around he had not a single
tooth.

"Wow your mother," said Ah Song, a hanger-on at the club
house. "Go sell your ass."

"Did you hear about the fight last night between a Lao Lim
and a Lao Ying in front of the Lotus Tea Shop?" This Lao
Lim accused Lao Ying of taking his wife out."

"Wow your mother. Why don't you go and die?" said Ah

Song, looking up from his newspaper, the Chinese *Compass,* at the mah-jong table.

"Later on the police came and separated the two men," Chong Loo continued. "Heh heh. Women nowadays are not to be trusted."

If the rent collector weren't so old, people might mistake him for a student, with his ever-present brief case. His head was big at the top and tapered off almost to a point at the chin. He had no hair on the dome, but sparsely-scattered long black hair mixed with gray on the circumference.

"Remember a year ago some Lao Tsuey ran down to South Carolina with Lao Ning's wife? She's the niece of the president of the Bank of Kwai Chow," Chong Loo persisted. "Have you heard the latest about . . . ?"

"Wow your mother," said Ah Song, this time a little louder than before.

Across from Ah Song, sitting on the couch, the proprietor, Wang Wah Gay, smiled his agreement. "You many-mouthed bird, go sell your ass."

"Heh heh. See you on the fifteenth, Mr. Wang."

His stooped shoulders and large head and brief case disappeared out the door and he began mounting the steep steps that led to the sidewalk. Wah Gay, from his half-reclining position on the sofa, could follow his exit until the rent collector's unpressed pants gradually ascended out of sight.

"Wow his mother," exclaimed Wah Gay, stretching himself. "He never fails to show up on the first of the month. You don't have to look at the calendar. When he arrives, you know it's the first." He crossed his legs and flicked the ash from his cigar on the tray.

"Chong Loo is all right," said Ah Song. He turned another page of the Chinese *Compass.* The circle of light from the overhanging lamp played on the newspaper. "Wow your mother. That's his job. It's his responsibility to show up on the first of every month to collect rent. Maybe he is a many-mouthed bird but he works for a living."

Ah Song let the newspaper drop flat on the table. Usually he read with glasses, but today he had been looking at the big letters in the advertisements. "Wow your mother, Wah Gay, do you think he's like you, never worked in your life?"

They both chuckled. "You dead boy," said Wah Gay. "You're still young yet. Why don't *you* go to work?"

"Who, me? I've worked more than you ever hope to work, you sonavabitch." Ah Song was a youthful-looking man in his mid-forties, with just a touch of gray at the temples. His neatly combed black hair had the effect of a crew-cut. A white handkerchief always adorned his breast pocket. Even on the hottest days he would never roll up his shirt sleeves or be caught without a necktie.

"When did *you* ever work?" replied Wah Gay. "I've known you for almost twenty years." He pointed a finger at Ah Song. "You sonavabitch, if you ever worked at all, you must have worked when you were a mere boy. Ever since I've known you, you haven't done a single day's work."

"Shut up your mouth. Do I have to tell you when I go to work?"

The basement club house was cool. Compared to the heat and humidity of the street, it was a refreshing paradise. The sudden intensity of the early summer heat had caught everyone unprepared. A few days before, it had been so damp and chilly and windy that Wah Gay had to turn on the gas heater.

The door creaked open.

"Nice and cool here," said the newcomer. He turned and made sure the door closed tight.

"Thought you went to the race track," said Wah Gay.

"I overslept," replied the man. "Might just as well. On a day like this." He looked around the room. "Where is everybody? Still early, huh?" He walked over to an easy chair in the corner and sat down. He took out a cigar and lit it. "You know, on a day like this, I think this is the best place in the city. Nice and cool, with natural air conditioning."

Lee Gong was slight of build, with silvery black hair. He continued puffing on the Admiration which had been given him at a banquet the night before. He and Wah Gay had come over to America from China on the *President Madison* together and had shared the confined quarters of Ellis Island as two teen-age immigrants many springs ago.

In his early days in the United States, Lee Gong worked in various laundries in New York. Later he, himself, owned one in the Bronx. In 1928, he went back to China. He remained there only long enough to marry. Then he returned to the Golden Mountain, leaving his wife in China. He received the news of the birth of his daughter, Mei Oi, several months after he had returned to the United States.

Some ten years later, he sold his laundry. With the proceeds from the sale of the laundry plus his small savings, he had planned to spend the late evening of his life in the rural quiet of Sunwei. The Sino-Japanese War had prevented him from realizing this long-cherished goal. The unsettled conditions of subsequent years in the Far East, which saw Mao Tse-tung grab control of the Central Government of China from Chiang Kai-shek, had weighed heavily in his decision not to return to Sunwei. While there were intermittent periods of peaceful travel in China for those who wanted it, Lee Gong could not bring himself to see anything permanently stable for a retired *gimshunhock* in China. So reluctantly he remained in New York.

"Ah Song, my boy," said Lee Gong from his easy chair. "You have good results lately?"

"What good results? I haven't been to the tracks for a whole week. No luck and no money."

"Ah Song is a smart boy," said Wah Gay. "He wouldn't go to the races unless he's lucky, heh heh."

"You go to hell." Ah Song folded his paper, got up and stretched his arms. He yawned. Yawning was a habit with him, almost as natural as breathing. "It's so hot you don't want to move."

"You just moved, you sonovabitch," said Wah Gay.

Ah Song ignored the remark and started toward the door.

"Where are you going to die?" Wah Gay called after him. "Be smart. Go get someone down here and start a little game. Where can you go in this hot weather?"

"To the race tracks!" Ah Song slammed the door behind him.

Lee Gong went over to the mah-jong table and sat in the chair that Ah Song had just vacated. He picked up the paper.

"That sonovabitch Ah Song eats good, dresses good, and he never works!"

"He's got what you'd call *Life of the Peach Blossoms,*" chuckled Wah Gay. "The women like him. He's a beautiful boy."

"Maybe he was born under the right stars."

"Three years ago he went to Canada and I've heard he married a rich widow from Vancouver and she bought him a car and gave him money."

"What has happened to the widow now?" Lee Gong asked, surprised that Ah Song was ever married. As far as he knew, Ah Song was living the life of a bachelor in New York.

"Nobody knows," the club house proprietor shook his head. "You know Ah Song's type. He never tells you anything. I heard he had some trouble with the police out in Portland when they caught him without proper registration for his car two years ago."

"I've never heard of that," said Lee Gong. "But you don't have to go back that far. Just a year ago he was mixed up with that Lao Woo's wife. Someone saw him and Woo's wife together around Times Square on a Saturday night. Soon the news got back to the husband, who took the matter up with the elders of the Woo Association. The chairman of the Woo Association sent a representative to see Ah Song . . ."

"What happened?"

"Ah Song was squeezed for $1,000."

"Did he pay?"

"Of course."

The afternoon was unusually quiet at the club house, and the two friends found this light talk helped pass the time away.

"This generation of girls is not what it used to be," lamented Wah Gay. "In nine cases out of ten, if the girl were good and honest, no trouble would come to her." Wah Gay got up and started pacing the floor. "You look at this generation of *jook sing* boys and *jook sing* girls. They have no respect for elder people. H'mn, they would call you by name. They would call you Lao Lee even though you are almost twice as old as their old man."

"Regardless what anybody might say," put in Lee Gong. The

words seemed to flow out of his mouth effortlessly. "Girls born in China are better. They are courteous and modest. Not like these *jook sings* born in New York. They can tell good from bad." He paused. The newspaper remained unread on the table. "Summer is coming. You'll see them running out on the streets almost naked. You could almost see their underpants."

They both chuckled.

The afternoon moved slowly. Even the sidewalk outside was deserted on this hot, sticky day. The perennial voices of children playing, the roar of their roller-skates against the pavement, were missing. An occasional rumble of passing trucks could be heard in the quiet retreat of the Money Come club house.

"A very deteriorating influence," continued Lee Gong dryly. "This Western civilization." He picked up the Chinese *Compass* again and tried to read it. The only illumination in the room was the circle of light that now played directly on the newspaper. "Nowadays girls go out and get a big belly before they get married."

"Heh heh," laughed Wah Gay. "What more do you want? One gets a grandchild with a brand new daughter-in-law at the same time."

The door swung open.

Chong Loo, the rent collector, had returned. This time he was without his brief case. Wah Gay had started walking back to the anteroom when he saw Chong Loo enter, and now he came out with an aluminum pot in one hand and a dollar bill in the other.

"Here," he said to Chong Loo, "go and get a few cents' worth of coffee."

Chong Loo, beaming, left with the pot and the dollar. In the meantime, Ah Song returned with two companions.

"You have lucky footsteps today," greeted Wah Gay. "I thought you said you were going to the race tracks?"

"I did," replied Ah Song. "I came back already."

"You big gun."

From the back room, the club house owner brought out six cups and placed them on the square mah-jong table, which was now covered with old Chinese newspapers serving as a table cloth. He rubbed his palms and bent his head forward a little. "You are lucky. You just walked in and we're going to serve you coffee!"

The two men who had just come in with Ah Song were Tuck King, a second cook on his day off, and his roommate, who, because of his generous proportions, was nicknamed Fat Man; but was politely referred to as the Kitchen Master in his presence.

"We were still sleeping when this sonovabitch Ah Song pounded on the door and woke us up," the Kitchen Master said. He removed his Panama hat and put it on a hook on the wall. His right hand automatically went up and smoothed his snow-white hair.

"That's why we came down . . . for coffee," Tuck King laughed. "Share the wealth."

The basement had a refreshing coolness. Not damp. Not muggy. None of the moldy smell of the unused cellar. After coffee, Ah Song spoke out, "Fifty dollars."

Lee Gong poured the mah-jongs on the table, some of them face up, others face down.

"Fifty dollars," echoed Tuck King, sitting down.

"Okay. Fifty."

Leaving the coffee cups unwashed in the sink, Wah Gay joined the others at the mah-jong table. When he walked, he took big steps and his whole body seemed to swing with them. From the sink to the mah-jong table it took him but three steps. In his place on the table were strips of ivory chips which had been divided equally by the others. The mah-jongs now all faced down. Wah Gay added his outstretched hands to the pairs that were already busily shuffling the tiny ivory tiles around. The old army blanket muffled the noise of the blocks clucking against one another. Quickly, deftly, hands moving, setting up the mah-jongs.

Lee Gong picked a pair of pea-sized dice from among the chips and rattled them in his palm. The dice bounced off the mah-jongs and onto the table, where the adhesive characteristics of the blanket acted as a dragging agent and the dice rolled reluctantly to a stop.

"Six."

Ah Song picked up the dice and threw them against the mah-jongs. "Ten."

Next came Fat Man. He watched the dice roll lazily to a two and a one. "Wow your mother!"

The dice rattled once more, this time in the fat palm of Wah Gay. The cubes danced, smacked against each other, and bounced off the stacked-up tiles.

"Eight."

"Ten has it."

Ah Song hit the dice again. "Twelve."

His right hand reached for the mah-jongs in front of him, counting to himself . . . two . . . four . . . six . . . eight . . . ten . . . twelve . . .

The mah-jongs thudded quietly against the blanketed table, all face up, in multi-colors of red, green, and blue. Someone let out a thirty thousand.

"Poeng powng!"

"So soon?"

"Wow your mother!"

XIII

Still unnerved by the prostitute's early morning call, Ben Loy got up at ten that morning to go to work for Chin Yuen, who was ill. He was not anxious to go back to work so soon after his return to New York, but Chin Yuen was a good friend. He did not want to leave Mei Oi.

"Are you sure you'll be all right?" he asked tenderly.

"I'll be all right," she said from her bed. "You go ahead and go to work."

"If anybody should come, just ignore him," he said. He was afraid someone else might come to the apartment. When he had shared the apartment with Chin Yuen, loose women came to the apartment at all hours. He was ashamed of his past and he certainly did not want his wife to learn about it.

Left alone, Mei Oi slept until noon. When she tried to get

up, the four walls of the bedroom whirled before her. The floor underneath her feet shook like a hog just out of a mud puddle in the village square. The effects of the plane ride from Hong Kong to New York were still with her. She had been ill the day before and had eaten little since. She sank down on the edge of the bed. Her elbows rested on her thighs, supporting her forehead with her hands. The ceiling swayed back and forth. Back and forth. Mei Oi closed her eyes tightly, holding back her tears.

The physical illness was just a temporary inconvenience, Mei Oi knew. In another day, or at most in a few days more, the dizziness from the plane ride would disappear. The giddiness came only when she stood up. As long as she remained in bed, she was relatively immune to the ill effects of the trip.

In the early morning when the buzzer had awakened her, she had been warmly receptive to Ben Loy's ardent kisses, hoping that they would lead to the act of love. Aside from the physical pleasure she would have derived from the union, it would have indicated to her that her man still loved her. When Ben Loy had turned away, she felt unwanted and useless. She had tried to console herself with the thought that her husband was being considerate and did not want to make demands upon her when she was still sick from the trip. But his monk-like behavior had begun even before she set foot on the airplane.

The first few weeks of her marriage had been happy; for Ben Loy was considerate, masterful and understanding in his role as a bridegroom. It was only when they had gone to the hotel in Hong Kong that the sudden change in him had occurred. The first night at the All Seas Hotel Ben Loy had failed miserably at making love. He was no more successful on subsequent nights. She had hoped his lack of ardor was only temporary and that soon she would again enjoy him as a husband.

After what seemed like the trekking of a thousand li, Mei Oi slowly opened her eyes. A relative calm had returned to the room. The walls no longer whirled and the water buffalo beneath the floor had gone. She could see the windows and the dresser clearly now. The bluish linoleum floor looked nice and smooth and shiny. The large pendulum that was their bedroom had run out of momentum. Soon it would be stilled completely and Mei Oi would see things in their true perspective.

She flopped over on her stomach and buried her head in the pillow. Sobs, like a baby's whimper, came to her freely and unashamedly in her solitude. Her heart had wanted to cry out for the past few weeks, but she did not want to cry in front of her husband.

A few short weeks ago she was still a girl. Her mother's daughter. Now she was a woman and a wife. She had looked forward to her marriage with excited anticipation. Like many girls of her own age, she had hoped to marry a *gimshunhock* and come to America to start a new family. Her mother had often said to her: "Mei Oi, I hope you will marry a *gimshunhock* and go to America with him. Then you will see him in the morning and at night."

It was obvious her mother was thinking of her own husband, Mei Oi's father, who had left her to return to America months before Mei Oi was born. Mei Oi was too shy to show any outward emotions during this discussion of marriage with her mother. But inwardly she had wanted very much to marry a *gimshunhock* and come to the Beautiful Country and raise a family. To her mother she would only say modestly, "I'm not that fortunate."

She knew she wouldn't marry a farmer. A farmer's wife worked from dawn till dusk out in the fields. She could see all around her farmers' wives toiling incessantly, gathering firewood, turning the earth, planting, harvesting, exposed to the elements in all sorts of weather. Cracked hands. Calloused feet. A face bronzed and lined and hardened by the wind and sun. Not a pretty picture, but a common one. Marry a school teacher? Not Mei Oi. There was this common observation. Unless you're poor, you would not be teaching.

After many months of anxiety and waiting, there had come a letter from her father, Lee Gong in New York, informing her mother that he was sending home a prospective son-in-law in the person of one Wang Ben Loy.

And now that she had married Wang Ben Loy and come to New York, the greatest and most beautiful city in all the world, she should be happy, very happy. A whole new panorama of fertile fields lay before her. Youth. Dreams. The future. All that a girl from New Peace Village in Sunwei could ever hope for.

But today her frustrations and heaviness of heart dwarfed even the discomforts of her illness from the plane. Mei Oi, the bride of two months, lay alone on her bed, troubled and un-communicative, separated by ten thousand li of oceans and mountains from her mother, whose love and encouragement she urgently needed now. Over and over she asked herself: What did I do to Ben Loy to make him stop loving me?

Finally, exhausted by tears and emotion, she fell asleep again.

When she awoke in mid-afternoon, she felt better. The ill effects of the plane ride seemed to have been washed away by her tears. She got up and stretched and yawned. Cry some more? How much can you cry? Who can hear you cry? And who cares when you are ten thousand folds of mountains away from home? Go ahead, Mei Oi, she told herself, go ahead and cry. And see who will pity you.

That night when Ben Loy came home from work it was al-most one o'clock in the morning. Mei Oi was waiting up for him. She had bathed and powdered her skin with talcum, in anticipation of her husband's return. When the lock on the door finally clicked, she was tense and full of expectation. Her heart pounded furiously against her ribs. But she wore a bright smile on her face. As she hurried from the bedroom, where she had been resting, to the living room to meet Ben Loy, she was like a little school girl let out for summer vacation.

"Loy *Gaw*," she said daintily, coming up to him and taking his coat and hat. "Was business good today?" She kissed him on the cheek.

"Not bad," replied Ben Loy, pleased with Mei Oi's atten-tions. "I was not familiar with where the things were and that made it difficult."

"I understand," said Mei Oi. She timidly took his hand and guided him to the sofa. "Today is the first time you went to work since you married me." She nestled closer to him, still holding his left hand with her right.

Mei Oi's mind flashed back to her wedding night when she

had stood before the brand new wash basin, which was part of her dowry, and washed her face and hands many times, wanting to delay the consummation of her marriage. Ben Loy was sitting by the edge of the bed, a ready and eager bridegroom. When he saw she was dallying, he had strolled over to her and carried her to the bed. With gentle hands, he had first unbuttoned her coat, and then untied her trouser string and, over her weak protestations, pulled off her pants.

"Do you remember our wedding night?" Mei Oi asked, full of excitement. She placed her head on his shoulder and wrapped her arms around him. "At first I was afraid but you made me very happy. Do you . . . Loy *Gaw* . . . do you want to make me very happy tonight?"

"I am tired," said Ben Loy. He took his wife in his arms and kissed her mechanically on the lips. He stroked her long black hair. "It was hard work at the restaurant. I am sleepy and tired."

Trying to fight back her tears, Mei Oi abruptly got up and walked to the bedroom. It took her a long time to fall asleep; but Ben Loy was snoring within minutes after he got into bed.

MOMOKO IKO
(1940-   )

Momoko Iko, born in Wapato, Washington, spent her childhood (1942–1945) in the Heart Mountain Concentration Camp and believes that mute time has colored her life more than any other experience. Her plays *The Old Man* and *The Gold Watch* won the East-West Players playwriting contests in 1970 and 1971. She received a B.A. degree from the University of Illinois in 1961 and attended the University of Iowa and Istitudo Allende in Mexico. She edited and contributed to the "Asian Liberation" newsletter in Chicago where she now lives. She has a novel in progress, *Second City Flat,* and her play *The Gold Watch* will be published by Inner City Press.

THE GOLD WATCH

CHARACTERS

MASARU MURAKAMI: A man in his forties, lean, hard-muscled, wiry. He's a farmer. His face is weathered and tanned. His arms to above his elbows are also tanned, his hands roughened. He uses his body when he talks and he's given to mimickry, expansive gestures, and displays of emotion. His loud displays are hardy, without meanness or real anger, the deliberately quieted voice is the dangerous one. He is sensible to the irony of his position.

KIMIKO MURAKAMI: A woman in her early thirties, slight, slim, with a body that moves as lithe as a girl's but quietly, almost imperceptibly. She is pale, in contrast to MASARU and her face shows age. She wears house dresses or baggy jeans and bandannas. Until the last act, her emotions are tinged with exasperation and sudden tirednesses.

TADAO MURAKAMI: Boy of thirteen, skinny, well-coordinated but face and body that of a younger boy. His movements are quiet and unintrusive but there is an underlying intensity or confidence which makes him an important part of any given scene.

CHIEKO MURAKAMI: A five-year-old, full of play and affection, direct in her expressions of feeling.

TANAKA: A man in his forties, owns the only Japanese trade store in the area. He tends to scurry along, duck his head before speaking, is somewhat formal in his manners, wears suits. With MURAKAMI, he is capable of honesty and shows himself to be a naturally courteous man.

HIROSHI TANAKA: A young, formal man.

FUMIKO TANAKA: A blooming woman who likes to gossip and visit. There are hints of meanness and roughness in her but she is a good-hearted woman.

The SCENES of the play are the house and yard of MURA-KAMI's forty-acre farm in the Pacific Northwest, fall of 1941 and summer of 1942, and a church basement.

The SETTING is a one-room house with attached lean-to bath. The door of the house faces the farmyard. There are steps leading to it and on either side of the door is a square un-curtained window. In the yard, downstage and off to the left is a packing shed, an outhouse, mountain and fields in the back-ground, fields downstage into audience. Both the exterior and the interior of the house will be used.
The interior reveals a faded carpet, 2 x 3, in front of the door. Stage left, a wooden table and four unmatched chairs. Directly back of the table stands a pot-bellied stove, pipe rising through the roof. Cooking is done on this stove. A stack of wood is on the floor to its left. Behind it, a pile of Japanese newspapers. On the left wall, a small laundry-tub–type sink, one faucet from the wall. Next to the sink, going downstage, a wooden icebox. Next to that two orange crates, unpainted, lined with jarred preserves, peaches, cherries, pears, corn, beans, egg plants, etc. On their tops and icebox top, vegetables, a couple of pots, utensils. Next to the sink, going upstage, a big vat on the floor and several gallon soy-sauce bottles filled with sake. Separated

from the main room are two sleeping areas, one for the children and one for the parents. Hanging cotton material denote the divisions. At the extreme right of the house is an overstuffed chair. Next to it, an old side table. On it, a radio.

That Japanese is the spoken language is to be assumed. Where I've actually used it, I've done so for dramatic effect or to define a sensibility poorly defined by English.

LIGHTING: I'd prefer no use of strong spots. The light should be somewhat subdued, quite like the natural light that comes into a house from a late afternoon sun. It is not realistic lights that I want but one that never pinpoints definitely the center of attention. If there is music, it can come from the radio or a slow koto or samisen music, faint, unintrusive, at its best, almost an echo for a land, a faint foreign sound off which this American action is to be played.

ACT I

SCENE I: Early evening, mid-November, 1941.

INTERIM: Audio-visual reference to bombing of Pearl Harbor.

SCENE II: Christmas Eve, 1941.

Act I, Scene I: House and forty-acre MURAKAMI *farm*
        KIMIKO *is setting up the table for dinner. She checks
        the soup, takes the rice pan from the stove, etc.* TAD
        is washing up at the sink. CHIEKO *is playing with a
        doll with cloth face and body. Wall-screen is down
        and these actions are seen as shadows.* MASU *is walking
        toward the house from left stage.* TANAKA *is coming
        from stage right, passing in front of the house. He is
        carrying the remnants of bolts of cloth, still wrapped
        around the cardboard spindles. He wears the slacks of
        a blue-serge suit and a Pendleton wool shirt. He carries a
        jacket.* MASU *wears workpants and a cotton flannel shirt,
        rolled just above the elbows. His hands and arms are
        dirty. He's carrying some potatoes in his hands. The*

rest of the family wears obviously worn out clothes.
The kids can be in stocking feet, KIMIKO *wears zori*
slippers. TANAKA *is approaching the front steps when*
MASU *notices him.*

MASU. Hoh' Tane-san, you're just in time for some sake. Before
supper. (*He stops, letting* TANAKA *pass the house to him,*
so that they can have a little chat before entering the house.
He drops some potatoes, swears.) Cocksacca' What have
you got there? (*He eyes the cloth bolts elaborately.*)

TANAKA (*Embarrassed, trying to change subject*). Potatoes?
This late?

MASU. Found them . . . clearing the fields. (*He handles them,*
from hand to hand.) They're still good. (*His sudden good*
humor at seeing TANAKA *has disappeared. He still eyes the*
bolts.) What's new in town?

TANAKA. It gets chillier every year. Let's go inside. I planned
to come earlier. . . . I didn't mean to bother you at dinner.
How are they? The daikon?

MASU *grunts and shakes his head.* TANAKA *goes up the*
steps ahead of MASU. *The wall rises, exposing the in-*
side of the house. MASU *grabs an edge of the material*
falling loose from a bolt and feels its texture. They are
inside the house.

MASU. Kimi' Get Tanaka sake!

KIMIKO *bows to* TANAKA *and prods* TADAO. TAD *goes*
gets the sake cups and little pitcher and begins to get
the bottle from the corner. MASARU *is at the sink,*
washing up. TANAKA *gives* KIMIKO *the cloth.* KIMIKO
takes a swift look at MASU *and retreats with the cloth*
into the bedroom. TAD *is filling the porcelain pitcher*
with sake. MASU, *washing up, takes large handfuls of*
water from the tap and splashes his face and arms with
it. He makes smacking sounds with his hands against
his face and arms. TAD *and* MASU *get in each other's*
way and MASU *playfully tousles the boy's hair with a*
wet hand. TAD *doesn't like it.* TANAKA *gives* CHIEKO
some candy and plays with her. CHIEKO *is delighted*
and begins to unwrap the pieces of candy when KIMIKO
re-enters and takes them away, chiding her about
dinner and manners. MASU *grabs a towel hanging from*
a nail and goes into the bedroom, to take off his shirt.

TANAKA *and* KIMIKO *exchange glances as* MASU *enters the bedroom.*

KIMIKO. Sa' sit down, Tanakasan.

(*She pulls a chair from the table and indicates that* TANAKA *should sit.* TANAKA *rises from the floor where he has been entertaining* CHIEKO *and bows and sits down.* TAD *takes the pitcher from the pan of water on the edge of the stove and pours some sake into the cup beside* TANAKA. *He leaves the pitcher by* TANAKA'*s cup.* TANAKA *tries to force some candy on* TAD *but* TAD *backs off.* MASARU *comes out from the bedroom in zori slippers, same pants, and a new shirt. He sits down across from* TANAKA, *slapping his thighs as he does. He takes the pitcher and pours himself a drink. He raises the cup, nods his head at* TANAKA *and drinks. Then he pours another cup and settles into his seat. He offers* TANAKA *another cupful.* TANAKA *refuses by putting his hand in front of the small cup.*)

TANAKA. No, no more . . . just one, I have to go back for dinner myself. (*He rises.*)

MASU (*Laughs*). Tanakasan, you come here, you ask how are the crops . . . you have our sake and now you are leaving. For a visit, it's too short. If it is business, it hasn't been stated.

TANAKA. You know the wife. . . . I must get going . . .

MASU. Besides that, you forgot your parcel . . . your large parcel. Kimi, get Tanakasan, his parcels.

TANAKA. E-yeeh . . . Masu I was clearing my summer stock. I found these clothes, yes? Who is going to buy cotton now, I say to myself . . . I am right, No? Perhaps Kimikosan might be able to use them. There's no harm in that? It's eehh my cu- i-s -ma-su pu-re-sants to you. (*Tanaka laughs.*) Yes, that's right. A early gift.

MASU. Kimi, give Tanakasan his parcel.

KIMIKO. Masu . . . I'll pay for them.

TANAKA. Kimi will pay me in the spring . . . next summer . . . with the money she will make at the road stand . . . this is good business, Masu.

MASU. Kimi, give Tanakasan his parcel.

TANAKA. Tanakasan, Tanakasan, we are now strangers, Masu?

KIMIKO. Tadao needs some clothes for school . . . you remem-

ber, we were going to buy him some in September . . .
remember. Chie-chan can use a new dress for church and
so can I . . . and you, you can use a shirt . . .

MASU. Kimi! (*He grabs Kimi by the arm and whips her around
toward the bedroom, then pushes ahead of her and goes in
himself to get the cloth.*)

TANAKA. Masu, listen, don't be stupid. This has got nothing to
do with pride . . . do you hear . . . nothing.

MASU *hands him the bolt.* TANAKA *won't take it.*

KIMIKO (*Disgust and anger*). Your pride . . . your pride . . .
is that all there is?

MASU *takes the cloth and begins to go out the door.*

KIMIKO. Masu . . . please.

TANAKA *goes outside. He looks toward stage center
and down at* MURAKAMI. *He sighs like a man who
has witnessed this scene too often to expect any different and yet as if he is always expecting a change to
occur. The interior of the house fades out.* MASU *is
headed toward wings of stage left.* TANAKA *steps
around the bolts that had been flung to the ground,
and approaches* MASU. *They sit.* TANAKA *offers cigarette.*

TANAKA. I always expect it will be different . . .

MASU. Maybe I do too. (*He picks up some soil and plays it
through his hands.*)

TANAKA. It isn't cheap cloth, you know.

MASU *snorts.*

TANAKA. IT isn't! Are you saying. . . .

MASU (*Laughing*). No Tane, I checked it.

TANAKA *ducks his head, a short smile of satisfaction.
The two are at ease.*

TANAKA. Masu, is it your fault that the summer crops brought
so little. No!

MASU. Goddamnsonnabitstsucocusaka! And then they don't let
you sell them. "Dig it under. Let it rot," they say. Goddamnsonnabitstsucocusaka'

TANAKA. That was last year . . .

MASU. It's just as bad this year. Tadao and me driving around
at night like we were the thieves! Good thing for that
Italian peddler!

TANAKA. Things are like that, we . . .

MASU. Tane, you are so sane, so level-minded . . . the rising sun would be proud of you.

> KIMIKO *comes out the door and takes the cloth in with her.* MASU *sees her.*

MASU. Give me another tobac. Why does she have to do it, like this?

TANAKA. You're too stubborn, a stupid mule, what else can she do?

MASU. Was I asking you?

TANAKA. Don't talk so loud within my hearing.

> *The two continue to smoke.* TANAKA *gets out his case and offers* MASU *another. He refuses.* TANAKA *looks for an opening.* MASU *is staring ahead, rocking on the crate.*

TANAKA. If you were just a little bit more reasonable. Masu . . . you know, you have credit with me.

MASU (*With joking irony*). Still? Is that so? I still do?

TANAKA (*Not liking the mock*). Masu.

MASU (*Jumping up, grabbing the crate and running upstage and back to place . . . gesturing*). To pay you off, all I need is a rainbow, stretching from waaay over there . . . to right here. And I will need that rainbow five years running.

TANAKA. You exaggerate. It's not your fault the crops brought in so little but it's not Kimiko's either . . . nor the children's, why should they do without?

MASU. How "reasonable."

TANAKA. Listen bozo-san, in Japan, you would have little to do with me. True? But this is America, Masu. (*Bitterness creeps into the voice.*) You don't owe me anything. I'm paying for this friendship. I'm the one. Isn't that so?

MASU (*Rises, slaps his thighs*). All right! Next year, you'll have the best vegetables in the valley . . . come back for a drink.

TANAKA. No, the wife. I have to go.

> *The two men return center stage.* MASU *scraps his foot on the ground where the bolt of cloth lay.*

MASU. Kimi is a very intelligent woman.

TANAKA. Then listen to her some times.

MASU (*Laughing*). I can't. She's got a mind of her own.

> TANAKA *exits stage right.* MASU *lingers on the porch and enters house.* TAD *is entering stage right, looking*

back because he notices TANAKA's *departure.* KI-
MIKO *looks up sharply at* MASU's *entry.*

KIMIKO. Chieko . . . dinnertime.

MASU. Tadao! Where's Tadao?

KIMIKO. He's not home yet. He said he was going to play . . .
football?

MASU. Football? What is that?

CHIEKO *enters with a book and goes to* MASU *and
gets put on his lap and asks that he read to her. He
tries to read, the book is in English so he can't read it.*
TADAO *enters, carrying some books. He is feeling kind
of good.*

MASU. You're late for dinner!

TADAO (*To everyone in general*). Sorry . . . got held up at
school. (TAD *takes his seat at the table, relaxed, fairly
pleased with himself. He doesn't know what took place.*)

MASU. Playing footsubalu?

TADAO (*Swift look to his mother*). Yes.

MASU. What is football?

CHIEKO (*Unmindful of the others*). Papa, will you read to me
after dinner?

MASU. Your brother will read to you. . . . What is football?

TADAO (*Still pretty much full of himself but apprehensive*). It's
a game . . . where . . .

MASU. With a foot and a ball?

TADAO (*Laughing but upset*). Right papa, with a foot and a
ball . . .

MASU *is uncertain now. Fact? Jest? Putdown? He does
not know what football is. So he shrugs it off and
grunts. He begins eating. He wolfs down the rice.*
CHIEKO *begins to copy him and gets a gentle repri-
mand from* KIMIKO. KIMIKO *begins to clear the table.*
CHIEKO *renews her attempt to get her father to
read to her. His embarrassment is getting him angry.
He sends her to the chair and she sits in it and tries
to read the book.* KIMIKO *presses some checks on*
TADAO. *He is angered and refuses. She presses.* MASU
is at the table drinking sake, looking at the paper.
KIMIKO *leaves.* TADAO *returns to the table and sits
down. He clears his throat, not overlarge.* MASU *looks
up.*

TADAO. There's some checks you have to sign, papa.

MASU (*Gruff*). What!

TADAO. Bills . . .

MASU. For what?

TADAO (*Looking over the three bills*). One's for the seed store . . . they won't give us any more credit. It's only eleven dollars. Mama talked to the man.

MASU *is responding to all this, grunts, expressions, etc.*

TADAO. This one . . . for the bank. Twenty-five dollars on account. Did you go talk to them about loan yet? Till next year.

MASU *takes the last check. Looks at it.*

MASU. Fifteen dollars. For what?

TADAO. For food, school . . . (*quieter, hesitant*) shoes.

MASU. Shoes? Food? We have everything right here.

TADAO. No we don't . . . papa. You have to buy meat and sugar and salt and eggs . . .

MASU. Who eats all these eggs?

TADAO. You do . . . over rice . . . in the mornings . . .

MASU (*No longer wants to be bothered*). Shoes?

TADAO. They're not regular shoes. . . . They're . . . I put some money down on some football shoes . . .

MASU (*He's tired of hearing about football*). Football shoes?

TAD (*Cutting him off*). You really can't play without shoes . . .

MASU. What is football? (foo-tsu-bal-lu)

TADAO (*Getting angry*). I told you. It's a game where . . .

MASU (*Getting angry*). You need special shoes for a *game?* Make your own!

TADAO. But papa . . . it's not like drawing or making models . . . I can't . . .

MASU (*Trying to explain*). Tadao . . . we don't have money for the feed store. We don't have money for the bank. They will have to loan us some in order to pay them back . . . same as usual.

TADAO. But papa . . .

MASU (*Cutting in*). We have food . . . we have a house . . . we have clothes because of Tanaka . . . but no money . . .

TADAO (*Doesn't really understand*). You don't have to go into town and face all those people. Mama does and me . . . You never do.

MASU. Mama won't let me . . .

TADAO (*Reverting to threats*). They'll throw you in jail . . .

MASU (*Laughing. He's genuinely amused*). Don't be a fool
. . . if they threw everyone like me in jail, who would they
loan money to . . . charge interest to . . . how would
they collect?

TADAO. Papa . . . lots of people aren't like you.

MASU. Don't be a fool, they are all like me.

CHIEKO *comes up to* MASU, *wants the story read.*

TADAO (*To himself*). I want those shoes . . . I'm going to
have them.

MASU *hears but doesn't respond. He indicates to*
TADAO *to read* CHIEKO *the book, and takes the*
checks and signs them. TADAO *rises and takes the*
book and begins to read to her as they both exit.

TADAO. So one night, he goes to this haunted house, on a dare,
and even though he tries to be brave, he's scared. He tries
to go to sleep but he can't sleep, thinking about the evil
rat. He finds a little corner and he gets his blanket and mat
and tries to go to sleep again . . .

KIMIKO *enters with sewing and sets up at the table.*
MASU *moves to chair.*

KIMIKO. I can make you a new shirt. You could have a nice
shirt for church gatherings. He must have so much left
over. It's leftover material, you know. So don't feel bad.
He could not sell it. That's the reason . . . Put a curtain
on the window. That will be nice. Then you could move
the cloth aside and look at the sky.

MASU. I can see the sky without a curtain. . . . The emperor
and his samurai thugs are doing all right.

KIMIKO. Don't tell me. I don't want to hear about such things.

MASU. Why not? Don't you have a samurai up your family tree
somewhere?

KIMIKO. Don't talk so vulgar.

MASU. Look around here: farmers, fishermen, peasants, serfs.
That's what they were and now, they are crawling around,
snuffing at holes, looking for a fierce nobel samurai buried
in their past. Cocusakas.

KIMIKO. Masu!

MASU (*Rising toward her*). All right, all right. Shimizu had
some trouble in town?

KIMIKO. Yes, Harukosan was so afraid. They said the men were
drunk. That's why I don't think you should drink so much.

MASU. You don't let up, do you Kimi!

KIMI. Please don't start a fight! I feel weak. . . (KIMI *sews more diligently.*) The teacher told Tadao that he is missing too much school. You would think, in farm country, the teacher would understand. Anyway, Masu, I have decided that we cannot take him out anymore. Starting next year, for sure . . .

MASU. That's next year. We will talk about it then. Besides, it's only a month or so, a few weeks in the spring and a few weeks in the fall.

KIMI. No . . . next year, I will go out, all day. . . I can do it.

MASU. No. That's no good. There's Chiechan. It's no good for her. Besides, you keep losing babies on me that way.

KIMIKO *falls silent and becomes very still.* MASU *rises and tries to placate her.*

MASU. Let's go to bed.

KIMIKO (*Continues stitching*). You go ahead. I have things to finish up.

MASU. Kimi, let's go . . .

KIMIKO (*Flaring up*). This isn't Japan! This is America! When are you ever going to understand that!

MASU (*Mimicking*). This isn't Japan. This is America. I know. I know! What do you want, obahan? You want me to go around with a wooden bowl? Would that make me more American? Tanaka's a friend. What friend makes you feel like a beggar? What friend? Your son is ashamed of me. You make him ashamed of me, and me, I make him hate me. I would rather have that.

KIMIKO (*All her frustration spilling over*). It would have been better for both of us if you had become a priest.

MASU. Next time you say that, just remember, what you say is true. It would have been better for both of us. For me too. For me too.

KIMIKO. Let's go to bed, come on, let's go!

KIMIKO *rises abruptly, upsetting her sewing and slamming it down on the table. She tries to take the sake from* MASU. *They struggle.* TADAO *enters. He has on a light jacket. He's going out. He interrupts them.* KIMIKO *goes to the sink and begins sorting the dishes to be washed. She is still angry.*

KIMIKO (*Sharp, transferring her anger to her son*). Where are you going?

TADAO (*With disrespect*). Out.

MASU (*Reprimanding*). TADAO!

TADAO (*Reprimanded but angry*). I'm going to Markie Goodrich's.

KIMIKO (*Frightened/Shimizu-angry*). It's too late . . . go study.

TADAO (*Exiting toward door*). It's not dark yet . . .

    KIMIKO *looks to* MASU *to stop* TADAO.

MASU (*Shrugging*). This is America.

    KIMIKO *turns back to dishes, angrier and hurt. Masu relents. He goes up to her and physically forces her to the chair and sits her down. He courts her. She does not respond, flings the newspaper onto the floor.* MASU, *now angered, rises to leave.* KIMIKO *stops him. They begin to make love and exit toward bedroom.* TADAO, *outside the home, a looser person, picks up stones, skips them/throws them.*

INTERIM: INTRODUCTION OF PEARL HARBOR

    ACT I, SCENE *II: Christmas Eve afternoon. Snow piles on the ground, against the porch. This scene is to be played with every sense of normalcy. Nowhere should a sense of doom or frenzy prevail. Whether Interim is used or not, its effect on the atmosphere of this scene is unexpressed.*

    MURAKAMI *walks in front stage right, lugging an evergreen to center stage. He goes offstage and lugs in another evergreen and goes offstage right, again he enters with an evergreen. The trees are in a pile center downstage, to the left of front door. He picks up each tree, smacks the trunk against the ground, freeing the snow and examines each tree. He chooses the best of the three and takes it into the house.* CHIEKO *and* TADAO *greet him at the door.*

CHIEKO. Pretty! Papa! That's the prettiest one!

TADAO. What's the others for?

MASU. For our cheap friends.

    All help or try to help in setting the tree upright in the stand. MASU *is happy decorating.*

CHIEKO. Now Mama, now. Let's put up the star right now. Please . . . come on. Popcorn . . .

    MASU *grabs* KIMIKO, *being playful, swinging her.*

KIMIKO. Stop it, stop it Masu. What will the children think?

MASU. They will think their mama and papa DID have a reason to get married. Hey, Kimi?
He releases her but is still playful. For the first time, some of her softness and gayness shows.

KIMIKO. Why did you get so many trees? What are they for?

MASU (*Expansive, mimicking*). One's for Tane. (*He likes the whole idea . . . but he needs an excuse.*) The other's for Jiro Yamada, that jackass. I saw him on the way to the pass and I offered him a lift. I thought he might want to get himself a tree too. He got on his high-tone. He said: "I'M Buddhist. I don't observe Cu-ris-mas." He doesn't observe. Bah! I said, "Who cares; it's a holiday and a nice one." "I don't observe any Cu-ri-shan holidays," he says. What a jackass! That man, Kimi, he didn't even know he was Buddhist until he came to this country. He says, "I'm surprised, shocked at you, Murakamisan, you, who almost became a Buddhist monk." I said, "Yamadasan, only a real Buddhist could appreciate Christmas as I do." Kimi . . . what do you think? I take a tree to him, present it, give him a short lecture and give him the hand of Buddha. Should I?

KIMIKO (*Laughing*). Oh Masu, no. You can't do that. That would be terrible.

MASU. Why not? The stuffedass.

CHIEKO. Papa, Tad say to put up the star.
CHIEKO *shoves the star into his hand and* MASU, *still expansive, clowning, puts up the tree's star.*

KIMIKO (*Helping him onto chair*). Come on, ojichan, put the star up.

MASU (*Surveying the tree*). Bi-u-ti-ful!

CHIEKO. I want a store doll . . . I want a Shirley Temple doll . . . Did Santa Claus get me . . .
KIMIKO *shushes* CHIEKO *and they exit.* MASU, *mellow, cocky, gets a bottle of sake and goes onto the steps.* TADAO *eyes him, goes gets himself a cup and joins him.*

TADAO. Can I have some papa?
MASU *sits down, screwing up his face against the wetness of the snow. It's night and only the porch light brings out the scene.* MASU *fumbles with the pitcher and cups.*

MASU. Sure . . . sure. (*He pours some sake into* TADAO'S *cup.*

*He laughs nervously. He is not quite sure how to handle
this situation.)* Women with women . . . men with men.
TADAO *downs his sake and eyeing his father, pours
himself another cupful.* MASU *is leaning on one arm,
watching* TADAO. *He seems a little disconcerted, seeing the way* TADAO *drinks his wine so easily. At the
same time, the act seems to end his nervousness. He
drinks his cup down and pours himself another.*

MASU. You are going to high school soon?
TADAO. Yeah Papa, next fall.
MASU. What kind of classes are you going to take?
TADAO. I don't care. What they give me, I guess.
MASU. You have no special interest? What do you want to do?
TADAO. I don't know.
MASU. You have to decide. What? You want to be a farmer,
like me?
TADAO. The farm's okay. But I don't really want to be a farmer.
(*He is not sure how his father will take this. Neither is
used to talking to the other.*) Is that okay?
MASU (*Reassuring*). Sure.
TADAO. I want to . . . I want to fly airplanes . . .
TANAKA *and his wife* FUMIKO *and son* HIROSHI *enter
from right wing or audience right.*
TANAKA. Masu! Hop-pi Cu-ris-mas!
MASU (*Stands to greet them*). Come in, come in! Tadao (*indi-
cating that* TADAO *should rise*).
A flurry of greetings. KIMIKO *is at the door.* CHIEKO,
on stage. HIROSHI *is a stiff young man, who obviously
does not want to be with his parents, at the Muraka-
mis, at such a childish gathering; a typical American
adolescent, yet his deportment is that of a military
man.*
MASU. This . . . Hiroshi? Big. Nineteen?
KIMIKO. He was just this tall the last time . . .
TADAO. Hi Hiro, how you been?
HIROSHI *gives* TADAO *a curt nod.*
MASU. Come in. . . . TADAO, some sake! (*His back to* TANAKA
and HIROSHI.) Four years, sa! A long time. A boy can
change in four years.
MRS. TANAKA. What do you think we sent him back for. Not
just to be hightone. Good thing too. Stay around here, just
become another dirt farmer . . . (*cuts herself off*) Anyway,

no monkey business for him over there. These American kids, no respect, no self-control, flighty . . . plain flighty. . . . Ah, Kimikosan understands what I'm talking about. Isn't that so, Kimikosan?

KIMIKO (*All graciousness*). Come in. Come in.

> KIMIKO, MRS. TANAKA, TADAO, *and* CHIEKO *enter house.* KIMIKO *sets out cups etc.*

FUMIKO TANAKA. You still using these old cups? Why don't you write home and have them send you some new ones.

KIMIKO. These were one of my mother's special sets. It was handed . . .

FUMIKO (*Eyeing the house, checking it out*). Don't look special to me. Tane said you made a nice embroidery with the left-over thread we had . . . where is it?

KIMIKO. Later, if you like. I will show it to you later. Chieko, go put on your nightgown. Then later you can go straight to bed.

> TANAKA, MASU and HIROSHI *enter the house.*

TANAKA. What do you think, Masu? Would Japan advance this far? Pearl Harbor is Pearl Harbor but . . . it doesn't make sense. (*Referring to son.*) He says the bombing was in retaliation for the embargoes.

HIROSHI. Last year scrap steel . . . before that . . . oil . . . Japan is slowly being starved.

FUMIKO. Look here, Murakamisan, see what we've brought.

> HIROSHI *is visibly annoyed by the petty interruption.* MASU *goes to the table. On it,* FUMIKO *has spread out rice cakes, smoked fish, other Japanese delicacies.* MASU *tries something.*

MASU. Not bad . . . not bad . . .

FUMIKO. What do you mean, not bad!

MASU. I don't see what I want . . .

FUMIKO. And what is that?

MASU (*Improvise/lewd remark in Japanese*).

FUMIKO (*Pleased, flustered*). Ah you bad boy!

KIMIKO. Tanakasan, the embroidery . . . if you would like to see it? I have it hanging in the other room.

> KIMIKO *leads* FUMIKO *off stage right.*

HIROSHI. It had to be the embargoes. Japan was slowly being starved to death.

MASU. Certain death to possible starvation, huh?

HIROSHI. The Imperial Way cannot be defeated. It is the only

way! Still, I was not prepared for Pearl Harbor. I believe
. . . Pearl Harbor was Japan's way of letting America
know that she will not be dallied with. What are these
white countries screaming about? We, I mean, Japan does
in Asia only what Westerners do all over the world. Asia
belongs to yellow people. The bitter struggle is with China.
Who will lead the yellow people of Asia?

During this entire exchange, TANAKA *is trying to take
pictures with his new camera so that* HIROSHI'S *lines
can be broken up.*

MASU. Asia belongs to yellow people or yellow rulers? *(Pose,
snap.)*

HIROSHI. Japan's rulers think only of their people.

MASU. That is what the ruling class always says.

HIROSHI. Are you questioning the sincerity of the Japanese
government?

MASU. What? Questioning? All governments lie . . .

HIROSHI. Murakamisan, do you question the integrity of the
emperor?

MASU *(More serious)*. If they do not lie, they never tell the
truth. . . .

HIROSHI. We must leave right now, father.

TANAKA *(Shaking his head)*. Masu, very patriotic . . .

MASU. To think, Tane, you sent him over there to be educated
. . . curious the process of education.

HIROSHI.

*The previous lines were said pompously and right-
eously, making* HIROSHI *a laughable character; beginning here, one begins to see he is young and sincere.*

Murakamisan, you do not truly believe that the emperor
lies?

MASU. Sa?

HIROSHI. Manchuria is important to us. China must learn that
we are entitled to our territorial integrity. China must not
swallow us up . . .

MASU *(Beginning to take* HIROSHI *seriously)*. Territorial integrity. . . Who taught you such clever words?

TANAKA. He was going to one of the best common schools in
Tokyo . . .

Both MASU *and* HIROSHI *dislike the interruption
. . . for different reasons.*

MASU. I'm sure he was, Tane.

HIROSHI. Murakamisan . . . do you question integrity for yellow people?

MASU. No . . . but what has integrity to do with the conquest of China?

HIROSHI. The Chinese will smother us to death if we . . . (*Realizes, perhaps, that he has no reasonable answer.*) They are worthless swine anyway. . . .

MASU (*No longer any hint of joking*). Then we must be swine too. They have been our teachers for centuries.

HIROSHI (*Outrage, puzzlement*). The Chinese . . . !
TANAKA *orders* HIROSHI *to stop. A discomfort settles over the table.*

TADAO. What is it like in Japan?

HIROSHI (*Angered, confused by* MASU). The best place in the world!

TADAO. Then you want to go back there?

HIROSHI (*Directed at* MASU). Of course.

MASU. Such confidence in the Imperial Way. You will join the Imperial Army then?

HIROSHI. Of course. If they will have me. . .

TANAKA (*Cut in*). Of course not. How can he go back?

MASU. If he wants to, he will. . . .

TANAKA. He will not go back.

MASU. How will you stop him?

TANAKA (*Bitter*). The young are ungrateful!

MASU (*Lighter*). Come on, we have business. Tadao, give Hiroshi some more sake. Anyone so certain he is a man needs more sake.
MASU *and* TANAKA *go outdoors, upstage left to bathhouse.* TADAO *and* HIROSHI *are left at the table.* TADAO *goes for the sake bottle . . . brings out glasses for the two of them rather than cups.* HIROSHI *smiles, boyish again.*

TANAKA. What do you think, Masu, could he be right?

MASU. The cock-worshipers are full of themselves again. Who knows. What do you think?

TANAKA. I think you are lucky Tadao is still too young . . . .

MASU. I won't deny that, Tane.
TADAO *fills the glasses. They sit, uncertain of each other.*

TADAO. What is Tokyo like?

HIROSHI. The Imperial Way, how can I explain it. . . . You

know what is happening. . . . Them, (*indicating* MASU *and* TANAKA) they are stupid, behind the times. . . . Japan was fated to rule Asia. There is no . . .

TADAO. I mean, if, if a guy went to Tokyo, what would it be like for him? What do you do at school? What's it like?

HIROSHI (*Hesitant about personal feelings*). Well . . . we have drills . . . and economics . . . history. . . . I am fluent in Japanese now. I didn't like it at first . . . lonely . . . and everyone always jumping to attention. (*Anger at revealing this.*) You become a real man. Now I can't believe that I could have been so weak!

TADAO. Do they have art? . . . I mean . . . I'm interested in airplanes. I like to draw them.

HIROSHI. The Zero is the best fighter plane in the world . . . even better than the Messerschmitt.

TADAO. Better than the Spitfire?

HIROSHI. Easy! Where are those drawings?

TADAO. Come on . . . I'll show you.

> TADAO *and* HIROSHI *exit stage right to children's bedroom.* TANAKA *and* MASU *are in the bathhouse.* MASU *is on his knees, trying to work the burner.*

TANAKA. Turn that handle . . . there.

> MASU *lights a match, warily tries to light the burner. The flames flare up and make him rear up.* TANAKA *is smoking and he offers* MASU *a cigarette.* MASU *accepts and lights it off the burner. He's on his haunches, staring at the flame.*

MASU. Do you think she will really be happy with it?

TANAKA. What a question! Of course . . . no pumping . . . no lugging pails . . . what a question, Masu.

MASU. I don't know. If I were a woman, I'm not sure how pleased I'd be.

TANAKA. Take my word. It will make her very happy.

MASU. It's not that it would save her much work. Tadao and I do the heavy carrying.

TANAKA. But she has to fill the pails and heat them. Besides, a Japanese should have a hot tub whenever he wants!

MASU. That's true. That's true. Still, not very pretty. Not beautiful, that. A fine piece of silk for a dress. She might like that better.

TANAKA. Give her silk next Christmas. What does she need silk for?

Masu (*Pensive*). Still this costs more in the long run. Having to buy gas and the air. Think of that! (*He slaps his thighs; he can't believe it himself.*) Buying air!

Tanaka. Take my word. . . .

Masu. Hah, you're right. If you say so, you're right. You two understand each other much better than I do. You should have married her. She would be much happier.

Tanaka (*Tinged with superior agreement*). Masu, don't talk stupid. I have a wife.

Masu. We will switch. How about that? Would you like that? Not for that! Tane! Not so solemn . . . it's Christmas.
Lights off them, on in the house. Kimiko *and* Fumiko *cross room toward the door.*

Kimiko. Oh and again, thank you for the han-pan, the mochigashi, the smoked salmon. Masu will enjoy that so much.

Fumiko. Nothing, it means so little to us . . . but . . .

Kimiko. The children are so happy.

Fumiko (*Displaying popcorn balls*). What are these called again?

Kimiko. Popcorn balls. Tadao wanted me to make them. But thank you again for . . .

Fumiko. So pretty and cheap to make. . . Oh it's nothing, nothing . . .
Masu *and* Tanaka *enter from upstage left downstage toward house.*)

Masu. Such a formal man you are. Don't you ever get drunk. Come on, Tane, we'll go back to the house and get you drunk! Do you know something, you only laugh when you are embarrassed or apologizing for something.
The boys now come out the door, the women are on the porch).

Masu. No time to get you drunk. (*He gets a tree, stands it up and presents it to* Tanaka. Tanaka *is visibly touched. He doesn't want to accept it.*) Happy Christmas, Tane!

Tanaka. Yes. . . Happy Christmas to you. Make sure to come for New Years. The best Japanese food anywhere.
Tanaka *hands the tree to* Hiroshi. Chieko *runs in the house and comes back with* Tanaka's *camera, handling it carelessly.* Kimiko *takes it from her. He and* Tanaka *are exiting offstage right.*

Kimiko. Tanakasan, your camera.
Tanaka *returns for the camera, bowing, calls his*

family back for one last picture. HIROSHI, *upset, and even* FUMIKO, *irritated. Everyone poses.* TANAKA *takes the picture. Goodbyes again.* TANAKAS *exit offstage right.*

CHIEKO. They're gone! They're gone! Goody! Come on Taddie, let's the mochi.

KIMI. Not tonight . . . Chiechan, you mustn't say such things. *The family enters the house. They admire the tree, relaxing from company.*

MASU. A fine tree . . . a fine tree.

CHIEKO. That's the best tree ever, Papa. Isn't that so, Taddie?

MASU. Tadao, what do you think, should we take a Christmas Eve bath?

TADAO. Yeah, come on Mom, let's take a bath. Are you tired? Papa and me will do the work. (*He exits to change.*)

KIMIKO. Oh, it will take all night . . . tomorrow, heh?

MASU. You and me, Chiepo. We'll take a bath then. (MASU *and* CHIEKO *exit*).

KIMIKO (*Cleaning up, sweeping*). You should have told me sooner. There's no water. Nothing. All right! It will be a cold bath! I will not stoke the fire!

Actors should return to stage as quickly as possible. Above lines can be cut wherever unnecessary. MASU *enters stage right with* CHIEKO. *He has a towel hanging from his neck and a kimono or his pants.* TADAO *is dressed the same.* MASU *swings* CHIEKO. *Tries to teach her a slowish Japanese bon-dance.* CHIEKO *wants more swinging.*

CHIEKO. No, no, on your shoulders Papa . . . on your shoulders.

MASU *grimaces, acts like a weary old man and swings* CHIEKO *on his shoulders, doing a slow bon odori with her on. She does not like it.*

CHIEKO. No . . . no . . . run . . . run . . .

MASU *gives her a mock disgusted look and she laughs.*

CHIEKO. Faster . . . faster . . .

KIMIKO *enters anywhere in this sequel. She is dressed in a cotton kimono that stops at the knee or thereabouts, has a towel hanging from her neck and carries a bar of soap. She begins to follow in the dance and they dance to the door to the porch where, because of the cold, they all begin to run upstage left to the bathhouse. The actors should be nude for bath scene. If they are not, the scene should light up with actors already in the tub. The tub should be an old, big, wooden, Japanese-style tub with an aluminum corru- gated-roofing bottom. If the actors are nude as called for, this scene is to be played leisurely.* KIMIKO *still sit- ting on the edge, slowly sinking into the tub.* TADAO *climbing in,* MASU *standing in the tub, holding* CHIEKO *above the water, slowly dropping her in, lifting her as she protests, dropping. They are in the water and re- laxing.*

TADAO. Mama is a good faker. When did you know about the heater?

MASU. So you knew after all.

KIMIKO. I didn't know for certain until now, but I heard you two splashing around in here. When the two of you con- spire, everyone knows.

TADAO. Papa, we need some cold water!

KIMIKO. NO! This is wonderful . . . wonderful . . .
   MASU *gets out of the tub.*

MASU (*An order*). Time to scrub!
   KIMIKO *refuses.* CHIEKO *protests but is lifted out of the water and* MASU *scrubs her back with a hitchimi or towel quickly. Both he and the child are cold again. He quickly deposits her back into the tub and gets back in himself. He lies out and begins to hum a Japa- nese tune. Then he begins looking leeringly at* KIMIKO. *She is amused and almost daring. He scoots deeper into the water and pinches her. She yelps.*

KIMIKO. Masu, the children!

MASU. It's Christmas . . . Kimi . . . for your own Je-su-us Cu-rist-s sake, let them see us happy.
   The bath scene darkens and the entire family is seen scurrying back into the house. Inside, KIMIKO *is getting* CHIEKO *to go to bed.*

CHIEKO. I don't want to go to sleep.

KIMIKO. Chiechan . . .

CHIEKO. I don't want to. Why does Tad get to stay up? Papa . . . I don't want to . . .

KIMIKO (*Cutting in*). Now be good or Santa Claus won't bring you anything.

MASU. Don't say that. (*He takes the child, sits on the floor and*

cradles her.) So . . . po-po, you don't want to go to sleep?
CHIEKO. Sing the song, Papa. I'll help you.
MASU. Will you go to sleep then?
CHIEKO. Maybe. . . .
MASU (*He sings the song, getting faster toward the end*). Now, will you go to sleep.
TADAO. Go on, Po-head! (CHIEKO *sticks out her tongue at him.*)
CHIEKO (*Taking* MASU'*s hand*). You come with me.
MASU (*Refusing*). You're a big girl. Mama will sleep with you.
CHIEKO. I don't want her. I want you!
MASU (*Warning*). Chie!
CHIEKO. I hate you Papa!
KIMIKO. Chiechan, mustn't say such things.
CHIEKO. Taddie said so . . . I can too! Taddie says you're a "dirty Jap."
    MASU *glances up at* TADAO. TADAO *glares at* CHIEKO.
    CHIEKO *does not understand what she has said, but she knows that everyone feels bad.* MASU *takes her in his arms again.*
MASU. Chie-po . . . wasn't it nice today? Don't you wish this nice day could be longer? Go on into tomorrow and tomorrow night? Then you have to do your part. You have to go to sleep. Okay, will you?
CHIEKO. Yes Papa. (*She rises to go, turns back, touches her father.*) Papa, goodnight.
MASU. Good night, Chie-po.
    KIMIKO *and* CHIEKO *exit stage right.* TADAO *has already exited to porch.* MASU *rises and gets some sake, looks toward the porch, begins to go toward bedroom or chair, decides to go on the porch, gets a jacket for himself and* TADAO. *He opens the door to the porch and stands there, holding the bottle of sake and considering his son.* TADAO *realizes he is there.*
TADAO. She's lying.
MASU. Is that so? You didn't say that? Sure you didn't. (*Comes out and sits down next to* TADAO. *Takes a drink. Offers some to* TADAO. TADAO *refuses.*) The years go by so fast. I don't feel any different but you . . . Sometimes I forget you are not a boy anymore. (*Takes another drink.*) I enjoyed myself this morning . . . when we filled the tub . . . you did most of it . . . then later, this evening, on the steps.

TADAO. I did too. I really did.

MASU. And I realized that the reason I was enjoying myself so much was that we haven't been like that for a long time. Years, I guess. That's strange, Tadao, to think, years.

TADAO. Papa . . . do you ever think about going back to Japan?

MASU. No . . . Why?

TADAO. Nothing, doesn't matter.

MASU. Tell me.

TADAO (*A sudden angry burst . . . or slow, deeply concentrated voice*). I hate it here.

MASU (*Thoughtfully*). You don't know Japan . . .

TADAO. That's not fair . . .

MASU. I wasn't making light of what you said. . . .

TADAO. You think you know so much Papa. You think I don't see anything. You think because you don't talk about things. . . . You think because I can't read the Japanese papers. . . . I can read (*He's ready to cry but can't stand the thought.*) the Herald . . . and those signs in town . . . and I can hear what they say. . . . If they hate us so much, why don't we go back to Japan.

MASU. Sa . . .

TADAO. We weren't . . . you weren't poor, in Japan, were you?

MASU. Hum . . .

TADAO. Mama says you come from a good family . . . rich . . . that you were going to be a priest . . . a Buddhist monk. . . . Why did you come here?

MASU (*Rising, moving off the porch*). You have grown up . . . right here, in this house. And I didn't even notice it. (*He walks around downstage, considers, walks.*) I was the black sheep in my family. Everyone who comes here is a black sheep . . . of their family, of their class . . . of their country. They were not wanted where they were. Strange . . . the only people who are not black sheep are black people; they didn't come here on . . .

TADAO (*Annoyed at his father getting off the point*). Papa!

MASU. It's true. . . . Before I married your mama, I worked on a ship. I worked with some black men and they told me. They didn't come here on their own. They came here but they didn't want to . . . .

TADAO. Papa! I'm not interested in "niggers!" Not now!

MASU (*Dealing with a new word*). "Ni-gas."

TADAO. Black people.

MASU. So . . . is that it?

TADAO. What?

MASU. On the boat, sometimes I'd hear Americans say "ni-gas" but I didn't understand. (*Turning on the son.*) You say it and I understand.

TADAO (*Frustrated*). Papa . . . sometimes you act like . . . like you live somewhere else . . . like you don't know anything?

MASU (*Cutting in*). I know well enough. I know enough. How do you know, Tadao? There are no black men around here. We are all "ni-gas." Everyone here! (*Angry now.*) Tanakasan and men like him came here because men like my father, my brothers, said, "If you don't want to starve, go somewhere else, but don't bother us!" So Tanaka came here and he stopped starving . . . but he can't forget . . . he can't forget he was a "ni-ga" in Japan and he want to forget. He want that very bad. So he does to other men what my father and brothers did to him. He thinks that will stop making him a "ni-ga" but that won't do it!

TADAO (*Fighting back*). If we go back to Japan, everyone would be happier. Mama and you wouldn't have to fight. And things would be nice! We belong there!

MASU. Things aren't nice there. Not before and certainly not now. (*He begins to calm down.*) If it was as before . . . that's right! Your mama and I wouldn't have to fight . . . we wouldn't know each other well enough to fight . . . or see each other.

TADAO. You hate Mama!

MASU. That's not true!

TADAO. Do you love her?

MASU. Sa, now that is a question.

TADAO. See. You don't love her. You hate her.

MASU. I don't know, Tadao. Your mama is a good mother. Not much of a wife . . . but a good mother. She has to bear a lot. It hasn't been easy for her. Sometimes she is so good, so fine, but she lives by so many rules. I can't keep track of all of them. Sometimes, it is hard to find the woman in her. (*Pats* TADAO's *chest.*) You smoke? Tell me. (TADAO *indicates no.*) Neither do I. You are right Tadao. In Japan, I'd have been a different man. I might not have married.

And you (*smacks* TADAO's *chest*), *you* wouldn't be here to worry about such things. I'd be a good man but no husband at all. Here . . . (*shrugs*) the problems are different. I wanted to be a monk. When I was fourteen, I entered under a master. When I was seventeen, I decided I didn't want to be a monk and I was sent to Hawaii to stay with an uncle . . . my uncle was like my father . . . so when I could, I came here. I worked as a lumberjack . . . and then I worked the fishing boats . . . up the Columbia River . . . the salmon jump . . . they jump high . . . their leap, a soft arch. They glistened but their color does not disturb the eye. At the lower reaches of the river where the spawning salmon begin their struggle upstream, they are lovely and full of wonder . . . they are not weary nor desperate in their race to be born again. Time is still immense and boundless. You like this watch (*shows him the watch*), one day I'll give it to you.

TADAO. Was it your father's?

MASU. No, I bought it in a pawnshop . . . off the wharf in Seattle. It's pure gold . . . see . . . pure gold. . . . When you were six, Mama went back to Japan. . . . Don't you remember?

TADAO. Sort of . . . I think I liked it there.

MASU. Because it was different. The same was true for me, here. I was freer. I could see what it was like to be a lumberjack . . . and a fisherman . . . and anything else that came my way. Try it out and forget it. Go where I wanted. This land was still uncivilized and unpopulated. It still is, Tadao. Every act still had no name and every piece of land and sky were still not spoken for. I guess it is different for you. You were born here and so when other people tell you that you don't belong, it must hurt. That didn't hurt me. I knew I didn't come from this land. I knew what I came from. It cannot be helped. We are born, Tadao, to different times, so our lives are different, must be different if we are to survive.

TADAO. I want to go back Papa . . . I hate it here.

MASU. How? There's a war on.

TADAO. Hiro's going back!

MASU. Yes, he does sound as if he is . . .

TADAO (*Cutting in*). He is! I mean it. I've thought it out. I

mean- it. I could . . . Hiro could . . . I could learn Japanese faster with him there and get used to . . . learn
Japanese ways.

MASU. I don't think it can be done. . . . Let me think about it.

TADAO. Hiro's going . . . I know he is.

MASU. Mama has relatives in Japan. It might be a good time.
. . . I'll talk to Tane . . . maybe he could lend me the
money. Even if I live to be a hundred years old . . . I will
never be able to pay off my debt to him . . . so maybe one
more won't upset the balance . . . maybe Tane will go
too . . . all of you . . . a present to my father . . . I must
be getting old, Tadao. I want you to understand me. It's
late. One more drink apiece. (*Drinks, offers* TADAO *one
which* TADAO *accepts.*)

TADAO. You're going to talk to him then?

MASU (*Returning to house*). What? Yes . . . I will.

TADAO. When we go back, we'll be a lot happier . . .

MASU. What? You, maybe you. Not me!

TADAO. But you said . . .

MASU. You wanted this man to man, now you have it. You,
Chie, maybe Mama . . . You can go back but not me. I
can't go back! I can't go back. . . .

*The two re-enter the house, cross stage and go off stage
right. Faint light of Christmas tree.* KIMIKO *enters stage
right and puts children's present under the tree.* MASU
*comes out, has a long white strip of paper, pauses to
check what he wrote: I am sorry about the football
shoes. Take this watch instead. In Japan, if you go, it
will be more useful. (The note is in Japanese and is to
be read in Japanese.)* MASU *places the watch and paper
under the tree. He exits stage right.* TADAO *enters stage
right, has some hand-crafted crude gifts. He notices the
watch, looks back toward the bedroom, takes the watch
and note, tries to read the note by the tree light, goes
outside, sits on the porch and tries to read the note
again as the curtain falls.*

WALLACE LIN
(1950-   )

Wallace Lin is fourth-generation thoroughbred Chinatown born in San Francisco. His family is famous for long fingers. He remembers being a child out with his parents and his brothers and sisters late at night. They walked up and down the hills of Chinatown and let their long fingers dangle and make shadows. Wallace is better known for overtaking people with his shadow than he is for his fiction and poetry. Lin recently married his childhood sweetheart and now lives in Phoenix, Arizona.

ROUGH NOTES
FOR MANTOS

THE LONELIEST MAN in the world. Also my friend. Stain of beer and cigarettes. Warm arm. I'm sweating. He eats, sleeps, sees. With arms, with all seeing eyes. With a clarity that numbs. A blinding light. Blind clarity.

Mantos woke up from his mother's womb. He knew what he wanted from the start. He was an antibody to himself. Red corpuscle against the white world. Sun in the dark sea. A pulse in silence. That was the thing, he was not born to bliss. Ever. Before. In his past life. No paradise, no hope or hint of one. He was bound from the start always to travel, to see whatever had to be seen. But he was no genius though he saw how things and people worked in absolute fidelity, every part of the engine, of the features.

But he would not go as far as to say it was a superconsciousness of being. No. It was supremely frustrating. He wasn't ashamed of his flexibility, but then he wasn't any christ either. He was just Mantos, all he could be to his friends and forever more. He was a lords prayer. Amen was the beginning and the end. By the grace of God. By no one's grace, no one's vision but his own. Sometimes he felt indelicate. No bliss for him. Not the happy innocence of ignorance. But not worn yet. Only twenty-six. Brought up on long lean limbs. Limber. Stalking. Rigorous, disciplined. Which he was of course. Mantos. Like Athena, Goddess of Wisdom, full sprung from Zeus's head, wholly formed. Whole but not complete. The fate of never finding a person to talk with, to share his irreducible sight.

His desire was in the mind, to make the full use of it. In physical action he forgot to some degree the frustration. But not for very long. Afterward it was all there again, flooding back, filling his pores and his blood and the waters welling within him. There was no space for bliss.

I knew Mantos before. A few times, I have run across him. Beer and cigarette smoke will stay in my mind with him. Through night stages. A gulf of mind. Mine is not so open yet, so strong. To have a strong mind. After all, strength is beautiful, is functional. Is new. To keep it smooth, and from breaking.

To run my fingers over this clear, subtle mind, like a hard pebble found upon the beach, formed by heat and pressure, the most intense violence and fury. For the stone suddenly to explode and surround you in a forest, and I am lost.

A tender violence. Violent tenderness. A mixture of his self impression, with regard, care. Violence to a point—tempered by love.

When thinking about Mantos I cry, laugh. I am angry, frustrated, mistrustful, unsure. In flux.

As I sit in back of a streetcar at night going through San Francisco streets in the end seat that hugs both aisles, Mantos is gone. The streetcar is vintage 1948 and the lights on the ceiling are flat half globed yellowish white disks in two rows on either side of the aisle. I smell someone's cigarette smoke, but not the sweet acrid scent of the night after, the odor of an ashtray full of soft gray stumps . . . this smoke is new. The streetcar is in front of me and I am behind all the moon-disked lights somewhere back in the darkness.

It's eight o'clock passing Reynolds Park, its massive trees clumped inert figures of silence. The streetcar goes on, rattling through the tunnel, and there are square niches on the walls with bare bulbs like the entrances to catacombs or tombs. The night was like a heavy bottle pressed unhaltingly upon my lips.

For My Quiet Friend Mantos
Silence is round
Like a sphere, like
A whole separate world
Curved between hands.
I ask: what is chosen by silence

What is shaped within
That is growing, brooding
Going to be born out of it?
May the word that is shining
In the center of silence
Be yours.
Cut to the core of silence
Like the flash of knives
Or one green plant in a houseful of rooms—
There is that sleeping flesh of yours
Shaping a cool sheath around warm dreams.
Silence has made a full circle
Around your life and mine.
So I ask you again
What do you mean
By that silence
Behind your teeth
And all the past around your body
Like a thousand layers of cloth?
My quiet friend:
When word and skin and time
Can finally meet and sing
I will ask everyone
I know to rejoice
With me, with you.

If handwriting could convey the touch of your body, the tenderness and breadth of your mind, I would have stuffed your
pockets with pencils before you went.

This is my dry town, of dusty buildings that stem from dry
rot, slacked on dust, with a dry ocean right beside lapping
dunes through my arms, sweating dry sweat; even my blood is
dry, a needle in arm will draw a hole that will finally empty
me, dry powder, like an old woman's rouge or mascara, the
stuffing of a pillow or a doll, dry powder will come tumbling
out in clouds and my eyes will fall out because there is no more
dust to keep them. This is my dry town, a heedless neutral color
between tan and gray, flickering below a gray sun. There is no
landscape of green leaves, it is a brown abstract of points; even
the animals, the rats and cockroaches that remain have lost
their oily sheen on fur and shell we crawl dry.

Somewhere there must be a tree, new growth pushing upon
the bark, upwards now, forcing exultation. I must train my body

to live a thousand miles away from you, to drink dry water, to inhabit a dry landscape like a desert rat: to harmonize into fate as a shifting dune. I ignite easily now; my face and arms and skin have become flaccid and layered with dust and I am growing old. And Mantos, I wonder whether you are still alive.

> Hot light that has blinded my eyes,
> That has gathered the darkness into black flames.
> Face that I have seen a few nights,
> Hands that I have fought and taken, and brown hair . . .

POSTSCRIPT

Acrobat in the middle of the air, encircled by lights and canvas sky, floating on the clouds of a million human breaths, with sad eyes narrows into one single tear, as a drop falls imperceptibly through the net to damp sawdust of the ring and the blind crowd storms the gates shouting cheated and money back; while I among them sits still, awed, feeling that one tear enter my mouth, drawn down my throat; it has turned as heavy as mercury, and as it slips through my flesh it burns my belly, and my skeleton must be coated with poison so I do not stand but sit, alone on the bench, smiling, letting the mercury warm my own heat, nourishing the fumes of your tear, letting it course and burn and destroy my cells and though I cannot see my own face I believe that I am radiant, as I sit on the wood being devoured, benign as I am burnt; my bones are stiffening, I cannot move my wrist, my calcium has turned to hard silver, my flesh to nephrite, my blood to pure water and my clothes are now gone to shreds.

And one man's death has happened, a fat, graying old man seems to have suffered a stroke or an attack of some sort, at any rate his heart has stopped beating . . . it is with Mantos.

> Sometimes, as I walk along
> The path that is here,
> Your low voice juts into my arm
> And raises me.
> Your words have turned
> To hard ladders in my head
> And I am climbing with them.

Notes from a Son to his Father.

There is nothing good about being a son. I know; I am a son. When you have to admit that you have a father, allowing people to think that you are a father and son, as if any relation existed between those two terms, when there is really nothing to say.

And yet I usually find myself talking about my father, telling my friends and any strangers what he does and where he has been, trying to describe with exactness his activities, trying to grasp his life through what little information I have of him. Doing this, I feel like a small child pressing a string of hard beads to my chest, a rosary of sorts, chanting the same phrases and images a thousand times in order to derive an order, a strength out of them. But the polished beads do not yield a thing; it is a repetition of uselessness. Nothing comes out of them.

I know my father like this. I see him working in his white apron, flashing and sharpening his cleaver on the back rim of a white Chinese pottery bowl. Zhap zhap zhap, the gray steel cleaver on the sturdy bowl. After arranging different vegetables on the table, I see him grasping the handle of the cleaver firmly, then nudging the jade bitter melon under the blade, at a slant, so that the pieces come out in even green crescents, like perfect waves of a green sea, at the same angle, and then the carrots, in thin narrow ovals, cut and dropped to boil lightly in a pot a while, and then the green bell peppers, the seeds and pale green mulch scooped out with a spoon, then cut in quarters and sliced. Then all the vegetables are arranged in neat piles on a large plate, ready to be cooked; the hardest, fibrous vegetables to be cooked first in a dash of oil, and then the more delicately flavored ones, with purple and orange-tipped spears of heat, sizzling them in the heart, while all along the rice is boiling on another part of the stove, each white grain destined to be firm and separate from his brother.

My father's hands were always busy preparing food and papers, writing and touching inanimate and ultimately useful things such as pencils and knives. Yet I do not know the real strength of my father's arm, I have never been lifted on his

hand, brought up to see any life outside of my own. As a child
I dreamed of my father.

Was this true, could he see his father dancing, away from the
stiff and solemn pace of himself as father, provider, and business-
man? Was it true, his father strong and bare, bravely dancing,
using the wind as rope to catch all the worlds, flinging his arms
and legs?

No, that is not him at all; his motions are never quick or
free, but formal, stern, and placid for every emotion except
rage.

At the door to my room, my father is glittering in anger, a
knife poised in his hand. His face is pulsing pink, the once pale
cauliflower flesh tinged with color and rage, and he is on one
side of the room, about to throw the knife into me. I am just
standing there, cringing; how can I defend myself against this
violence, this dark pearl which I have struck? So this is what is
beneath my father's calmness, his layered dispassion, his view
of my foolishness and ignorance and youth, it is this seething
fury, not really his, but an inherited bitterness from some vague
source, from a life not his, a frustration that has finally found its
point in a knife, a silver gleaming tooth that will draw blood
from my chest. My father, I screamed inside, but outside I tried
to remain calm and rather disinterested in any personal aspect
of the situation, as if his piercing my body was an event apart
from the two of us, beyond any relation of father and son, as if
my death or any son's death could happen like this, if the son
did not observe and obey the rules—the correct way of doing
things. During these moments I appeared calm, waiting for the
blade to fall, and I despised him even more when his arm suddenly dropped down and the knife fell to the floor; he was not
strong enough to go through with his convictions—he could not
even kill his own son. I had heard the story about Abraham and
Isaac, how Abraham would have killed his own son for God,
because of his trust in God, but my father was not as good as
that, because he does not believe in God in the first place. He
will just kill me for no god at all.

At a later age, when one is a little older, one begins to strike
back against his father with a vengeance, with a force akin to
hatred or love, with the urge utterly to destroy all images of

men or seek all images of them wherever and whenever possible.

Because one is a son himself he must realize his peculiar tendency to be i.e. manly and so he searches. I went out into the streets to look for this, this peculiar stuff of which pictures, pride, and parades are made of. Now I am in the middle of it, sunk into it. With love to the Father and to the Son.

TOSHIO MORI
(1910-   )

Toshio Mori stopped short a career as a professional base-ball player with the Chicago Cubs to help in his parents' business. He turned his ambitions toward writing in the twenties. Now in his sixties, he has the manuscripts of four novels on his shelf written in the English that Japanese-Americans of the thirties and forties happened to speak. His collection of short stories, *Yokohama, California,* about Oakland and San Leandro in the twenties and thirties was published in 1949. His work has appeared in several anthologies, including *New Directions* and *Best American Short Stories of 1943,* and in periodicals such as *Pacific Citizen, Public Welfare, Common Ground, The Coast, Writer's Forum, Current Life, Clipper, Matrix,* and *Iconograph.* Toshio Mori has lived in the San Francisco Bay area all his life with the exception of three years in Topaz Center, Utah, during the evacuation and exclusion of Japanese-Americans on the West Coast. During that time, Mori along with other writers and artists of Topaz Center started the camp magazine *Trek.*

THE WOMAN WHO MAKES SWELL DOUGHNUTS

THERE IS NOTHING I like to do better than to go to her house and knock on the door and when she opens the door, to go in. It is one of the experiences I will long remember—perhaps the only immortality that I will ever be lucky to meet in my short life—and when I say experience I do not mean the actual movement, the motor of our lives. I mean by experience the dancing of emotions before our eyes and inside of us, the dance that is still but is the roar and the force capable of stirring the earth and the people.

Of course, she, the woman I visit, is old and of her youthful beauty there is little left. Her face of today is coarse with hard water and there is no question that she has lived her life: given birth to six children, worked side by side with her man for forty years, working in the fields, working in the house, caring for the grandchildren, facing the summers and winters and also the springs and autumns, running the household that is completely her little world. And when I came on the scene, when I discovered her in her little house on Seventh Street, all of her life was behind, all of her task in this world was tabbed, looked into, thoroughly attended, and all that is before her in life and the world, all that could be before her now was to sit and be served; duty done, work done, time clock punched; old-age pension or old-age security; easy chair; soft serene hours till death take her. But this was not of her, not the least bit of her.

When I visit her she takes me to the coziest chair in the living room, where are her magazines and books in Japanese and English. "Sit down," she says. "Make yourself comfortable. I will come back with some hot doughnuts just out of oil."

And before I can turn a page of a magazine she is back with a plateful of hot doughnuts. There is nothing I can do to describe her doughnut; it is in a class by itself, without words, without demonstration. It is a doughnut, just a plain doughnut just out of oil but it is different, unique. Perhaps when I am eating her doughnuts I am really eating her; I have this foolish notion in my head many times and whenever I catch myself doing so I say, that is not so, that is not true. Her doughnuts really taste swell, she is the best cook I have ever known, Oriental dishes or American dishes.

I bow humbly that such a room, such a house exists in my neighborhood so I may dash in and out when my spirit wanes, when hell is loose. I sing gratefully that such a simple and common experience becomes an event, an event of necessity and growth. It is an event that is a part of me, an addition to the elements of the earth, water, fire, and air, and I seek the day when it will become a part of everyone.

All her friends, old and young, call her Mama. Everybody calls her Mama. That is not new, it is logical. I suppose there is in every block of every city in America a woman who can be called Mama by her friends and the strangers meeting her. This is commonplace, it is not new and the old sentimentality may be the undoing of the moniker. But what of a woman who isn't a mama but is, and instead of priding in the expansion of her little world, takes her little circle, living out her days in the little circle, perhaps never to be exploited in a biography or on everybody's tongue, but enclosed, shut, excluded from world news and newsreels; just sitting, just moving, just alive, planting the plants in the fields, caring for the children and the grandchildren and baking the tastiest doughnuts this side of the next world.

When I sit with her I do not need to ask deep questions, I do not need to know Plato or The Sacred Books of the East or dancing. I do not need to be on guard. But I am on guard and foot-loose because the room is alive.

"Where are the grandchildren?" I say. "Where are Mickey, Tadao, and Yaeko?"

"They are out in the yard," she says. "I say to them, play, play hard, go out there and play hard. You will be glad later for everything you have done with all your might."

Sometimes we sit many minutes in silence. Silence does not bother her. She says silence is the most beautiful symphony, she says the air breathed in silence is sweeter and sadder. That is about all we talk of. Sometimes I sit and gaze out the window and watch the Southern Pacific trains rumble by and the vehicles whizz with speed. And sometimes she catches me doing this and she nods her head and I know she understands that I think the silence in the room is great, and also the roar and the dust of the outside is great, and when she is nodding I understand that she is saying that this, her little room, her little circle, is a depot, a pause, for the weary traveler, but outside, outside of her little world there is dissonance, hugeness of another kind, and the travel to do. So she has her little house, she bakes the grandest doughnuts, and inside of her she houses a little depot.

Most stories would end with her death, would wait till she is peacefully dead and peacefully at rest but I cannot wait that long. I think she will grow, and her hot doughnuts just out of the oil will grow with softness and touch. And I think it would be a shame to talk of her doughnuts after she is dead, after she is formless.

Instead I take today to talk of her and her wonderful doughnuts when the earth is something to her, when the people from all parts of the earth may drop in and taste the flavor, her flavor, which is everyone's and all flavor; talk to her, sit with her, and also taste the silence of her room and the silence that is herself; and finally go away to hope and keep alive what is alive in her, on earth and in men, expressly myself.

JOHN OKADA
(1923-1971)

In a letter to the Charles E. Tuttle Co., dated February 14, 1956, John Okada wrote:

> While I am primarily interested in finding a market for my work in the United States, I feel that the subject matter with which I naturally concern myself would be of interest to the Japanese. This is my first novel and I am now at work on a second which will have for its protagonist an immigrant Issei rather than a Nisei. When completed, I hope that it will to some degree faithfully describe the experiences of the immigrant Japanese in the United States. This is a story which has never been told in fiction and only in fiction can the hopes and fears and joys and sorrows of people be adequately recorded. I feel an urgency to write of the Japanese in the United States for the Issei are rapidly vanishing and I should regret it if their chapter in American history should die with them. Providing my efforts are unsuccessful, I pray equally fervently that there is another like myself who is creating a similar work which will find its way into publication.

John Okada's widow, Dorothy Okada, offered the University of California at Los Angeles all of Okada's stories, notes, papers, and the unfinished novel about the Issei. They had never heard of John Okada and were not interested in the novel. She believed that no one would be interested in the novel and in a fit of grief burned his papers. UCLA's lack of insight mirrored sentiments about *No-No Boy* when it was published in 1957.

The *Hokubei Mainichi* on June 2, 1957, stated: "This is a story with a purpose, a purpose so insisted upon, and so repeatedly, that it overwhelms the plot and the characters. The style and tone of the book range from slang coarseness to sonorous nobleness, from barking invectives to resonant self-pathos . . . It is better not to blame it for what it is not: literature."

Colleges and universities did not recognize *No-No Boy* as American literature as recently as 1971 to 1972. They refused to accept a study of all Asian-American literature, including *No-No Boy*, on the grounds that it lacked literary value. It was not American enough. Students who enrolled in a class in Asian-American literature offered by the Ethnic Studies Department at Mills College and who wanted credit toward their English major were turned down, while others received credit in related fields such as history, philosophy, drama, and black literature. The English department wrote:

> Many of the books are not of high literary quality, however interesting and valuable they are as records of the experience of an ethnic minority in America. . . . The department discussed the matter at great length before coming to this decision, but agreed in the end that the cross-referencing had better wait until a more substantial body of material has been produced. As soon as the young Asian-American writers do produce a body of material comparable in size and caliber to black literature, we will be delighted to add such a course to the offerings of the English department.

Obviously, sincerity and the real language that Okada heard in the streets of Seattle, where he grew up, was not literature. Of all the reviewers of *No-No Boy,* Earl Miner in the *Saturday Review* was most sensitive to Okada's skill as a writer: "*No-No Boy* is an absorbing, if often strained, melodrama based on injustice and the immemorial problem of harmonizing the guilt of a society with the lesser guilt of the individual. The modern American, of whatever descent, is truly both the hero and the villain of the piece. The heroine is 'that faint and elusive insinuation of promise' which is the American's heritage. The problem itself is tragic, and *No-No Boy* comes as close as anything in recent fiction to exploring the nature of this tragedy."

John Okada was raised in Seattle, Washington. He received two B.A. degrees from the University of Washington, one in English and one in library science and later received a master's degree in English from Columbia University, where he met his wife, Dorothy. He served as a sergeant in the U.S. Air Force during World War II.

From
NO-NO BOY

No! No! No! No! No! No! No! No!

AN HOUR LATER Ichiro was at home with a promise from Kenji to pick him up early the next morning. As he walked into the store, his mother looked up from a sheaf of bills and receipts. If there was any indication of relief, he didn't notice it.

"Where have you been?" she said accusingly.

"Out." On the way home he had felt a twinge of guilt for having spent the night away without telling his folks, but whatever regrets he might have had were quickly dispelled by the tone of her voice.

"Where have you been?" she repeated harshly.

"With Kenji, Kanno-san's boy." He approached the counter and faced her. "You know him."

"Ahh," she said shrilly and distastefully, "that one who lost a leg. How can you be friends with such a one? He is no good."

He gripped the counter for fear of having his hands free. "Why?" he rasped.

His discomfort seemed strangely to please her. She raised her chin perceptibly and answered: "He is not Japanese. He fought against us. He brought shame to his father and grief to himself. It is unfortunate he was not killed."

"What's so good about being Japanese?" He felt the pressure of the wood against his nails.

She seemed not to hear him. Quite calmly, she continued,

talking in the tone of mother to son: "You can be a good boy, a fine son. For my sake and yours do not see him again. It is just as well."

Pushing himself away from the counter, he let his arms drop to his sides. "I'm going to Portland with him tomorrow."

Her face, which had dropped to regard a column of figures on an invoice from the wholesale grocer, jerked up. For a moment, it glared at him, the twisted mouth contorting the slender, austere face into a hard mass of dark hatred. "Do as you will," she cried out. Then the tension drained just as quickly from her face and she was putting her mind to the figures once more.

Through his anger crept up a sudden feeling of remorse and pity. It was an uneasy, guilty sort of sensation which made him want almost to take her into his arms and comfort her, for he saw that the sickness of the soul that was Japanese once and forever was beginning to destroy her mind. Right or wrong, she, in her way, had tried harder than most mothers to be a good mother to him. Did it matter so much that events had ruined the plans which she cherished and turned the once very possible dreams into a madness which was madness only in view of the changed status of the Japanese in America? Was it she who was wrong and crazy not to have found in herself the capacity to accept a country which repeatedly refused to accept her or her sons unquestioningly, or was it the others who were being deluded, the ones, like Kenji, who believed and fought and even gave their lives to protect this country where they could still not rate as first-class citizens because of the unseen walls?

How is one to talk to a woman, a mother who is also a stranger because the son does not know who or what she is? Tell me, Mother, who are you? What is it to be a Japanese? There must have been a time when you were a little girl. You never told me about those things. Tell me now so that I can begin to understand. Tell me about the house in which you lived and of your father and mother, who were my grandparents, whom i have never seen or known because I do not remember your ever speaking of them except to say that they died a long time ago. Tell me everything and just a little bit and a little bit more until their lives and yours and mine are fitted together, for they surely must be. There is time now while there

are no customers and you and I are all alone. Begin from the beginning when your hair was straight and black and everyone
was Japanese because that was where you were born and America was not yet a country beyond the ocean where fortunes
were to be made or an enemy to hate. Quick, now, quick,
Mother, what was the name of your favorite school teacher?

While he wrestled with the words which cried to be spoken,
the mother glanced up and looked surprised as if to say: Oh, I
thought you had gone. She riffled through the papers and dug
out an envelope arrayed with an assortment of expensive-looking
stamps. It was similar to the other ones from Japan which he
had seen in his father's hands two nights previously.

"For Papa," she sneered, flipping it across the counter at him.

He snatched it as it was about to slide over the edge. If he
had been about to say something, the moment was gone.
Wretchedly, he turned and stumbled into the kitchen.

The father turned from the cutting board, where he was
chopping up a head of cabbage for pickling. Around his waist
was a bright plastic apron and his wide, stubby, stockinged feet
were crammed into a pair of shapeless reed slippers.

"Ichiro, my son," he chuckled, "you are home." He gazed
fondly at him and added: "Had a nice time, yes?"

He looked up at his father, not immediately understanding
what the old man meant. "Sure," he said, interpreting the sly,
friendly smile, "not enough to make up for two years, but I had
a big time."

"Ya," the father said gleefully and brought his hands together
as might a child in a brief moment of ecstasy, "I was young once
too. I know. I know." He picked up the broad, steel blade and
sank it energetically into the cabbage.

Whatever the old man thought he knew was probably wilder
and lewder and more reckless than the comparatively gentle
night he had spent with Emi. It bothered him to have his father
thinking that he had spent the night carousing when such was
not the case. He could imagine what it must have been like for
the young Japanese new to America and slaving at a killing job
on the railroad in Montana under the scorching sun and in the
choking dust. Once a month, or even less, the gang of immigrants would manage to make it to town for a weekend. There

would be gambling and brawling and hard drinking and sleeping with bought women, and then the money would be gone. Monday would find them swinging their sledge hammers and straining mercilessly against the bars to straighten the hot, gleaming strips of railing while the foul smell of cheap liquor oozed out of their listless bodies. Occasionally, one of them would groan aloud with guilty resolve that he would henceforth stay in camp and save his money and hoard and cherish it into a respectable sum, for was that not what he had come to America for? And there would be murmurs of approbation from those who harbored the same thoughts and were thinking what foolishness it is to work like an animal and have nothing but a sick faintness in the head to show for it. If it is not to work and save and go back to Japan a rich man, which is why one comes to America, it is better never to have left Japan. The will is there and, in this moment when the shame and futility is greatest, the vow is renewed once and for always. No more gambling. No more drinking. No more whoring. And the ones who had long since stopped repeating the vow snickered and guffawed and rested their bodies by only seeming to heave when the gang boss commanded but by not really heaving at all so that the younger ones had to exert themselves just that much more and thereby became more fervent in their resolution to walk a straight path.

"I got pretty drunk," he said vaguely.

"Ya, I drink pretty good too." He bent over the cabbage, mumbling: "Pretty good—pretty good."

Ichiro laid the letter on the table and pressed it flat with his hands. "Another letter, Pa. Just came."

Laying down the knife and wiping his hands on a dish towel, the old man sat at the table and took the letter. Holding it at arm's length, he examined the envelope curiously. "So much money to send such a tiny piece of paper. Still, they write. For Mama, this one. From her sister. They would die with happiness if they saw our little store so full of cans and bottles and boxes of things to eat."

He inserted a pudgy finger under the flap and ran it through from end to end. The thin sheets of rice paper crackled softly as he removed them. He read the letter slowly and deliberately, his eyes barely moving and his mouth silently forming words. After he had finished, he sat staring at the last page for a long time without moving, looking extremely thoughtful. Slowly, he shook his head several times.

"Mama!" he shouted suddenly in a loud voice.

The mother stuck her head through the curtain, looking unhappy about being disturbed.

"Sit down, Mama."

"Who will watch the store?"

"Please. I say sit down."

She did so but not without making it obvious that she disapproved. "What is it?"

The old man shoved the letter before her. "It is from your sister for you. Read."

"I do not have to read it," she said flippantly. "Is this why you ask me to leave the store unattended and sit in the kitchen?" She started to rise.

"No," he said and pushed her roughly back into the chair. "Then I will read."

She glared stubbornly at him, but was momentarily too surprised to defy him.

Ichiro was watching his father, who continued to speak: "It is from your sister who calls you Kin-chan. She has not written before."

"Kin-chan?" voiced the mother stupidly, hardly believing the sound of her own diminutive, which she had almost forgotten.

" 'Many, many pardons, dear Kin-chan,' " the father read, " 'for not having written to you long before this, but I have found it difficult to write of unpleasant things and all has been unpleasant since the disastrous outcome of the war which proved too vast an undertaking even for Japan. You were always such a proud one that I am sure you have suffered more than we who still live at home. I, too, have tried to be proud but it is not an easy thing to do when one's children are always cold and hungry. Perhaps it is punishment for the war. How much better things might have been had there been no war. For myself, I ask nothing, but for the children, if it is possible, a little sugar, perhaps, or the meat which you have in cans or the white powder which can be made into milk with water. And, while I know that I am already asking too much, it would be such a comfort to me and a joy to the children if you could somehow manage to include a few pieces of candy. It has been so long since they have had any. I am begging and feel no shame, for that is the way things are. And I am writing after many long years and immediately asking you to give assistance, which is something that one should not do in a letter until all the niceties have been covered, but, again, that is the way things are. Forgive me, Kin-chan, but the suffering of my children is the reason I must write in this shameless manner. Please, if you can, and I know not that you can, for there have been no answers to the many letters which brother and uncle and cousin have written, but, if you can, just a little will be of such great comfort to us—' "

"Not true. I won't listen." She did not, however, move. Nervously, she rubbed her palms against her lap.

"One more place I will read," said the father and, casting aside the first sheet, searched along the second until he found the place he wanted. "Here she writes: 'Remember the river and the secret it holds? You almost drowned that day for the water was deeper and swifter than it looked because of the heavy rains. We were frightened, weren't we? Still, they were wonderful, happy times and, children that we were, we vowed never to tell anyone how close to dying you came. Had it not been for the log on the bank, I could only have watched you being swallowed up by the river. It is still your secret and mine for I have never told anyone about it. It no longer seems important, but I do think about such things if only to tell myself that there were other and better times.' "

He laid the sheets on the table and looked firmly at his wife as he had not done for a long, long time. Then, as if sensing the enormity of the thing he had been trying to prove, his mouth trembled weakly and he retreated timidly to the cabbage, which he began industriously to stuff into a stone tub partly filled with salt water. On the cabbage he placed a board, and on the board, a large, heavy stone weight. Not until then did he fearfully cock his head and look askance at the woman who was his wife and the mother of his sons.

She sat stonily with hands in lap, her mouth slightly ajar in the dumb confusion that raged through her mind fighting off the truth which threatened no longer to be untrue. Taking the letter in her hands finally, she perused it with sad eyes which still occasionally sparked with suspicious contempt.

Ichiro watched wordlessly, having understood enough of the letter to realize what was taking place. The passive reaction of his mother surprised him, even caused him to worry uncomfortably.

"Oh, they are so clever," she suddenly said very clearly in a voice slightly nasal, "even to the secret which I had long forgotten. How they must have tortured her to make her reveal it. Poor, poor sister." With letter in hand, she rose and disappeared into the bedroom.

The father glanced nervously at Ichiro and shoved the cabbage-filled stone tub under the sink. "It is happening, ya? She is beginning to see how things are?"

"I don't know, Pa. I think so."

"What is it you think?"

"She didn't look too happy. Maybe it means she's not so sure any more about Japan winning the war."

Muttering under his breath, the father hastened to get the bottle from the cupboard and tilted it hungrily to his mouth. Taking more than he had intended, he gagged noisily and stamped his foot on the floor until the agony passed. Tears streaming down his beet-red face, he stumbled to the table and flopped down hard on the chair. "Aagh," he grunted hoarsely, "good stuff, good stuff."

Ichiro fetched a glass of water, which the old man downed promptly. He nodded gratefully to his son. When his discomfort had passed, he uttered with obvious embarrassment: "I do not mean to hurt her, Ichiro. I do not mean to do any wrong. It is not right for her to go on hugging like a crazy woman to her dreams of madness when they are not so, is it? Is it, Ichiro?"

"No, it's not right."

"I am not wrong, no?"

"No, you're not wrong. She should know."

"Ya," he said, greatly relieved, "I do only what is right. A woman does not have the strength of a man, so it is I who must make her see the truth. She will be all right."

When Ichiro did not answer, the old man, looking concerned again, repeated: "She will be all right, ya, Ichiro?"

"Sure, Pa, sure. Give her time."

"Ya, time. We have plenty time. She will be all right, but look anyway."

"What?"

"Look. Look in the bedroom. See that she is all right, now."

His disgust mounting rapidly, Ichiro peeked into the bedroom doorway. In the semi-darkness of the room, the mother sat on the edge of the bed, staring blankly at the sheets of paper in her hand. Her expression was neither that of sadness nor anger. It was a look which meant nothing, for the meaning was gone.

"How is it?" asked the father anxiously. "What is she doing, Ichiro?"

"Sitting," he replied.

"Only sitting?"

"Maybe thinking too. How should I know?"

"I make lunch. After she eat, she be fine. You watch the store, ya?"

"Sure." Ichiro settled himself on a stool behind the cash register and lighted a cigarette. He thought of the trip to Portland the following day and wished that he were already on his way. Then it occurred to him that he might look for work down there without returning home.

I haven't got a home, he said to himself, smiling ironically. Why should I come back? Too many people know me here. Best I can do around Seattle is knock my head against the wall. The sensible thing to do would be to find work in Portland, mind my own business, keep away from the Japs, and there's no reason why things couldn't work out. It's the only chance I've got. I've got to start clean. I've got to get away from Pa and Ma and forget the past. To forget completely would be impossible, but I don't have to stay here where I'll be reminded of it every moment of the day. I don't owe them a thing. They loused up my life for me and loused up their own in the process. Why can't they be like other people, other Japs, and take things as they are? . . . They? Ma's the one. Pa, he's just around. Still, his weakness is just as bad as Ma's strength. He might have prevented all this. He saw what was going on. He could have taken her in hand and straightened her out long ago. Or could he? No, I guess not. Pa's okay, what there is of him, but he missed out someplace. He should have been a woman. He should have been Ma and Ma should have been Pa. Things would have worked out differently then. How, I don't know. I just know they would have.

I won't be running away. I'll be getting away from them and here, but I won't really be running away because the thing that's inside of me is going along and always will be where it is. It's just that I've got to do things right and, in order for things to be right, I've got to be in a new place with new people. I'll talk to Pa about it. Somebody ought to know and I certainly can't tell Ma. She wouldn't understand. She never has and never will. Pa won't really understand either, but he'll agree. Maybe it'll make him happy. He should have been a woman, dammit. Poor Ma. Wonder what kind of hell she's going through now.

The door latch clicked, the bell tinkled, and a small boy walked in. He gaped at Ichiro with the doorknob still in his hand and said: "Who are you?"

"I work here," he said.

"Oh." The boy closed the door and proceeded to the bread rack, where he methodically squeezed each loaf of bread. "Day-old stuff," he grimaced and reluctantly selected a small loaf. He placed it on the counter and examined the coins in his hand. "Gimme two black-whips too," he said.

"Black-whips? What are they?"

"If you work here, how come you don't know? I know more'n you."

"Yeah, you're smart. What are black-whips?"

"Lik-rish. Them over there." He pointed behind Ichiro at the assortment of candy, indicating the long strips of red and black licorice. "I want the black ones."

Without further comment, Ichiro took two strips from the box and handed them to the boy, who put his coins on the counter and departed after again eyeing him skeptically.

He was telling himself that he'd better pack his suitcase, when his father called to say that lunch was ready.

Somehow, he knew that his mother wouldn't be in the kitchen, and she wasn't. After they had been eating for a while, the father got up and looked into the bedroom. "Mama," he said, trying to sound cheerful, "Mama, come and eat. I made fresh rice and it is good and hot. You must eat, Mama."

Rocking hesitantly from one slippered foot to the other, he suddenly made as if to go in but quickly stepped back and continued to watch, the sad concern making the puffiness of his cheeks droop. "Mama," he said more quietly and hopelessly, "one has to eat. It gives strength."

And still he stood and watched, knowing that no amount of urging would move the beaten lump on the edge of the bed and vainly searching for the words to bring her alive. He brushed an arm to his eye and pressed his lips into a near pout. "The letter," he continued, "the letter, Mama. It could be nothing." Hope and encouragement caused his voice to rise in volume: "Your own sister would never write such a letter. You have said so yourself. It is not to be believed. Eat now and forget this foolishness."

Enraged by his father's retreat, Ichiro swore at him: "Goddammit, Pa, leave her alone. Feed your own stupid mouth."

"Ya, ya," he mumbled and returned to the table. He picked distractedly at the food, jabbing the faded chopsticks repeatedly into the plate only to pinch a tiny bit of food, which he placed unappetizingly on his tongue.

"I'm sorry, Pa."

"Ya, but you are right. I do not know what I am doing."

"She'll work it out okay."

"What is she thinking? She is like a baby dog who has lost its mother."

"It'll be all right, Pa," he said impatiently. "It isn't anything she won't live through."

The father weighed his words carefully before answering: "You can say that, but, when I see her sitting and not moving but only sitting like that, I am afraid."

"Can it, Pa," he lashed out angrily. "Nothing's going to happen. Things like this take lots of time. Look at me. Two years, Pa, two years I've thought about it and I'm not through yet. Maybe I'll spend the rest of my life thinking about it."

The old man looked at him, not understanding how it was that his problem could be compared to the mother's. "You are young," he said. "Old minds are not so easily changed. Besides, if it was wrong that you went to prison, it is over, all done. With Mama, it is deeper, much harder."

Hardly believing what his father had said, Ichiro reared back in his chair, then leaned far forward, at the same time bringing his fists down on the table so viciously that the dishes bounced crazily. "You really think that?"

"What is that?"

"About me. About what I've done. I've ruined my life for you, for Ma, for Japan. Can't you see that?"

"You are young, Ichiro. It does not matter so much. I understand, but it is not the same."

"You don't understand."

"Ya, I do. I was young once."

"You're a Jap. How can you understand? No. I'm wrong. You're nothing. You don't understand a damn thing. You don't understand about me and about Ma and you'll never know why it is that Taro had to go in the army. Goddamn fool, that's what you are, Pa, a goddamn fool."

The color crept into the father's face. For a moment it looked as if he would fight back. Lips compressed and breathing hastened, he glared at his son who called him a fool.

Ichiro waited and, in that tense moment, almost found himself hoping that the father would strike back with fists or words or both.

The anger drained away with the color as quickly as it had appeared. "Poor Mama," he mumbled, "poor Mama," and he had to slap his hand to his mouth for he was that close to crying out.

At the tinkle of the doorbell, the father hastily dabbed his eyes with a dishcloth and rose heavily from his chair.

"I'll go," said Ichiro to the man who was neither husband nor father nor Japanese nor American but a diluted mixture of all, and he went to wait on the customer.

OSCAR PEÑARANDA
(1944-   )

Oscar Peñaranda describes himself as the fastest busboy in Las Vegas in 1962, the most valuable player in the Filipino-American Basketball League in 1964, and the honorary mayor of South Naknek, Alaska. His short stories have been anthologized in *Asian-American Authors*. He was born in Barvgo, Leyte, Philippine Islands. He lives in San Francisco with his wife and two children.

DARK FIESTA

COMING HOME from school that day (well, it was not really from school because he had met Totoy on the way to school in the morning and went with him instead of continuing to school and in spite of his mother's constant warning against Totoy's company), Amador sensed an ominous silence in the house as he opened the screen door. Like the silence of a vast shell put close to the ear.

—How was school today, Amador? his mother asked, not looking at him for she was busy with preparing dinner, filling bowls with vegetables, dishes and plates with raw meat, its blood still trickling. Now and again she would wipe her apron and look around.

—Fine, Mother, he lied.

What is it like in school? Totoy had asked just today.

He had not answered him.

Well, then. You'd better go now. You will be late, Totoy said, I'll see you tomorrow at the fiesta.

And then he looked at the climbing sun. I think I am late for class, anyway. I will just go with you, I might as well. Let's take the long way.

Just give her an apple to make up for it, Totoy had laughed.

—What is that behind your back, Amador? Come show your mother.

Just give her an apple.

—No it is nothing, Mother. It is just another worm I caught. You told me never to show you worms.

Just today on his way to school he had tried to catch the worm but it had gnawed its way into the freshness of the green grass. Brushing his fingers off his pants, he had wiped the mud and deeply inhaled the crisp air rising from the clear waters of the island Leyte. The wind was whistling through lyres of green hills and trees. Green sea. Ominously silent, like the silence of a vast shell. The mud-grasses oozed up between the toes of his naked feet and felt cool and refreshing. Sunshine and dew had seeped in the early mornings of November to make them moist and fresh.

—But what are you holding with your two hands behind your back, Amador? Why did you not put it in your pouch like the rest of them?

She was teasing again. He could tell, for the servants were giggling and his mother was trying to hold back a smile. But he dashed into his room and no one saw it. He did not know he had been carrying the apple in his hand when he entered the house, the green apple for teacher.

Just give her an apple, Totoy had said this morning, she will forgive you right away.

—Come out from there, Amador, he heard his mother shout. You didn't go to that old bridge, did you? You did not go to that old bridge? Keep away from there, Amador. There are ghosts there and it is dark on the other side.

In his room he put the apple, the apple for teacher, on the back of the bird cage, and then he came out. No, Mother, I did not go there, he answered. Where is Father?

—Why, did you not see him? He went to fetch you. Did you get out early or something?

—Yes . . . in fact I did, we did, get out early, he smiled.

Wanna ride, schoolboy? Totoy's voice had really startled him earlier today. Just about when he was to cross the river, he was feeling his steps gingerly looking for a stable path to walk on, when he heard him. He knew it was him before he even turned around to look. Straw hat, torn pants, vest-like garment clinging to his bare trunk. Totoy was something. A fishing pole hung from his right hand, and from his left a rope leading a huge gray water buffalo.

They stood awhile in silence on the banks of the rushing river.

Thanks, Totoy, he had said, remembering that his parents and elders had insistently forbade him to associate with Totoy, but never quite understanding why. What was there to fear from him?

Here, take this, he had said, handing him a green and yellow butterfly, about six weeks dead. Or would you rather have this? Come on, take it. This is the biggest bullfrog in town and you know it. Listen, Totoy.

He had put his mouth half a millimeter from the frog's. Croak—Croak, Samson. And it croaked. They had both looked at each other in astonishment and laughed, Totoy and he.

—It is no wonder you missed him, his mother said. But your father will be in shortly. He probably walked teacher home first.

They were always a threesome when his father came to fetch him—Father, teacher, and he.

—Teacher says you are naughty, Amador. Don't you like teacher?

—No I don't like teacher, Mother.

—She is very pretty, is she not?

—Yes she is. A cold tremor chilled his body. His father by now knew he did not go to school. And he would be home soon. Dinner is already at the table.

The door flung open and his father walked in with Bruno, their servant. His father was still looking at Bruno after they had entered.

Are you sure it was Watcher, Bruno?

—Yes, Mr. Ante. Many people saw it. The little ones were piercing broomsticks into the dog's rear end, while it was sleeping, that's why.

—And what did the boy's father say?

—What I told you, Mr. Ante. Bruno looked at him.

His father turned to his mother and said, Watcher bit some boy today. Now the parents want the dog's blood. Claims that that is the only thing that can cure the boy. These superstitious bastards! They're only after the dog's meat, that's all.

—But did you tell them we would buy the anti-rabies shot for them or something?

—I bought the stuff already, and I gave it to them, and they threw it on the ground. They want the dog's liver—and by tomorrow night at the fiesta. It must be brought to them there, like a gift or something, so people won't get suspicious.

I'll see you tomorrow night at the fiesta. Tomorrow night. Tomorrow night the Feast of John the Baptist. Everyone will be throwing bucketsfull of water on anyone and it would be considered a joke and a lot of fun. All part of the festivities. To remember the baptism of Jesus, of course.

Bruno was leaving quietly while Amador swallowed his food, staring at him. They must have the liver by tomorrow night, the servant said. And we must be the one to—to do it. They don't want the neighbors to know that they—

—You are not going to let them, are you Father? he asked quietly. He was going to cry. There was no way of hiding it. He could feel it. His voice was already broken.

His father turned to his mother. Better the dog than the child, he said. Bruno, come outside for a moment.

The next morning he awoke, thinking. He jumped from his bed and ran to the living room where Watcher sleeps. The dog was still there, sleeping, breathing.

He was early for school but he did not care. He hurried to dress, shined his apple and turned to the green parrot in the cage. Dulce, sing me a song, he said in rapture, a sweet song. The bird chirped and fluttered its wings as he swung the cage like a pendulum and left the room.

He was eating breakfast when his father and mother approached him.

—Why did you not go to school yesterday, his father asked.

They stood awhile, they were standing on the banks of the rushing river, Totoy and he. He had said then: I'm late for class, anyway. I will just go with you, I might as well; let's take the long way.

—Why did you not go to school yesterday? his father asked again.

—Because I . . . fell . . . crossing the river, Father—and all my clothes got wet.

—You did not go with that Totoy again, did you? his mother
asked.

—Yes, I met him.

He had put his mouth half a millimeter from the frog's.
Croak—Croak Samson. It had croaked and they had both
laughed, Totoy and he. It was then that Totoy asked him,
What is it like in school, Amador?

He had not answered.

Well you had better go now, he had said. You're going to
be late. And added, You seem to like school. You have
never been absent, have you?

I learn many things in school.

What is it in school your father can not teach you?

For a fellow who can't read or write, Totoy knew some
things, he thought.

What shape is the world, Totoy? he had asked him. That,
he knew he could not know. And what color is it? I bet you
do not know. He had not waited for an answer. It is round
and it is green. I remembered what teacher had told class
one day.

I know what shape it is, Totoy had answered.

What then?

It is crooked.

It was then that they had mounted the boy's water buffalo.
Why don't you go school, Totoy? It must be fun not to
go to school.

Cause my mother don't want me to and I don't want me to.
Besides—all grown-ups want children to go to school.

Not my mother. She says it crups kids' minds, somehow.
Says schools make kids go away and leave their mothers
sooner or later. Says I'll learn a lot more by just being
around rivers and trees and birds and stuff. And I won't
get to leave. Why do you go to school, Amador?

Cause I told you, silly. Grown-ups and parents. Especially
my father, likes for me to go. So I can be grown-up, too,
like him, handsome and brave.

Totoy, he was something . . .

—Yes, I met him—

--Good Lord, you did not go to that old bridge, did you?

(She turned to his father.) He lives near there, you know.

—No, we did not; I told you, Mother.

—I wish they'd get rid of that old bridge. It is ready to fall apart. And it spells nothing but trouble for children.

—I am sorry for yesterday, Father, he said—But I am making up for it today. He held up the green apple. This is for teacher.

—Well, now.

—How thoughtful of you, Amador. You do just that, his mother said. Your father will fetch you again tonight, and maybe he'll take you to the fiesta.

Fiesta John the Baptist Tomorrow night, no tonight. Watcher Liver Blood To remember the Baptism of Jesus of course.

At school that day, his mind wandered somewhere outside. He looked out the window and saw the shadows of trees already growing long. The afternoon was almost over. His father should be around any minute now. Totoy should be on his way home now, perched on his water buffalo, or leading it by the nose. Then they all stood up and sang "What Shall We Do" and after that "Let Us Put Our Books Away" and then "I Have Eyes":

> I wear a sword that cuts
> But can not cut itself.
> I have eyes that see
> But cannot see itself.

Then he knew that class was over. But his father had not come yet. He ought to wait for him. But he filed out of the room just the same.

Outside the late afternoon was cool and soft. Carding, the boy behind him, was chasing a grasshopper. Amador ran after him. They kept at it for a while, until Carding finally caught it.

—Here, he gave it to Amador.

—Thanks, Carding. He opened the pouch to put the big grasshopper in.

—There's an apple inside, Amador!

—Oh, I forgot, the apple is for teacher.

Amador and Carding ran back to the classroom to find teacher.

Teacher was not there anymore. And his father was not there yet. He did not know whether to wait for him or try to head for the fiesta celebrations to find teacher. He decided to run after teacher, toward the fiesta center. Carding followed from behind.

Far away Amador saw teacher enter a door of a booth or a small hut of some sort. He rushed down from the hillside to catch her. The celebrations have already begun because he saw the big searchlight being lighted. He ran a little faster trying to leave Carding behind. But Carding was too fast for Amador. He sped by him laughing and they raced down the hill. In waves, in surges, Amador's breath came up on him. He tried to slow down a little but could not. The world beneath his feet was spinning. Suddenly the hill rose up and hit his face. The blades of grass speared into his forehead, and bright whirling shapes danced around him.

A pair of feet stared at him. The air filled with fiesta noise, and shouts, and lights.

—Are you all right, Amador? Carding said from somewhere. We're sorry Mister; we fell running down the hill. Is your sack all right? Apologize to the man, Amador.

The sack behind the pair of feet was bulky and heavy, for he saw the deep tracks it made on the dust. The smell nauseated him, a decaying stench.

But before Amador got on hands and knees to get up, the pair of shoes had quickly moved away, and was swallowed by the glaring lights and crowds of the fiesta. But he noticed the man's gait, strikingly familiar.

He picked up his pouch and rushed through the maze of legs and pants and skirts, looking for the booth or hut that teacher had entered. He heard Carding shouting his name behind him. Through a momentary opening Amador had a glimpse of it, the little hut. He rushed, fearful of being lost again in the current of the crowd. And then, there it was! the hut, with the door still a little open.

He stopped by the door and looked into the room to see if teacher was still there. Teacher was still there and so was his father, and they were very close together. His father and teacher were alone in the dim room, and he did not know if he should go inside or not, or if he should go home or not.

Near them was a bulky sack, resting where deep winding tracks on the dust ended. The nauseating smell pushed his heavy head away, and he turned from the small hut with the decaying stench. He leaned on a post beside the door of the hut and embraced it tightly. His hand felt something warm. On the post where he clung he felt it, something warm and thick. Blood. Lower along the post an ax was planted, its handle craning skyward, its blade dripping with blood.

Amador took out the apple from his pouch. Carding looked at it and said,

—It is rotten, Amador! Your apple is rotten!

The door opened and teacher came out with his father. They both saw Amador as he flung the apple far and hard into the dust where the shadows were growing long.

It was then that he started to run. He left Carding and father and teacher and Totoy and everything behind him. He ran. Out there where there was no one. His knees were shaking and his legs were carrying him towards the old bridge, the taboo bridge. He ran. As fast as he could, for he felt the world spinning beneath his feet, and he had to keep his legs going in order to stay up.

SAM TAGATAC
(1939-   )

Sam Tagatac is a film-maker active in the Filipino community and emphasizes the media as an organizing tool. Among the films he has made is *P.O.C. Filipino Community Organizing*. He was graduated from California State University at San Francisco with a B.A. and a M.A. in Film. He taught film in the Asian-American Studies Department of his alma mater. He is presently at work on a script based on the history of the Filipino in America. He is also an accomplished poet and short-story writer and his work has appeared in several anthologies. He married recently and now lives in Santa Barbara with his wife.

THE NEW ANAK

So what is it.
So what is it!
So what is it?

The echo

of the moonlight fell upon his soft heel that he was, himself in his shoes, hip boots, acid of himself. He heard. The grating of himself, against the wood leaf shingle of the neighborhood where Minna Street ended. Where he would have liked for it to end. Not in the bare light where he saw last night's cat, the light of its eyes as bright as his own, all seeing beyond the windows, beyond these conjured images of his hearing.

Whrrrrrrrrrrrrrrrrrrrrrrrrrrrrrrrrrrrrrrrrrrrrrrrrrrrrrrrrrrrrrrrrrrrrrrrrrrrr

"Say,
Man."

Whrrrrrrrrrrrrrrrrrrrrrrrrrrrrrrrrrrrrrrrrrrrrrrrrrrrrrrrrrrrrrrrrrrrrrrrrrrrr

"That
A
Cam
Era
Man."

I'm

goinggoinggoinggoing

to
be
in
a movie a movieamovieamovieamovie."

". . . usssssst oi ano ba ito

pilm me, please pilm me.
What is this? Pictiure?"

rrrrrrrrrrrrrrrrrrrrrrrrrrrrrrrrrrrrrrrrrrrrrrrrrrrrrrrrrrrrrrrrrrrrrrrrrrrrrrrrrrrrrrrr

"My manong, Elpidio, GI now in
Nam. News. They pilm him too
Pilipino in Nam . . . ai he's
lonely. He writes."

The echo

of the moonlight fell upon his soft heel that he was, himself in his shoes, hip boots, acid of himself. He heard. The grating of himself, against the wood leaf shingle of the neighborhood where Minna Street ended. Not in the bare light where he saw last night's cat and dreamt. . . .

"It was after the *tudo* of the world, the monsoon rains when the roads, just as suddenly as typhoon clouds appear during seasonal cyclones, turn to parchment, dust rising after each footfall, pervading as death in their slow fall. I saw her, a silent shadow growing. She did not falter in the dust, and the heat of the *Ifugao* sun seemed to make her image in my soul dance. Behind her, and beyond the central plains of my dreams where the palay, wild with ancestral spirits, crest the wind, rose the blue *Ifugao* mountains, guarding since the beginning of time the soil the Ilokanos break each season with their steel plows and carabaos. Such a frail little girl, thing, almost as substanceless as her shadow. Her dust rose and fell, nearer, edge to edge the confrontation of our shadows.

"Our eyes met."

"Your friends," she said, her finger pointed beyond my eyes, in back of me to the children who seemed separated by her appearance. They jeered at her, fearful of what she was, the smell of rotting flesh which was clear, and not clear, for what did they know then of death. We had climbed the *salamagi* tree at sunrise, eaten its fruit and played war among its branches. "I know why they are afraid of me," she whispered, touching her breast.

"I'm not. You're just a girl, a little girl." She began to walk, and my eyes followed, my body rooted in the dust which rose and fell around her.

"Wait. Where are you going?"

"To join the *tao*."

I did not understand, and the dust settled in my hair. The children began to laugh, scuffing up dust with their shoes for they too did not understand. You smell like rot. They chanted, and clambered up the *salamagi* and began pelting the little girl with fruit. But still the dust rose and fell, and she did not turn even then, being so close to the earth. Now the children ceased their chatter and began to shout and chirp like birds. The pealings of the *salamagi* struck the dust, instantly drying, choked. "Wait," I shouted and ran to her.

"Don't you know my kind of smell," she said, touching her breast.

I lied. I said I did not know.

"Haven't you had those nightmares?"

I said, I did not know, thinking I was lying.

"You should go. Please go." She did not turn, her eyes seeing only what I could not see beyond the road.

"If you don't," how childish she was all at once, not what she was an instant before, "my smell will follow you. It will. I'm warning you . . . it will be with you for the rest of your life, all of it with you before your time."

"But I want to walk with you."

And with that, she turned, baring her breasts, the wounds in her chest clear as day.

                                                    CRACK
rrrrrrrrrrrrrrrrrrrrrrrrrrrrrrrrrrrrrrrrrrrrrrrrrrrrrrrrrrrrrrrrrrrrrrrrrrrrrrrrr

                                        . . . . my brother
                                        Ragadio, he

still sings. I remember the bandaria of the field when he sang
by moonlight against the oaks. San Luis Obispo. Ai, Macario,
one day sang also of his wounded heart . . . Clara of the *waig,*
Bacara, the little town across the mountains where the sweet rise
kissed the *Ifugao* sun where she was born, pouring water over
her . . . magic words. She no can wait. Married man from
state . . . navy. I come here . . . San Francisco . . . you know
Kearney . . . in depression, I get sick, Macario's cousin die
eating the moss of the oak.

The echo

"Paris! Paris!"

"Yon." He laughs, his luck turning, the ball falling into his
wish, the ivory hope of a long felt table.

"DITO!
DITO!"

RRRRRRRRRRRRRRRRRRRRRrrrrrrrrrrrrrrrrrrrrrrrrrrr

The echo of
other voices

are

continually

rrrrrrrrrrrrrrrrrrrrrrrrrrrrrrrrrrrrrrrrrrrrrrrrrrrrrrrrrrrrrrrrrrrrrrrrrrrrrrrrr heard

the room full of prayers, and players . . . the figure of a man
enters the eye, but he is too close, hard to see, lack of accom-
modation. Someone said he remembers him, once in the field
of his memory in a competition of crates. Dust . . . dust upon
the spirit, under the sand of cultivation, finally having tired of
it, having no place to go . . . all the *waigs* of youth, risen to
clouds on other lands he is here, strikes the balls with his stick.
Gradually the face of this man sharpens . . . he is in his late
fifties, sixties? In spite of the sun . . . he is a Filipino face
. . . what age is he? No one knows, except the continent of his
new footing. Is it Ragadio . . . Elpidio of Nam? He stares into
his sight quite naturally as though he is just another pool
player. He moves aside where he has come from, always going
from the wall to another wall lined with the ornament of his
being . . . old men, shadows of himself, following the action
of the tables.

ai hindi mo ma
tama . . .

ai along this wall . . . along this wall of men, more than the
photograph of their thoughts, eyes of a yellowing pose, watching the cue ball . . . money, voices . . . as of another time,
the loud craaaaaaack!

. . . the bright eyes of a winner . . . when
was the time the last harvest of palay touched the kernel of
each sunrise, the ancestral eyes of forefathers when land bridges
fell to the water and legends, myths fell from the sky. The sun
islands of the south where Mecca's rays penetrated the minds
and souls of the Mindanao merman maidens, came the reptiles
of the sea, crocodiles born from the center of the sea, the Philippine Deep, bottomless where all being evolved. These croco-

diles, with bamboos growing in their backs, traveled with the
seasonal wind, along rivers where they gathered children of
these rivers and forests, beyond the *salamagi* and pinia, beyond
the dream of the beetle nut and beyond the blue haze of the
Ifugao mountain range. Finally to a land of joy and perfection
these reptiles of the first tao brought these special children to
be nurtured in the deeds of what is godlike.

. . . the pay off, a bet. Doming pays off, seemingly accustomed
to giving.rrrrrrrrrrrrrrrrrrrrrrrrrrrrrrrrrrrrrrrrrrrrrrrrrrrrrrrrrrrrrrrr

RRRRRRRRRRRRRRRRRRRRRRRRRRRRRRRRRRRRRR

                                        Quite animated, he

                squints
                peers into

what he cannot see, his face forming in the latent image of a
memory. This is not real life . . . echoes, he echoes.

rrrrrrrrrrrrrrrrrrrrrrrrrrrrrrrrrrrrrrrrrrrrrrrrrrrrrrrrrrrrrrrrrrrrrrrrrrrrr

                            If you want the real life of me
                            here, you go down to the Stock-
                            ton, he says. Last season when he
                            wrote . . . he cannot remember,
                            last season was yesterday's thirty
                            years, Marzo to May. Doon, he
                            says, still glazed with the touch of
                            dust, remembering how the dream
                            of the real palay fell in a land
                            without water, where the land
                            turned white, mornings when
                            ducks filled the sky with shadows.
                            He says

then you can make all kinda piln; you want doon . . . then
pg ka tapos, you go down to Presno. But now you arerrrrrrrrrrr
                                        taking the

picture
here

This is bad por me. He moves his hands.rrrrrrrrrrrising above
his eyes

and sees
her . . . the *waig* of life where he left Clara, above
the women's washing stones when he touched her with his
hands, his eyes, his soul, for the last time . . . and sees a room
of his youth.

From what time are you here?

Sun up to sundown.

What do you guys do?

Well . . . he laughs . . . we're starting up a casino.

With what?

Money . . .
Work?
Youguys

RRRRRRRRRRRRRRRRRRRRRRRRRRRRrrrrrrWork? . . .

What the hell, shit.

No work, man.

He's a veteran.

Who?

Elpidio.

Is that right?

Yeah . . . rrrrrrrrrrrrrrrrrrrrrrrrrrrrrrrrr

He's retired

They laugh.

The string from the light bulb, twenty-five watts, hangs in such a way that it looks like a hangman's noose. Seventy-five . . . retired in a room of the International Hotel . . . knowing no one. The whores, bodies, stray in the hall light on the first of each month and with unmistakeable woman voice, faithful always.

> Clear as day . . .
> baring, the wounds
> in her chest, clear
> as day where
> the bayonet entered . . . "I want to walk with you."

At the end of the road, winding beyond sight, the hard clearing, ancestral landscape of winged angels . . . guardians . . . she entered, my shadow trailing this strange procession of a vision . . . where she touched wood, the wood of her ancestry. She was the only one left of that family of her memory where the brooks, *waigs* of her dreams, touched by moonlight tide, when the kawayan rise, not from the wind, but from the power of the universe, the moon long before the starfighter with golden tires riding that rock reality broadcast the image of a golf ball shattering the mirror of the universe. And she would leave this world, my presence which has tasted the sweet wrappers of hershey bars . . . blue eyes, I saw them too before understanding, raising their eyes from their steel helmets, through the wood, bamboo slats of Dinnee's floor, where his wife became a whore. Each night. Morning. The endless procession . . . I knew, the whole town with its marble town square where friars once heard the soul of a town . . . the sugar of America's soldiers paid, souring the *salamagi* . . . knew of Dinnee's wife becoming a whore, hating her and themselves finally. In the north the rising sun fell . . . I thought I

saw her heart through the flake of the wound, the edge healing
what it could not really heal. The wind wept . . . I thought
and whispered to her . . . children, what did we know of it, the
love. I have searched for you all my life, not knowing from the
million winds which one. . . . Had I seen you when you had
become a woman perhaps it would have been different, the scar
healing what had been, but as it is the memory remains, the
open wound of you clear as day, see the ducks grace the light
with their wings, the quack, not from wings, but from love
which you cannot feel, hear, so tranquil to hear. How many
times had you escaped, their meaning as clear as day, wounds.
We are children from memory. You're a child. I saw mine too
across the stillness of a black lake. The crossing before stars, the
eyes of that black lagoon disturbed by a single raft, reed bamboo perhaps from the backs of mythical crocodiles. At the helm
of a long bamboo pole pushed Putin, the man servant, grandfather's nephew. A town lay burning at the horizon . . . a
husband and wife, later recounted after the war over dinner
watching television, the fire and color of another asian war,
blue eyes, who were tired of their tranquillity, refused to leave,
proud of their home and burned to death in their . . . I remember the light of that lagoon, the mythical sound of the
flying dragon, spitting fire, one pass, one strafing run across
water for what is water from the sight of the gods, the crosshair
splitting the forming of a real image, so distant the face of . . .
your face, my face. There was no clenching from the cold spray
of water where the sting, greater than the barb of a thousand
bees, of bullets cried among our cry. And the steel bird whirled
to the light of stars, the moon, and the sunrise still to come.
Lightning, I said later in a village of fishermen where there
were no men. Finally the bank of that infinite lagoon. Beyond
the sand and into the dark line of jungle we entered . . . our
hearts rising still with the swell of the water, the wind in our
breaths swept by steel wings, the lightning entered the light of
stars. We entered. Across the starlight, the burning village
danced. Stifle their cries . . . someone said. "They will make
noise." But they were already frightened by the baptism of
steel wings. "They will hear." The soldiers made silhouettes of
their being across the lake, their eyes burning . . . how the

palay roof the peasants' souls quickly caught the night, over-powering the moon and starlight. What cold suns. In antarc-tica the winter tropic light falls on a test sight of the future, long after the cloud of Hiroshima and Mon Amour, a white chick getting fucked by a . . . "Hold their mouths!" "Their breathing will give us away." The woman explains as gently as . . . such fears, her man at the beginning of these, things of value and a thousand islands where typhoons spawn across the China Sea, and died dies for the future and dreams of the blue eyes where Bulosan wrote of the blue sky and his first teacher, a blond woman who felt . . . "Hold their eyes." Later, after this memory, a boy still in memory, he enters a wooden stair-way of a hotel at the Fillmore above the streets where the Jews sell the polished wood of ancestors. He could not remember the gentle breathing of that woman who brought him his first child, and writing of seagulls and men who were not of his own until he flashed on to the light of that vintage year and felt the water. "Hold their mouths. They mustn't cry. Por dios." And they began to crawl through the forest of thorns they could not see, their bodies burning with the points of barbs meant for ani-mals. All night they crawled on their hands and knees, the chil-dren's cry held by their hands. Then it was morning, silent morning after the peace of waking, that certain acquiescent mo-ment when dream and time touch one another, finally the open-ing of eyes. An owl crowed. A forest of tall trees, a land of giants. Here where the rice cooked, the children felt the legend of fear their elders saw in their eyes, their souls. Putin said it was a safe place. The soldiers of their people sang of the morning and of the *Ifugao* sun and recounted how they had emasculated an enemy soldier under the *salamagi* tree where it now weeps. The ghosts of the soldiers brothers and friends went home to the hills of their coming. Serafin, the young medical student of Santo Tomas of the Dominicans, told of how his hands . . . once the fathers told him how he would be a great surgeon be-cause of his delicate hands and steady eye, how he topped all exams in chemistry, knowing all the chemical compounds of the body . . . looped the knot over the dead soldier's head and pulled, being afraid of booby traps, grenades, the head rolling softly from a month's decay where the worms of flies

touched his eyes, how he, for the first time, could not eat for
days. And Doming, lost, ran into a small camp . . . how their
eyes met, knowing what it was they wanted to avoid, finally
. . . Doming fired first hitting the one eating rice in the belly,
the other running without his gun, running away from his
blood. Friendly soldiers entered this forest of tall trees. Together they ate rice and said for the women and children to go
south to the hacienderos. And they left that place . . . came
to a village and a school yard where a steel bell black with the
soot of fire marked its final message. She stood clear on concrete and hard eyes. Her name, he was to know at another
place of memory, grown and beautiful woman . . . told of her
loss, how the priest had died in front of his students, how they
had burned the flag of his belief, cut his ears and finally pierced
his belly and heart when he would not eat. She remembered
the eyes of his teaching, his soul impressed in the latent image
of her eyes which she is to tell to her love one day at another
place of her memory. She will fly, her dreams told her years
later, on steel wings from the land of crocodiles to a forest of
tall trees and tall buildings where you will have a surgeon's
hands, touching life, the breath of babies and your own. But
having no time . . . the image is always latent of the road,
dust birthing her figure growing . . . "I want to walk with
you." Her odor . . . "I want to walk with you." She does not
protest, only . . . "I will be with you all your life." The echo.

RRRRRRRRRRRRRRRRRrrrrrrrrrrrrrrrrrrrrrrrrrrrrrrrrr

rrrrrrrrrrrrrrrrrrrrrrrrechoOOO of the moonlight falls upon his
soul, Minna Street bagoong, fish scent but unlike any American
fish scent, or Fisherman's Wharf. The salt of ancestral dreams
preserved the fish which fights the sting of onions at Fosters.
He sees the cameraman. "I see you before . . ." "Maybe." "My
name is Doming . . . long time I'm top cook, there. I make
the best soup." "Are you TV?" "No." "What outpit." "No one."
"I have no one too. What the hell. . . . I drink and think. I
remember my niece she die, little girl . . . you want to come
to my place, eat pakbet bagoong. Oh but you born here, maybe
you no like pish . . . you american boys, you have white girl
friends, I remember Carlos he had big, like this big, blonde

. . ." Up Minna, Doming walks, bright under the street lamps, finally entering the night, fades where a cat falls on padded feet . . . how strong the scent, even the salt air riding the fog from the Pacific does not intrude the secret door. Doming of the haunted look, walking like the ancient cat of his memory, mounts the stairs and sees the light at the top of the stairs, hears the cry of a cat, he knows better, a woman in the making of that odorrrrrrrrrrrrrrrrrrrrrrrrrRRRRRRRRRRRRRRRRRRRR RRRRRRRRRRRRRRRRRRRRRRRRRRRRRrrrrrrrrrrrrrrrrrrrrrr silent yyyyyyyyyyyyyyyyyyyyyyyy beyond the memory of eyes, latent images, beyond the confrontation of touching Doming goes to a landscape of . . . the branches were delicate, almost bare where he first stood and saw her across the stark white sky, walking across the horizon as though across the moon of another future. Raptured by her image, he rested somewhat against the tree trunk . . . old and a strange thing happens as though the world in this place, this hill restores the color of Doming's youth. It is brief, dashing against a flow of landscapes, a boy running a flooded field, palay dancing in the wind where a carabao pulls a steel plow . . . and the grass is sprouting on the hill, green and yellow where the light has seeped through. Juana's face is soft, out of the horizon, her face and eyes, her presence as the grass itself, the flowers greeting the sky. They are making love, or about to make love, or in that twilight of exhaustion when body and spirit separate, stare at their indifference. Doming feels saddened by what has passed. Juana's eyes open to the sky . . . birds flying, a hawk. She turned away when the spoken words intruded, perhaps her mind, or Doming's dream already dying, tortuous and twisting, the spires of a distant church perhaps, passing just as her passing . . . Clara of the women's washing stones in the *waig* of life in the light of another world. When he left her, he felt saddened. He had touched her for the first time, a small token, a solemn promise that both their souls were one. Always, he remembered the saying that the Ilokanos of the palay were a free spirit. He spoke of love, but not the words of lovers, but from ancestral instinct of man-woman. She heard him speak of riding the crocodiles whose kawayan flourished across the sea . . . and he would send for her, dream of her until that final touching.

And he sailed. The engine seems to drown his words. The hawk flies across the field where he sees her on the horizon, the tractor creating a small cyclone of dust.

"I don't want much."
She reaches out, her hand touching his shoulders, his back carefully as one does perhaps with a map, tracing the veins pulsing with her spirit.

"I don't want much."
The engine drowns his words. The hawk flies.

"Yesterday I saw Onor's children running down the road . . . what dust they made. I saw their eyes . . ."

She has drawn back, away from his eyes, touch, away from the sunlight beside the tree where she puts on her blouse, back pale . . . "isn't it plain and natural to want . . . to feel ambition . . ."

He sees something, perhaps the field, or beyond the field. A small figure rising out of the road, a pale apparition forming of dust the little girl intruded the space of safety. They let her enter their circle, smiling as though from lack of manners, still learning as one speaks meaningless sounds at first. She intruded the room of their own making, the odor saturating their simple world.

"Come in, come in. This is my room." He smiles proudly, just as the smiles of the photographs on the dresser greet Doming. "The best room in the Hotel. Go ahead, take picture. I paint it myself." On the dresser, the picture of a girl under a tree. Is she dead? The grass grows around her. The shadows of the tree enfold her. The morning of a photograph enfolds a field of corn . . . it's impossible, you'll leave, and she turns and sees autumn caressing the surface of pumpkins. Her hands stroke grass. In the distance a dog begins to bark. An engine starts. whrrrrrrrrrrrrrrrrrrrrrrrrrrrrrrrrrrrrrrrrrrrrrrrrrrrrrrrrrrrrrr rrrrrrrrrrrrrrrrrrrrrrrrRRRRRRRRRRRRRRRRRRRRRRRRRRRRR

RRRRRRRRRRRRRRRRRRRRRRRRRRRRRRRRRRRRRR
RRRRRRRRRRRRRRRRRRRRRRRRRRRRRRRRRRRRRR
RRRRRRrrrrrrrrrrrrrrrrrrrrrrrrrrrrrrrrrrrrrrrrrrrrrrrrrrrrrrrr
rrrrrrrrrrrrrrrrrrrrrrrrrrrrrrrrrrrrrrrrrrrrrrrrrrrrrrrrrrRRRR
RRRRRRRRRRRRRRRRRRrrrrrrrr

There had been too many nights under the stars. She watched
her children in this black forest of thorns, thinking that when
this thing was done, finished . . . but where is the end of
stark presence, fears of the soul having no goals, only the essence of that fear when time has no time and it does not matter.
Where had her song left its wings . . . on a clear *waig*, rip-
pling and gone with the waters of the sea, across the myth of
crocodiles. Her song came across the crackle tank threads, unseen, and was it by the grace of God they had heeded the warn-
ings of the messenger, come to tell of the enemy patrol. Now
only the cold swirls around the glow of the burnt village across
the lagoon. How much more efficient these steel horse . . . what
foolish bravery her men showed, massing in a distant town, the
oaths and promises with their wooden arms across their chests,
how they somehow remembered from their ancestral instinct
which bamboo made the best spear. Now the threads searched
and the engines drowned even the proud monkeys of the forest
who knew nothing yet of warrrrrrrrrrrrrrrrrrrrrrrrrrrrrrrrrrrrrrrrr
rrrrrrrrrrrrrrrrrrrrrrrrrrrrrrRRRRRRRRRRRRRRRRRRRRRR
RRRRRRRRRRRRRRRRR

And the tractor raced against time, against spring, steam from
the seasonal rain rising from the broken earth. The man
perched on the steel seat, Macario with the red bandana across
his face, an outlaw of another sort. On the horizon, that which
he steadily plows toward, he sees the tree he planted, and still
beyond it, the windmill and pale house. Una the beautiful
Mexican girl has married Roman of Visaya . . . she is considered white and he has no tail. She learns to speak English
and some Philipino. Ai anako, Roman says to his son when

Nam is created for his children and they leave to seek their ancestry.

                                   "They pilm him. News.
rrrrrrrrrrrrrrrrrrrrrrrrrrrrrrrrrrrrrrrrrrrrrrrrrrrrrrrrrrrrrrrrrrrrrrrrrrrrr
                                   Manong Elpidio of Nam.
                                        . . . ai, he writes . . .

                    By day still

a silent bridge made of bamboo frequented by wheels, bicycle
riders and carabaos. Nam has them too. Sentry . . . I'm told
by my superior this wooden bridge is mine, own it with my
whole heart, soul. And night comes quickly here, racing it seems
before its inhabitants . . . one night the flame from my fear,
the training in short bursts for there was no password for bicycle riders in black. A little girl, teen-ager, a woman . . . what
great wounds you made in her chest, ripped right off, took her
away a wagon . . . told him later for he did not know until
spring came quickly.
RRRRRRRRRRRRRRRRRRRRRRRRRRRRRRRRRRRRRR
rrrrrrrrrrrrrrrrrrrrrrrrrrrrrrrrrrrrrrrrrrrrrrrrrrrrrrrrrrrrrrrrrrrrrrrrrrrr
                                   After the rain, spring
                                   comes quickly in

the valley of Lodi . . . across the delta, above the sky where the
ducks sift sunlight. Onor walks with Baldo, squat, the brown
teeth of toscani in his mouth, he spits and surveys the flat land
with his soul, the eye not being enough. In the brown delta the
fishermen begin their exodus for the waters of strippers.

"Ni. Na caro met ti molam." Spits Baldo.

At another time . . . long after the memory of their children, they might have said, "Your plants are baaaaad."

"Ai wen ah . . . naka suerte ka ita."

"Easy thousan deta."

"Kasta?"

"Wen."

"Apay, nag talao ni kasinsin mo?"

They turn their backs, the beets still ripening in their starch before the sugar of their harvest when, if the market stays level, they have estimated that it would bring at least a thousand. Baldo spits the toscani away, noting the pale empty house at the top of the horizon . . .

"Napanan na?"

"To the city."

"Kasta?"

"Dina kano kayat degitoy rogiten."

He will remember the winter sunrises and the dust of his making, long after the morning crows of his rooster. The tractor lies rusting where he left it when he fell sick . . . telling no one at last of his parting, only his back which they saw and did not understand. And now he will not see the death of Macario in the eyeing of dew when the soil of his own making broke beneath his feet. Once there was another soil, earth, but from the true feeling of bare feet testing the tension of soil and water . . . what do prayers know of a sight of palay racing against the wind, like the sea of crocodiles, and finally even the falling, the suffering which transcends the words, when in the end wood is selected. They remember what is bright . . . Ragadio's death, the castration under a tree, terribly ashamed under the blue eyes of the sheriff who came still not to understand these . . . without tails bearing gifts of strawberries and of themselves . . . every morning during morning rituals of washing, of dreams, touching of face by fingers and still the need for

reassurance even when only the fingers, finally, are felt . . .
"how will I know Clara when I return . . ."

". . . dear francisco I've touched the barb wire again . . . how
red the rust falls each day now . . . each day now I've twisted
the line of the fence taut, this barb which surrounds our hearts,
the land. The knife flash. I remember each morning the pet
rooster you set against . . . the knife flash. It had arrived in a
wire cage and we had called it Canta for its pure song . . . how
the hens in the barn perked their feathers . . . we all swore,
also the plants in the fields suspected, growing suddenly with
souls out to the sun.

SHAWN HSU WONG
(1949-   )

Shawn Hsu Wong spent most of his childhood traveling in airplanes and cars. As soon as he was able to see, his father made him drive home to Berkeley in their old black Ford. His mother and father raised him in Berkeley, the islands of the Pacific, and in the Sierra Nevada Mountains. He co-edited a special issue of the *Bulletin of Concerned Asian Scholars* on Asian America, an issue of the *Yardbird Reader*, and is presently completing a novel, *Night Driver,* about three generations of one Chinese-American family. He is a co-director of the Combined Asian-American Resources Project, Inc., and has published poetry, essays, and reviews in various periodicals and anthologies. He was born in Oakland, California.

EACH YEAR GRAIN

I AM THE SON of my father and I have a story to tell about my history and about a dream. I had the dream inside of a tree. I was child, walking through a forest of giant shade and I found a huge stump of a once giant redwood burned hollow so that you could step inside and look up and see the sky. I suddenly shouted into the charcoal darkness, into the soft charred soul of this tree. My shout was absorbed so quickly, I knew the tree was listening. And I spoke to the tree in my dream. The tree showed me its rings of growth and as I ran my fingers over each year grain, the tree showed me the year I was born and my history.

I asked the tree to show me the year I was born and the year of my father's birth and the tree said that it would not only show that year but would begin farther back in my history and show me my great-grandfather's country, the country that he came to, the land where he toiled day after day and the land where he was buried.

I came running down the grassy hills as fast as the wind moves down the waves of grass from shade to light. I came running down the long meadow of tumbling yellow greens racing wind across drifting grasses. I came running into a dream Appoloosa-like.

"Your great-grandfather's country was a rich land, the river's sand had gold dust in it. The water was fresh and clear, the sand sparkling beneath the surface of the water like the shiny skin of the trout that swam in the deep pools. This was California's gold country of the 1850's and your great-grandfather was there to reap the riches that California offered and to return home a rich man to live in comfort with his family."

I knew by the feeling of the land in my dream that great-grandfather did not live to return to China, nor to reap any riches. Instead he died here in northern California buried in the dark moist earth. And I heard my great-grandfather's voice in the wind speak, "Do not send my bones back to China. Bury me here beneath my tears."

> The hawk glides in hot drafts of summer dust wind and drops the furry body of his meal into the brittle meadow grasses below and the body becomes the grass of next spring growing wet from light snow. And the land that makes each spring birth again is held moist in my hands. California north.

"Your great-grandfather was humiliated by the land and the people to which he gave his life. But unlike the other Chinese who died here and had their bones sent back to China, so that at least that much of them would return home away from the land that humiliated them and the life they loathed, your great-grandfather felt that since this land was important enough for him to give his life to, he should not leave and that his sons should follow him to this country, and his soul would protect them."

> Woodsmoke drifts from Shasta, Trinity, Siskiyou, north to the wild Klamath River. Drift woodsmoke, bend and fall with the river near the people that live in your California heart! Klamath, Salmon, Eel, river running to a space where woodsmoke lives in the deep clover and moss on the breath of wind that passes down through the unmoving redwoods. California northcoast. Woodsmoke dissolves in a forest of mist from the sea cold, falling from jagged cliffs wearing by age. Points and coasts like Reyes, Bolinas, Monterey, take Sur Country energy into the black night ocean and repeat over and over the same silence.

I could see the gold country land in my dreams and I loved its sun, its wood, and the dark, loose and cool earth where my feet could dig in like roots. Then another vision came into my dream. It was not the same land. And the tree spoke to me, "One of the men you see working here was your great-grandfather building the railroad. It was the work that broke him and the work that he desperately held on to—to make a little place in this country. His brother was murdered."

My great-grandfather who drove rail spikes and laid track was speaking to me. "I left for San Francisco one month before my brother. In those days some ships were bringing us in illegally. They would drop a lifeboat outside the Golden Gate with the Chinese in it. Then the ship would steam in and at night the lifeboat would come in quietly and unload. If they were about to be caught, my people would be thrown overboard. But, you see, they couldn't swim because they were chained together. My brother died on that night and now his bones are chained to the bottom of the ocean. No burial ever. Now I am fighting to find a place in this country.

"We do not have our women here. My wife is coming to live here. We are staying. Nothing was sweet about those days I lived alone in the city, unless you can find sweetness in that kind of loneliness. I slept in the back of a kitchen by the grimy window where the light and noises of the wet city streets were ground in and out of me like the cold. The bed was so small I could hardly move away from my dreams. And when I awakened with the blue light of the moon shining in, there would be no dreams. That one moment when I wake, losing my dreams, my arms and heart imagining that she was near me moving closer and I float in her movements and light touch. But the blue light and the noise was always there and I would have nothing in my hands."

Great-grandfather's wife was a delicate, yet a strong and energetic lady. Insisting in her letters to Great-grandfather to let her come and join him. The loneliness was overpowering him, yet he resisted her pleas, telling her that life was too dangerous for a woman. "The people and the work move like hawks around me, I feel chained to the ground, unable even to cry for help. The sun blisters my skin, the winters leave me sick, the cold drains us. I look into the eyes of my friends and there is nothing, not even fear."

Upon receiving his letter, Great-grandmother told her friends that she was leaving to join her husband, saying that his fight to survive was too much for a single man to bear. And so she came and was happy and the hawks had retreated.

She lived in the city and gave birth to a son while Great-grandfather was still working in the Sierras building the railroad. He wrote to her, saying that the railroad would be finished in six months and he would return to the city and they would live together again as a family.

During the six months, the hawks came back into his vision. "The hawks had people faces laughing as they pulled me apart with their sharp talons, they had no voices just their mouths flapping open, a yellow hysteria of teeth." He knew that this was the beginning of sickness for his lover, he sensed her trouble and moments of pain, no word from her was necessary. "Your wounds are my wounds," he would say in the night, "the hawks that tear our flesh are disturbed by the perfect day, the pure sun that warms the wounds, I am singing and they cannot tear us apart."

She saw the sun as she woke that morning after waking all night long in moments of pain. The sun was so pure. She thought that this could not be the city, its stench, its noise replaced by this sweet air. She knew that this air, this breath, was her husband's voice. The ground was steaming dry, the humus became her soul, alive and vital with the moving and pushing of growth. She breathed deeply, the air was like sleep uninterrupted by pain, there was no more home to travel to, this moment was everything that loving could give and that was enough. She was complete and whole with that one breath, like the security of her childhood nights sleeping with mother, wrapping her arms around her, each giving the other the peace of touch, pure sun. There was a rush of every happiness in her life that she could feel and touch and as she let go, she thought of their son, and the joy of his birth jarred her and she tried desperately to reach out to wake, to hold on to that final fear, to grasp his childhood trust, but the smell of the humus, the moist

decaying leaves struck by sunlight and steaming into her dreams
was too much and she was moving too fast into sleep.

Great-grandfather had dreams, making vows to his son, seeing dark legends that moved on him like skeletons stomping
down the metal spiral staircase of her grave. The hollow sounds
of their white silk capes flapping in an updraft of hot dust.

"I shall take my son away from these hawks who cause me to
mourn. I cannot cry. My tears leave scars on my face. There is
no strength in pity. I will take my son away, move deeper into
this country. I have heard stories about the South that there is
no winter, only sun."

The images were strength for him. He had dreams of the
South and they moved upon him like legends of faith. The hot
dry dust and heat cleansing his skin, warming his back. The
swamps were the visions of life's blood, there was something
vital and deep red in the hiss of hot animal mouths and the
humid steaming life that rose up to embrace him. There was a
julep woman there for him, cool and she was the touch of
green. She was silence, soft as meadow loam, sweet as a stream
that he could lie in, letting her waters rush over his body, hearing the sound of leaves in the wind. The dream always ended
with the scream of white fire. It was the magnolia. A huge
magnolia tree afire, branches of flames moving around each
white magnolia blossom. He saw them drop into the dust, a
ball of white fire. The smell of the magnolia burning always
woke him that smell lingering into morning like charred flesh,
so cold.

> Magnolia, magnolia your white blood
> Is the fire of moons.
> Your flower is winter to my flesh.

For Great-grandfather it was not enough anymore to say he
was *Longtime Californ'*. He had lost faith in the land. He fell
into deeper depressions, not from mourning his wife's death,
but more from his loss of faith in the country. He had been defeated when he had vowed not to lose ground to the harsh land
and cruel people. It was his son that finally carried him through,
helped return the faith so that at least he would die at peace.

Slide, tumble down wide open tall grass hills, feel the warm sun on your face as you spin from earth to sky, fingers reaching into the moist earth and laugh uncontrolled or cry, it doesn't matter, just keep tumbling down that steep hill and finally when you roll slowly to a stop stained green stained brown and exhausted you will notice while catching your breath that you may have startled a blue heron which lifts its great wings up then down again rising from the meadow loam down the sun washed valley of tall trees. Watch until the low sun engulfs its silent flying guest. The moment is yours, take it with you into your own loneliness where sight becomes feeling. Instantaneously.

"The country that accepted your great-grandfather and his son now rejected them. The railroad was finished and the Chinese were chased out of the mines. They were allowed to live but not marry. The law was designed so that the Chinese would gradually die out, leaving no sons or daughters."

HISAYE YAMAMOTO
(1921-   )

Between the years 1948 and 1961 Hisaye Yamamoto wrote
and published seven short stories. She was born in Redondo
Beach, California. Since 1961 the duties of wife and mother
have kept her from writing any new fiction. Today her
writing is confined to poetry for the holiday edition of the
Rafu Shimpo. Her modest body of fiction is remarkable for
its range and gut understanding of Japanese America. The
questions and themes of Asian-American life are fresh.
Growing up with foreign-born parents, mixing with white
and nonwhite races, racial discrimination, growing old, the
question of dual personality—all were explored in the seven
stories of Hisaye Yamamoto. Technically and stylistically,
her writing is among the most highly developed in Asian-
American writing. Her sense of humor is distinctly funny
and precisely Japanese-American. Unlike better known
Asian-American writers, her sense of humor does not reinforce the reader's sense of the superiority of white culture.
Her jokes about an Issei's garbled understanding of American slang do not demean the foreign-born, as when the Issei
asks the young Japanese girl about her mother. He is told
she "took a powder." "Oh, poison?" the Issei asks. Instead of crudely illuminating the ignorance of the old man

from Japan, she illuminates a whole linguistic process. In her work we see how language adapts to new speakers, new experience, and becomes new language. Hisaye Yamamoto's people speak a fluid language that is in a constant state of change. Her seven stories form the only portrait of prewar rural Japanese America in existence. She now lives in Los Angeles with her husband and five children.

YONEKO'S EARTHQUAKE

YONEKO HOSOUME became a free-thinker on the night of March 10, 1933, only a few months after hes first actual recognition of God. Ten years old at the time, of course she had heard rumors about God all along, long before Marpo came. Her cousins who lived in the city were all Christians, living as they did right next door to a Baptist church exclusively for Japanese people. These city cousins, of whom there were several, had been baptized en masse, and were very proud of their condition. Yoneko was impressed when she heard of this and thereafter was given to referring to them as "my cousins, the Christians." She, too, yearned at times after Christianity, but she realized the absurdity of her whim, seeing that there was no Baptist church for Japanese in the rural community she lived in. Such a church would have been impractical, moreover, since Yoneko, her father, her mother, and her little brother Seigo, were the only Japanese thereabouts. They were the only ones, too, whose agriculture was so diverse as to include blackberries, cabbages, rhubarb, potatoes, cucumbers, onions, and canteloupes. The rest of the countryside there was like one vast orange grove.

Yoneko had entered her cousins' church once, but she could not recall the sacred occasion without mortification. It had been one day when the cousins had taken her and Seigo along with them to Sunday school. The church was a narrow. wooden building mysterious-looking because of its unusual bluish-gray paint and its steeple, but the basement schoolroom inside had been disappointingly ordinary, with desks, a blackboard, and

erasers. They had all sung "Let Us Gather at the River" in
Japanese. This goes:

> *Mamonaku kanata no*
> *Nagare no soba de*
> *Tanoshiku ai-masho*
> *Mata tomodachi to*
>
> *Mamonaku ai-masho*
> *Kirei-na, kirei-na kawa de*
> *Tanoshiku ai-masho*
> *Mata tomodachi to.*

Yoneko had not known the words at all, but always clever in
such situations, she had opened her mouth and grimaced non-
chalantly to the rhythm. What with everyone else singing at
the top of his lungs, no one had noticed that she was not making a peep. Then everyone had sat down again and the man
had suggested, "Let us pray." Her cousins and the rest had
promptly curled their arms on the desks to make nests for their
heads, and Yoneko had done the same. But not Seigo. Because
when the room had become so still that one was aware of the
breathing, the creaking, and the chittering in the trees outside,
Seigo, sitting with her, had suddenly flung his arm around her
neck and said with concern, "Sis, what are you crying for? Don't
cry." Even the man had laughed and Yoneko had been terribly
ashamed that Seigo should thus disclose them to be interlopers.
She had pinched him fiercely and he had begun to cry, so she
had had to drag him outside, which was a fortunate move, because he had immediately wet his pants. But he had been only
three then, so it was not very fair to expect dignity of him.

So it remained for Marpo to bring the word of God to
Yoneko, Marpo with the face like brown leather, the thin
mustache like Edmund Lowe's, and the rare, breathtaking
smile like white gold. Marpo, who was twenty-seven years old,
was a Filipino and his last name was lovely, something like
Humming Wing, but no one ever ascertained the spelling of it.
He ate principally rice, just as though he were Japanese, but he
never sat down to the Hosoume table, because he lived in the
bunkhouse out by the barn and cooked on his own kerosene
stove. Once Yoneko read somewhere that Filipinos trapped wild

dogs, starved them for a time, then, feeding them mountains of rice, killed them at the peak of their bloatedness, thus insuring themselves meat ready to roast, stuffing and all, without further ado. This, the book said, was considered a delicacy. Unable to hide her disgust and her fascination, Yoneko went straightway to Marpo and asked, "Marpo, is it true that you eat dogs?", and he, flashing that smile, answered, "Don't be funny, honey!" This caused her no end of amusement, because it was a poem, and she completely forgot about the wild dogs.

Well, there seemed to be nothing Marpo could not do. Mr. Hosoume said Marpo was the best hired man he had ever had, and he said this often, because it was an irrefutable fact among Japanese in general that Filipinos in general were an indolent lot. Mr. Hosoume ascribed Marpo's industry to his having grown up in Hawaii, where there is known to be considerable Japanese influence. Marpo had gone to a missionary school there and he owned a Bible given him by one of his teachers. This had black leather covers that gave as easily as cloth, golden edges, and a slim purple ribbon for a marker. He always kept it on the little table by his bunk, which was not a bed with springs but a low, three-plank shelf with a mattress only. On the first page of the book, which was stiff and black, his teacher had written in large swirls of white ink, "As we draw near to God, He will draw near to us."

What, for instance, could Marpo do? Why, it would take an entire, leisurely evening to go into his accomplishments adequately, because there was not only Marpo the Christian and Marpo the best hired man, but Marpo the athlete, Marpo the musician (both instrumental and vocal), Marpo the artist, and Marpo the radio technician:

(1) As an athlete, Marpo owned a special pair of black shoes, equipped with sharp nails on the soles, which he kept in shape with the regular application of neatsfoot oil. Putting these on, he would dash down the dirt road to the highway, a distance of perhaps half a mile, and back again. When he first came to work for the Hosoumes, he undertook this sprint every evening before he went to get his supper but, as time went on, he referred to these shoes less and less and, in the end, when he left, he had

not touched them for months. He also owned a muscle-builder sent him by Charles Atlas which, despite his unassuming size, he could stretch the length of his outspread arms; his teeth gritted then and his whole body became temporarily victim to a jerky vibration. (2) As an artist, Marpo painted larger-than-life water colors of his favorite movie stars, all of whom were women and all of whom were blonde, like Ann Harding and Jean Harlow, and tacked them up on his walls. He also made for Yoneko a folding contraption of wood holding two pencils, one with lead and one without, with which she, too, could obtain double-sized likenesses of any picture she wished. It was a fragile instrument, however, and Seigo splintered it to pieces one day when Yoneko was away at school. He claimed he was only trying to copy Boob McNutt from the funny paper when it failed. (3) As a musician, Marpo owned a violin for which he had paid over one hundred dollars. He kept this in a case whose lining was red velvet, first wrapping it gently in a brilliant red silk scarf. This scarf, which weighed nothing, he tucked under his chin when he played, gathering it up delicately by the center and flicking it once to unfurl it—a gesture Yoneko prized. In addition to this, Marpo was a singer, with a soft tenor which came out in professional quavers and rolled r's when he applied a slight pressure to his Adam's apple with thumb and fore-finger. His violin and vocal repertoire consisted of the same numbers, mostly hymns and Irish folk airs. He was especially addicted to "The Rose of Tralee" and the "Londonderry Air." (4) Finally, as a radio technician who had spent two previous winters at a specialists' school in the city, Marpo had put together a bulky table-size radio which brought in equal proportions of static and entertainment. He never got around to building a cabinet to house it and its innards of metal and glass remained public throughout its lifetime. This was just as well, for not a week passed without Marpo's deciding to solder one bit or another. Yoneko and Seigo became a part of the great listening audience with such fidelity that Mr. Hosoume began remarking the fact that they dwelt more with Marpo than with their own parents. He eventually took a serious view of the matter and bought the naked radio from Marpo, who thereupon put away his radio manuals and his soldering iron in the bottom of his steamer trunk and divided more time among his other interests.

However, Marpo's versatility was not revealed, as it is here, in a lump. Yoneko uncovered it fragment by fragment every day, by dint of unabashed questions, explorations among his possessions, and even silent observation, although this last was rare. In fact, she and Seigo visited with Marpo at least once a day and both of them regularly came away amazed with their findings. The most surprising thing was that Marpo was, after all this, a rather shy young man meek to the point of speechlessness in the presence of Mr. and Mrs. Hosoume. With Yoneko and Seigo, he was somewhat more self-confident and at ease.

It is not remembered now just how Yoneko and Marpo came to open their protracted discussion on religion. It is sufficient here to note that Yoneko was an ideal apostle, adoring Jesus, desiring Heaven, and fearing Hell. Once Marpo had enlightened her on these basics, Yoneko never questioned their truth. The questions she put up to him, therefore, sought neither proof of her exegeses nor balm for her doubts, but simply additional color to round out her mental images. For example, who did Marpo suppose was God's favorite movie star? Or, what sound did Jesus' laughter have (it must be like music, she added, nodding sagely, answering herself to her own satisfaction), and did Marpo suppose that God's sense of humor would have appreciated the delicious chant she had learned from friends at school today:

> *There ain't no bugs on us,*
> *There ain't no bugs on us,*
> *There may be bugs on the rest of you mugs,*
> *But there ain't no bugs on us?*

Or, did Marpo believe Jesus to have been exempt from stinging eyes when he shampooed that long, naturally wavy hair of his?

To shake such faith, there would have been required a most monstrous upheaval of some sort, and it might be said that this is just what happened. For early on the evening of March 10, 1933, a little after five o'clock this was, as Mrs. Hosoume was getting supper, as Marpo was finishing up in the fields alone because Mr. Hosoume had gone to order some chicken fertilizer, and as Yoneko and Seigo were listening to Skippy, a tremendous roar came out of nowhere and the Hosoume house began shuddering violently as though some giant had seized it in his two hands and was giving it a good shaking. Mrs. Hosoume, who remembered similar, although milder experiences, from her childhood in Japan, screamed, *"Jishin, jishin!"* before she ran and grabbed Yoneko and Seigo each by a hand and dragged them outside with her. She took them as far as the middle of the rhubarb patch near the house, and there they all crouched, pressed together, watching the world about them rock and sway. In a few minutes, Marpo, stumbling in from the fields, joined them, saying, "Earthquake, earthquake!", and he gathered them all in his arms, as much to protect them as to support himself.

Mr. Hosoume came home later that evening in a stranger's car, with another stranger driving the family Reo. Pallid, trembling, his eyes wildly staring, he could have been mistaken for a drunkard, except that he was famous as a teetotaler. It seemed that he had been on the way home when the first jolt came, that the old green Reo had been kissed by a broken live wire dangling from a suddenly leaning pole. Mr. Hosoume, knowing that the end had come by electrocution, had begun to writhe and kick and this had been his salvation. His hands had flown from the wheel, the car had swerved into a ditch, freeing itself from the sputtering wire. Later, it was found that he was left permanently inhibited about driving automobiles and permanently incapable of considering electricity with calmness. He spent the larger part of his later life weakly, wandering about the house or fields and lying down frequently to rest because of splitting headaches and sudden dizzy spells.

So it was Marpo who went back into the house as Yoneko screamed, "No, Marpo, no!" and brought out the Hosoumes' kerosene stove, the food, the blankets, while Mr. Hosoume huddled on the ground near his family.

The earth trembled for days afterwards. The Hosoumes and Marpo Humming Wing lived during that time on a natural patch of Bermuda grass between the house and the rhubarb patch, remembering to take three meals a day and retire at night. Marpo ventured inside the house many times despite Yoneko's protests and reported the damage slight: a few dishes had been broken; a gallon jug of mayonnaise had fallen from the top pantry shelf and spattered the kitchen floor with yellow blobs and pieces of glass.

Yoneko was in constant terror during this experience. Immediately on learning what all the commotion was about, she began praying to God to end this violence. She entreated God, flattered Him, wheedled Him, commanded Him, but He did not listen to her at all—inexorably, the earth went on rumbling. After three solid hours of silent, desperate prayer, without any results whatsoever, Yoneko began to suspect that God was either powerless, callous, downright cruel, or nonexistent. In the murky night, under a strange moon wearing a pale ring of light, she decided upon the last as the most plausible theory. "Ha," was one of the things she said tremulously to Marpo, when she was not begging him to stay out of the house, "you and your God!"

The others soon oriented themselves to the catastrophe with philosophy, saying how fortunate they were to live in the country where the peril was less than in the city and going so far as to regard the period as a sort of vacation from work, with their enforced alfresco existence a sort of camping trip. They tried to bring Yoneko to partake of this pleasant outlook, but she, shivering with each new quiver, looked on them as dreamers who refused to see things as they really were. Indeed, Yoneko's reaction was so notable that the Hosoume household thereafter spoke of the event as "Yoneko's earthquake."

After the earth subsided and the mayonnaise was mopped off the kitchen floor, life returned to normal, except that Mr. Hosoume stayed at home most of the time. Sometimes, if he had a relatively painless day, he would have supper on the stove when Mrs. Hosoume came in from the fields. Mrs. Hosoume and Marpo did all the field labor now, except on certain overwhelming days when several Mexicans were hired to assist them. Marpo did most of the driving, too, and it was now he and Mrs. Hosoume who went into town on the weekly trip for groceries. In fact, Marpo became indispensable and both Mr. and Mrs.

Hosoume often told each other how grateful they were for
Marpo.

When summer vacation began and Yoneko stayed at home,
too, she found the new arrangement rather inconvenient. Her
father's presence cramped her style: for instance, once when her
friends came over and it was decided to make fudge, he would
not permit them, saying fudge used too much sugar and that
sugar was not a plaything; once when they were playing paper
dolls, he came along and stuck his finger up his nose and pre-
tended he was going to rub some snot off onto the dolls. Things
like that. So, on some days, she was very much annoyed with
her father.

Therefore when her mother came home breathless from the
fields one day and pushed a ring at her, a gold-colored ring with
a tiny glasslike stone in it, saying, "Look, Yoneko, I'm going to
give you this ring. If your father asks where you got it, say you
found it on the street." Yoneko was perplexed but delighted
both by the unexpected gift and the chance to have some secret
revenge on her father, and she said, certainly, she was willing to
comply with her mother's request. Her mother went back to the
fields then and Yoneko put the pretty ring on her middle finger,
taking up the loose space with a bit of newspaper. It was similar
to the rings found occasionally in boxes of Crackerjack, except
that it appeared a bit more substantial.

Mr. Hosoume never asked about the ring; in fact, he never
noticed she was wearing one. Yoneko thought he was about to,
once, but he only reproved her for the flamingo nail polish she
was wearing, which she had applied from a vial brought over
by Yvonne Fournier, the French girl two orange groves away.
"You look like a Filipino," Mr. Hosoume said sternly, for it
was another irrefutable fact among Japanese in general that
Filipinos in general were a gaudy lot. Mrs. Hosoume immediately came to her defense, saying that in Japan, if she remembered correctly, young girls did the same thing. In fact, she
remembered having gone to elaborate lengths to tint her fingernails: she used to gather, she said, the petals of the red
tsubobana or the purple *kogane* (which grows on the underside
of stones), grind them well, mix them with some alum powder,

then cook the mixture and leave it to stand overnight in an envelope of either persimmon or sugar potato leaves (both very strong leaves). The second night, just before going to bed, she used to obtain threads by ripping a palm leaf (because real thread was dear) and tightly bind the paste to her fingernails under shields of persimmon or sugar potato leaves. She would be helpless for the night, the fingertips bound so well that they were alternately numb or aching, but she would grit her teeth and tell herself that the discomfort indicated the success of the operation. In the morning, finally releasing her fingers, she would find the nails shining with a translucent red-orange color.

Yoneko was fascinated, because she usually thought of her parents as having been adults all their lives. She thought that her mother must have been a beautiful child, with or without bright fingernails, because, though surely past thirty, she was even yet a beautiful person. When she herself was younger, she remembered, she had at times been so struck with her mother's appearance that she had dropped to her knees and mutely clasped her mother's legs in her arms. She had left off this habit as she learned to control her emotions, because at such times her mother had usually walked away, saying, "My, what a clinging child you are. You've got to learn to be a little more independent." She also remembered she had once heard someone comparing her mother to "a dewy, half-opened rosebud."

Mr. Hosoume, however, was irritated. "That's no excuse for Yoneko to begin using paint on her fingernails," he said. "She's only ten."

"Her Japanese age is eleven, and we weren't much older," Mrs. Hosoume said.

"Look," Mr. Hosoume said, "if you're going to contradict every piece of advice I give the children, they'll end up disobeying us both and doing what they very well please. Just because I'm ill just now is no reason for them to start being disrespectful."

"When have I ever contradicted you before?" Mrs. Hosoume said.

"Countless times," Mr. Hosoume said.

"Name one instance," Mrs. Hosoume said.

Certainly there had been times, but Mr. Hosoume could not

happen to mention the one requested instance on the spot and
he became quite angry. "That's quite enough of your inso-
lence," he said. Since he was speaking in Japanese, his exact
accusation was that she was *nama-iki,* which is a shade more
revolting than being merely insolent.

"*Nama-iki, nama-iki?*" said Mrs. Hosoume. "How dare you?
I'll not have anyone calling me *nama-iki!*"

At that, Mr. Hosoume went up to where his wife was ironing
and slapped her smartly on the face. It was the first time he had
ever laid hands on her. Mrs. Hosoume was immobile for an
instant, but she resumed her ironing as though nothing had
happened, although she glanced over at Marpo, who happened
to be in the room reading a newspaper. Yoneko and Seigo forgot
they were listening to the radio and stared at their parents,
thunderstruck.

"Hit me again," said Mrs. Hosoume quietly, as she ironed.
"Hit me all you wish."

Mr. Hosoume was apparently about to, but Marpo stepped up
and put his hand on Mr. Hosoume's shoulder. "The children
are here," said Marpo, "the children."

"Mind your own business," said Mr. Hosoume in broken
English. "Get out of here!"

Marpo left, and that was about all. Mrs. Hosoume went on
ironing, Yoneko and Seigo turned back to the radio, and Mr.
Hosoume muttered that Marpo was beginning to forget his
place. Now that he thought of it, he said, Marpo had been increasingly impudent towards him since his illness. He said just
because he was temporarily an invalid was no reason for Marpo
to start being disrespectful. He added that Marpo had better
watch his step or that he might find himself jobless one of these
fine days.

And something of the sort must have happened. Marpo was
here one day and gone the next, without even saying good-bye
to Yoneko and Seigo. That was also the day the Hosoume family
went to the city on a weekday afternoon, which was most unusual. Mr. Hosoume, who now avoided driving as much as
possible, handled the cumbersome Reo as though it were a nervous stallion, sitting on the edge of the seat and hugging the
steering wheel. He drove very fast and about halfway to the city

struck a beautiful collie which had dashed out barking from someone's yard. The car jerked with the impact, but Mr. Hosoume drove right on and Yoneko, wanting suddenly to vomit, looked back and saw the collie lying very still at the side of the road.

When they arrived at the Japanese hospital, which was their destination, Mr. Hosoume cautioned Yoneko and Seigo to be exemplary children and wait patiently in the car. It seemed hours before he and Mrs. Hosoume returned, she walking with very small, slow steps and he assisting her. When Mrs. Hosoume got in the car, she leaned back and closed her eyes. Yoneko inquired as to the source of her distress, for she was obviously in pain, but she only answered that she was feeling a little under the weather and that the doctor had administered some necessarily astringent treatment. At that, Mr. Hosoume turned around and advised Yoneko and Seigo that they must tell no one of coming to the city on a weekday afternoon, absolutely no one, and Yoneko and Seigo readily assented. On the way home, they passed the place of the encounter with the collie, and Yoneko looked up and down the stretch of road but the dog was nowhere to be seen.

Not long after that, the Hosoumes got a new hired hand, an old Japanese man who wore his gray hair in a military cut and who, unlike Marpo, had no particular interests outside working, eating, sleeping, and playing an occasional game of *goh* with Mr. Hosoume. Before he came Yoneko and Seigo played sometimes in the empty bunkhouse and recalled Marpo's various charms together. Privately, Yoneko was wounded more than she would admit even to herself that Marpo should have subjected her to such an abrupt desertion. Whenever her indignation became too great to endure gracefully, she would console herself by telling Seigo that, after all, Marpo was a mere Filipino, an eater of wild dogs.

Seigo never knew about the disappointing new hired man, because he suddenly died in the night. He and Yoneko had spent the hot morning in the nearest orange grove, she driving him to distraction by repeating certain words he could not bear to hear: she had called him Serge, a name she had read somewhere, instead of Seigo; and she had chanted off the name of the tires they were rolling around like hoops as Goodrich Silver-TO-town, Goodrich Silver-TO-town, instead of Goodrich Silvertown. This had enraged him, and he had chased her around the trees most of the morning. Finally she had taunted him from several trees away by singing "You're a Yellow-streaked Coward," which was one of several small songs she had composed. Seigo had suddenly grinned and shouted, "Sure!", and walked off, leaving her, as he intended, with a sense of emptiness. In the afternoon, they had perspired and followed the potato-digging machine and the Mexican workers, both hired for the day, around the field, delighting in unearthing marble-sized, smooth-skinned potatoes that both the machine and the men had missed. Then, in the middle of the night, Seigo began crying, complaining of a stomach ache. Mrs. Hosoume felt his head and sent her husband for the doctor, who smiled and said Seigo would be fine in the morning. He said it was doubtless the combination of green oranges, raw potatoes, and the July heat. But as soon as the doctor left, Seigo fell into a coma and a drop of red blood stood out on his underlip, where he had evidently bit it. Mr. Hosoume again fetched the doctor, who was this time very grave and wagged his head, saying several times, "It looks very bad." So Seigo died at the age of five.

Mrs. Hosoume was inconsolable and had swollen eyes in the morning for weeks afterwards. She now insisted on visiting the city relatives each Sunday, so that she could attend church services with them. One Sunday, she stood up and accepted Christ. It was through accompanying her mother to many of these services that Yoneko finally learned the Japanese words to "Let Us Gather at the River." Mrs. Hosoume also did not seem interested in discussing anything but God and Seigo. She was especially fond of reminding visitors how adorable Seigo had been as an infant, how she had been unable to refrain from dressing him as a little girl and fixing his hair in bangs until he was two. Mr. Hosoume was very gentle with her and when Yoneko accidentally caused her to giggle once, he nodded and said, "Yes, that's right, Yoneko, we must make your mother laugh and forget about Seigo." Yoneko herself did not think about Seigo at all. Whenever the thought of Seigo crossed her mind, she instantly began composing a new song, and this worked very well.

One evening, when the new hired man had been with them a while, Yoneko was helping her mother with the dishes when she found herself being examined with such peculiarly intent eyes that, with a start of guilt, she began searching in her mind for a possible crime she had lately committed. But Mrs. Hosoume only said, "Never kill a person, Yoneko, because if you do, God will take from you someone you love."

"Oh, that," said Yoneko quickly, "I don't believe in that, I don't believe in God." And her words tumbling pell-mell over one another, she went on eagerly to explain a few of her reasons why. If she neglected to mention the test she had given God during the earthquake, it was probably because she was a little upset. She had believed for a moment that her mother was going to ask about the ring (which, alas, she had lost already, somewhere in the flumes along the canteloupe patch).

WAKAKO YAMAUCHI
(1924-   )

"My mother and father were immigrants from Japan. They farmed in a desert basin euphemistically called Imperial Valley near the southern border of California. I was born in the township of Westmoreland, the third of four children, in 1924. The depression of the twenties followed us everywhere, even when it was over for everyone else. Life was frugal and isolated. My mother was a beautiful woman; my father was a quiet man.

"We subscribed to a Japanese paper and I used to enjoy Hisaye Yamamoto's column in the English section. I remember when I first discovered the column, I frantically searched through back issues to see if I'd missed any. She was very young but she wrote with wit and whimsy even then.

"When I was fifteen, Providence dealt my father such a blow, he finally threw in his hand and we moved to Oceanside for a fresh start. It was probably the only way we would have left the Valley. And Si and her family also meandered through several years and little known communities and we met in Oceanside. It was like Providence at work again, but we didn't become friends. Perhaps I was too effusive.

"During the war with Japan, we were shunted off to

Poston, Arizona. There I joined the Poston *Chronicle* as a staff artist and met Si again. I was seventeen and green and dumb. She opened my eyes to more things in heaven and earth than I'd dreamed of in my philosophy. We have been close friends since.

"By the late fifties, Si had already embarked on a fine literary career, but because of her burgeoning family and/or other priorities, she stopped writing. I felt at least one of us should always be writing and perhaps I ought to carry on until she was ready to start again. I was like a cripple in a foot race dragging a gimpy leg. And I found there was no easy open sesame: the only way to the promised land was through hard work, practice, clear thinking, and absolute honesty. And there's another reason I wanted to write: years ago when my mother passed away, she left a diary in Japanese that I was unable to read. I realized I never really knew her nor would I ever now know her, and it became important to me to leave something of myself that my daughter could read and perceive the person I really was, so she could know who she was and why.

"I have been married to Chester Yamauchi for 25 years. We now live in Gardena with our daughter Joy."

AND THE SOUL
SHALL DANCE

It's all right to talk about it now. Most of the principals are
dead, except, of course, me and my younger brother, and
possibly Kiyoko Oka, who might be near forty-five now, because,
yes, I'm sure of it, she was fourteen then. I was nine, and my
brother about four, so he hardly counts at all. Kiyoko's mother
is dead, my father is dead, my mother is dead, and her father
could not have lasted all these years with his tremendous appe-
tite for alcohol and pickled chilies—those little yellow ones, so
hot they could make your mouth hurt; he'd eat them like
peanuts and tears would surge from his bulging thyroid eyes
in great waves and stream down the dark coarse terrain of his
face.

My father farmed then in the desert basin resolutely named
Imperial Valley, in the township called Westmoreland; twenty
acres of tomatoes, ten of summer squash, or vice versa, and the
Okas lived maybe a mile, mile and a half, across an alkaline
road, a stretch of greasewood, tumbleweed and white sand, to
the south of us. We didn't hobnob much with them, because
you see, they were a childless couple and we were a family:
father, mother, daughter, and son, and we went to the Buddhist
church on Sundays where my mother taught Japanese, and the
Okas kept pretty much to themselves. I don't mean they were
unfriendly; Mr. Oka would sometimes walk over (he rarely
drove) on rainy days, all dripping wet, short and squat under
a soggy newspaper, pretending to need a plow-blade or a file,
and he would spend the afternoon in our kitchen drinking sake

and eating chilies with my father. As he got progressively
drunker, his large mouth would draw down and with the stream
of tears, he looked like a kindly weeping bullfrog.

Not only were they childless, impractical in an area where
large families were looked upon as labor potentials, but there
was a certain strangeness about them. I became aware of it the
summer our bathhouse burned down, and my father didn't get
right down to building another, and a Japanese without a bathhouse . . . well, Mr. Oka offered us the use of his. So every
night that summer we drove to the Okas for our bath, and we
came in frequent contact with Mrs. Oka, and this is where I
found the strangeness.

Mrs. Oka was small and spare. Her clothes hung on her like
loose skin and when she walked, the skirt about her legs gave
her a sort of webbed look. She was pretty in spite of the boni-
ness and the dull calico and the barren look; I know now she
couldn't have been over thirty. Her eyes were large and a little
vacant, although once I saw them fill with tears; the time I insisted we take the old Victrola over and we played our Japanese
records for her. Some of the songs were sad, and I imagined the
nostalgia she felt, but my mother said the tears were probably
from yawning or from the smoke of her cigarettes. I thought
my mother resented her for not being more hospitable; indeed,
never a cup of tea appeared before us, and between them the
conversation of women was totally absent: the rise and fall of
gentle voices, the arched eyebrows, the croon of polite surprise.
But more than this, Mrs. Oka was *different*.

Obviously she was shy, but some nights she disappeared
altogether. She would see us drive into her yard and then lurch
from sight. She was gone all evening. Where could she have
hidden in that two-roomed house—where in that silent desert?
Some nights she would wait out our visit with enormous forbearance, quietly pushing wisps of stray hair behind her ears
and waving gnats away from her great moist eyes, and some
nights she moved about with nervous agitation, her khaki
canvas shoes slapping loudly as she walked. And sometimes
there appeared to be welts and bruises on her usually smooth
brown face, and she would sit solemnly, hands on lap, eyes

large and intent on us. My mother hurried us home then: "Hurry, Masako, no need to wash well; hurry."

You see, being so poky, I was always last to bathe. I think the Okas bathed after we left because my mother often reminded me to keep the water clean. The routine was to lather outside the tub (there were buckets and pans and a small wooden stool), rinse off the soil and soap, and then soak in the tub of hot hot water and contemplate. Rivulets of perspiration would run down the scalp.

When my mother pushed me like this, I dispensed with ritual, rushed a bar of soap around me and splashed about a pan of water. So hastily toweled, my wet skin trapped the clothes to me, impeding my already clumsy progress. Outside, my mother would be murmuring her many apologies and my father, I knew, would be carrying my brother whose feet were already sandy. We would hurry home.

I thought Mrs. Oka might be insane and I asked my mother about it, but she shook her head and smiled with her mouth drawn down and said that Mrs. Oka loved her sake. This was unusual, yes, but there were other unusual women we knew. Mrs. Nagai was bought by her husband from a geisha house; Mrs. Tani was a militant Christian Scientist; Mrs. Abe, the midwife, was occult. My mother's statement explained much: sometimes Mrs. Oka was drunk and sometimes not. Her taste for liquor and cigarettes was a step in the realm of men; unusual for a Japanese wife, but at that time, in that place, and to me, Mrs. Oka loved her sake in the way my father loved his, in the way of Mr. Oka, the way I loved my candy. That her psychology may have demanded this anesthetic, that she lived with something unendurable, did not occur to me. Nor did I perceive the violence of emotions that the purple welts indicated—or the masochism that permitted her to display these wounds to us.

In spite of her masculine habits, Mrs. Oka was never less than a woman. She was no lady in the area of social amenities; but the feminine in her was innate and never left her. Even in her disgrace, she was a small broken sparrow, slightly floppy, too slowly enunciating her few words, too carefully rolling her Bull

Durham, cocking her small head and moistening the ocher tissue. Her aberration was a protest of the life assigned her; it was obstinate, but unobserved, alas, unheeded. "Strange" was the only concession we granted her.

Toward the end of summer, my mother said we couldn't continue bathing at the Okas'; when winter set in we'd all catch our death from the commuting and she'd always felt dreadful about our imposition on Mrs. Oka. So my father took the corrugated tin sheets he'd found on the highway and had been saving for some other use and built up our bathhouse again. Mr. Oka came to help.

While they raised the quivering tin walls, Mr. Oka began to talk. His voice was sharp and clear above the low thunder of the metal sheets.

He told my father he had been married in Japan previously to the present Mrs. Oka's older sister. He had a child by the marriage, Kiyoko, a girl. He had left the two to come to America intending to send for them soon, but shortly after his departure, his wife passed away from an obscure stomach ailment. At the time, the present Mrs. Oka was young and had foolishly become involved with a man of poor reputation. The family was anxious to part the lovers and conveniently arranged a marriage by proxy and sent him his dead wife's sister. Well that was all right, after all, they were kin, and it would be good for the child when she came to join them. But things didn't work out that way; year after year he postponed calling for his daughter, couldn't get the price of fare together, and the wife— ahhh, the wife, Mr. Oka's groan was lost in the rumble of his hammering.

He cleared his throat. The girl was now fourteen, he said, and begged to come to America to be with her own real family. Those relatives had forgotten the favor he'd done in accepting a slightly used bride, and now tormented his daughter for being forsaken. True, he'd not sent much money, but if they knew, if they only knew how it was here.

"Well," he sighed, "who could be blamed? It's only right she be with me anyway."

"That's right," my father said.

"Well, I sold the horse and some other things and managed to buy a third-class ticket on the Taiyo-Maru. Kiyoko will get here the first week of September." Mr. Oka glanced toward my father, but my father was peering into a bag of nails. "I'd be much obliged to you if your wife and little girl," he rolled his eyes toward me, "would take kindly to her. She'll be lonely."

Kiyoko-san came in September. I was surprised to see so very nearly a woman; short, robust, buxom: the female counterpart of her father; thyroid eyes and protruding teeth, straight black hair banded impudently into two bristly shucks, Cuban heels and white socks. Mr. Oka brought her proudly to us.

"Little Masako here," for the first time to my recollection, he touched me; he put his rough fat hand on the top of my head, "is very smart in school. She will help you with your school work, Kiyoko," he said.

I had so looked forward to Kiyoko-san's arrival. She would be my soul mate; in my mind I had conjured a girl of my own proportions: thin and tall, but with the refinement and beauty I didn't yet possess that would surely someday come to the fore. My disappointment was keen and apparent. Kiyoko-san stepped forward shyly, then retreated with a short bow and small giggle, her fingers pressed to her mouth.

My mother took her away. They talked for a long time—about Japan, about enrollment in American school, the clothes Kiyoko-san would need, and where to look for the best values. As I watched them, it occurred to me that I had been deceived: this was not a child, this was a woman. The smile pressed behind her fingers, the way of her nod, so brief, like my mother when father scolded her: the face was inscrutable, but something—maybe spirit—shrank visibly, like a piece of silk in water. I was disappointed; Kiyoko-san's soul was barricaded in her unenchanting appearance and the smile she fenced behind her fingers.

She started school from third grade, one below me, and as it turned out, she quickly passed me by. There wasn't much I could help her with except to drill her on pronunciation—the "L" and "R" sounds. Every morning walking to our rural school: land, leg, library, loan, lot; every afternoon returning home: ran, rabbit, rim, rinse, roll. That was the extent of our communication; friendly but uninteresting.

One particularly cold November night—the wind outside was icy; I was sitting on my bed, my brother's and mine, oiling the cracks in my chapped hands by lamplight—someone rapped urgently at our door. It was Kiyoko-san; she was hysterical, she wore no wrap, her teeth were chattering, and except for the thin straw zori, her feet were bare. My mother led her to the kitchen, started a pot of tea, and gestured to my brother and me to retire. I lay very still but because of my brother's restless tossing and my father's snoring, was unable to hear much. I was aware, though, that drunken and savage brawling had brought Kiyoko-san to us. Presently they came to the bedroom. I feigned sleep. My mother gave Kiyoko-san a gown and pushed me over to make room for her. My mother spoke firmly: "Tomorrow you will return to them; you must not leave them again. They are your people." I could almost feel Kiyoko-san's short nod.

All night long I lay cramped and still, afraid to intrude into her hulking back. Two or three times her icy feet jabbed into mine and quickly retreated. In the morning I found my mother's gown neatly folded on the spare pillow. Kiyoko-san's place in bed was cold.

She never came to weep at our house again but I know she cried: her eyes were often swollen and red. She stopped much of her giggling and routinely pressed her fingers to her mouth. Our daily pronunciation drill petered off from lack of interest. She walked silently with her shoulders hunched, grasping her books with both arms, and when I spoke to her in my halting Japanese, she absently corrected my prepositions.

Spring comes early in the Valley; in February the skies are clear though the air is still cold. By March, winds are vigorous and warm and wild flowers dot the desert floor, cockleburs are green and not yet tenacious, the sand is crusty underfoot, everywhere there is the smell of things growing and the first tomatoes are showing green and bald.

As the weather changed, Kiyoko-san became noticeably more cheerful. Mr. Oka who hated so to drive could often be seen steering his dusty old Ford over the road that passes our house, and Kiyoko-san sitting in front would sometimes wave gaily to us. Mrs. Oka was never with them. I thought of these trips as the westernizing of Kiyoko-san: with a permanent wave, her straight black hair became tangles of tiny frantic curls; between her textbooks she carried copies of *Modern Screen* and *Photoplay,* her clothes were gay with print and piping, and she bought a pair of brown suede shoes with alligator trim. I can see her now picking her way gingerly over the deceptive white peaks of alkaline crust.

At first my mother watched their coming and going with vicarious pleasure. "Probably off to a picture show; the stores are all closed at this hour," she might say. Later her eyes would get distant and she would muse, "They've left her home again; Mrs. Oka is alone again, the poor woman."

Now when Kiyoko-san passed by or came in with me on her way home, my mother would ask about Mrs. Oka—how is she, how does she occupy herself these rainy days, or these windy or warm or cool days. Often the answers were polite: "Thank you, we are fine," but sometimes Kiyoko-san's upper lip would pull over her teeth, and her voice would become very soft and she would say, "Drink, always drinking and fighting." At those times my mother would invariably say, "Endure, soon you will be marrying and going away."

Once a young truck driver delivered crates at the Oka farm and he dropped back to our place to tell my father that Mrs. Oka had lurched behind his truck while he was backing up, and very nearly let him kill her. Only the daughter pulling her away saved her, he said. Thoroughly unnerved, he stopped by to rest himself and talk about it. Never, never, he said in wide-eyed wonder, had he seen a drunken Japanese woman. My father nodded gravely, "Yes, it's unusual," he said and drummed his knee with his fingers.

Evenings were longer now, and when my mother's migraines drove me from the house in unbearable self-pity, I would take walks in the desert. One night with the warm wind against me, the dune primrose and yellow poppies closed and fluttering, the greasewood swaying in languid orbit, I lay on the white sand beneath a shrub and tried to disappear.

A voice sweet and clear cut through the half-dark of the evening:

> Red lips press against a glass
> Drink the purple wine
> And the soul shall dance

Mrs. Oka appeared to be gathering flowers. Bending, plucking, standing, searching, she added to a small bouquet she clasped. She held them away; looked at them slyly, lids lowered, demure, then in a sudden and sinuous movement, she broke into a stately dance. She stopped, gathered more flowers, and breathed deeply into them. Tossing her head, she laughed—softly, beautifully, from her dark throat. The picture of her imagined grandeur was lost to me, but the delusion that transformed the bouquet of tattered petals and sandy leaves, and the aloneness of a desert twilight into a fantasy that brought such joy and abandon made me stir with discomfort. The sound broke Mrs. Oka's dance. Her eyes grew large and her neck tense—like a cat on the prowl. She spied me in the bushes. A peculiar chill ran through me. Then abruptly and with child-like delight, she scattered the flowers around her and walked away singing:

> Falling, falling, petals on a wind . . .

That was the last time I saw Mrs. Oka. She died before the spring harvest. It was pneumonia. I didn't attend the funeral, but my mother said it was sad. Mrs. Oka looked peaceful, and the minister expressed the irony of the long separation of Mother and Child and the short-lived reunion; hardly a year together, she said. We went to help Kiyoko-san address and stamp those black-bordered acknowledgements.

When harvest was over, Mr. Oka and Kiyoko-san moved out of the Valley. We never heard from them or saw them again and I suppose in a large city, Mr. Oka found some sort of work, perhaps as a janitor or a dishwasher and Kiyoko-san grew up and found someone to marry.